# MY SIDE OF *Life*

# SHANE FILAN
## MY SIDE OF *Life*

With **Ian Gittins**

1 3 5 7 9 10 8 6 4 2

Virgin Books, an imprint of Ebury Publishing,
20 Vauxhall Bridge Road,
London SW1V 2SA

Virgin Books is part of the Penguin Random House group of companies
whose addresses can be found at global.penguinrandomhouse.com

First published by Virgin Books in 2014
This edition first published in Great Britain by Penguin Random House in 2015
www.eburypublishing.co.uk

A CIP catalogue record for this book is available from the British Library

ISBN: 9780753556047

Designed and typeset by K. DESIGN, Winscombe, Somerset
Printed and bound by CPI Group (UK) Ltd, Croydon CR0 4YY

Penguin Random House is committed to a sustainable future for our
business, our readers and our planet. This book is made from Forest
Stewardship Council® certified paper.

*To Gillian,*
*Together Girl Forever*

# CONTENTS

# INTRODUCTION

## SNOOKERED IN THE RED

There was a bit of history to that basket.

It had been around for a long time. My wife, Gillian, had first had it in her family home when she was a girl. She used to throw her spare change and her tips from her teenage waitressing job into it. When she and I got together and married, her basket had come with her. Now, it lived inside a wardrobe in our bedroom in Castledale, our big family home just outside Sligo.

That house was our pride and joy. We had designed it ourselves, just as Westlife were getting huge, and then spent four years watching it go up before we moved in. We had lived there as happy as could be with our daughter, Nicole, and son Patrick. We had another kid on the way.

Gillian and I used the basket for the same purpose that she always had. We threw our spare coins in there. Every time I was in the bedroom getting dressed and had change in my pocket, or I came home from a Westlife tour laden down with euros, I chucked them in there.

We had done it for years. God knows how much was in there;

we had never counted. We always laughed that the money would come in handy for a rainy day.

Not that rain ever seemed likely. I was the multi-millionaire singer of one of the biggest boy bands the world had ever seen. Everything I touched turned to gold. I led a charmed life.

That was what the outside world thought, anyway. The reality was very different – and a lot darker.

For the last five years, I had been leading a double life. It was a dual existence that was about to result in despair… and disaster.

Westlife had always had our ups and downs, and I had often worried how I would provide for my family when the band eventually came to an end. I had hit on the idea of a sideline in the property business.

At the time, everybody was doing it. Ireland was booming and bricks and mortar were the way forward. My brother, Finbarr, and I had started up a company. We called it Shafin Developments.

We had started small, and were happy to stay that way. But when I felt forced into buying a huge plot of land to protect my home (it's a long story, but I will tell it here), we had somehow turned into major property developers.

It had never been our intention. And, to say the least, it had not gone well.

We had fallen into debt. Trying to spend our way out of it, we had got in way over our heads just as the global economy was crashing. We owed millions of euros – and, today, our bank had demanded all of the money back.

A multi-millionaire pop star? I was worse than destitute. I had always said that my change basket was for a rainy day. Well, right now it was a very, very rainy night in Sligo.

In fact, it was one of the worst nights of my life. Gillian was heavily pregnant and was lying on the couch, feeling sick. I was tending to her – but my thoughts were also on that basket.

My brother and I pulled it out of the wardrobe and lugged it downstairs to my snooker room. I had spent many happy hours knocking balls around that snooker table. Once, I had even played with two world champions: Ken Doherty and Steve Davis. Now I needed it for a rather more unpleasant purpose.

Finbarr and I tipped the contents of the basket onto the table and hunched over it, counting.

Counting, and panicking. *How much was there?*

It took us fifteen minutes: '€100... €200... €600... €800... €1,000...'

It came to €1,400. Finbarr and I pocketed half of it each. It would see us through the next few days. But after that... What would I do then? Where was all this going to end?

It was going to end in tragedy, heartache, public humiliation, misery... and the loss of the home that Gillian and I adored.

It was going to end in bankruptcy.

So how did I go from fronting one of the world's biggest pop bands, travelling the globe and entertaining millions, to this? And, after Westlife imploded, how would I begin my long, slow journey to recovery and redemption?

Believe me, it's an extraordinary story – and it begins thirty-five years ago in the heart of Sligo, Ireland, with a spectacularly happy childhood in a place called the Carlton Café.

# I

# LIVING OVER THE CAFÉ

The cliché of an Irish childhood is being born into a huge, loving family, with firm but easy-going parents, and running around with loads of brothers and sisters, playing mad games, getting into sports, messing about with horses and generally having brilliant craic.

Well, I guess I must have had a very clichéd childhood. It was wonderful.

I was lucky to get the chance to enjoy it, though. Before I was born, I almost died. I have never been one to do things in the straightforward way, and my path to life wasn't easy. My mum had complications in her pregnancy and nearly miscarried me twice, at ten weeks and twelve weeks. She had to get a stitch put in her womb to hold me in.

Despite this, or maybe because of it, I was clearly desperate to get out and arrived four weeks early, at 8.45 a.m. on 5 July 1979, at Sligo General Hospital. Like a lot of premature kids, I was tiny and weighed in at just under five pounds. It took me a long time to catch up: I was loads smaller than other kids my age right until my mid-teens.

Having made my arrival, I found I was joining quite the crowd scene. My mum and dad had always wanted a big family, and I was the youngest of seven kids with only eleven years between the lot of us: Finbarr, Peter, Yvonne, Liam, Denise, Mairead and me. You have probably worked out by now that my parents were Catholic.

My dad, Peter Filan, was from Castleplunkett in County Roscommon while my mum, Mae MacNicholas, was from Kiltimagh in Mayo. They had met in the 1950s at a dance in Carrick-on-Shannon. My mum was a very beautiful girl with jet-black hair and she was a great dancer, and my dad was transfixed the second he set eyes on her.

He kept going back to the same dance week after week and eventually worked up the courage to talk to her. Mum was working as a clerk in the town hall at Carrick-on-Shannon and sharing an apartment with a couple of other girls, and she invited him round for tea and biscuits one afternoon. They are still together close on fifty years later. They must have been great biscuits.

My dad's parents had tried to encourage him to go into the priesthood, but he had managed to swerve that one. Instead, he had got together with a brother and a sister – my Uncle Luke and Aunty Lily – and they bought a café in Castlerea, close by Castleplunkett.

They ran the place for a bit but when my dad married my mum, the two of them and Uncle Luke bought another café called the Mayfair in Sligo. I think they chose Sligo just because it was halfway between her home and his. Then a year or so later my parents went off and upgraded to a bigger café, the Carlton, which was just around the corner in Castle Street, in the middle of Sligo.

That was where I grew up; my home for more than twenty years. The Carlton was a proper old-fashioned diner-style Irish café with long wooden tables and a big counter at the side of the room where everything got cooked. Mum did the books, she and Dad were the chefs and we all lived on the two upstairs floors.

We had four bedrooms between seven kids and so we took it in turns to share. A lot of kids might have kicked off about this, but it was just how it was and we never really minded. We were always chopping and changing: I think I must have shared with every one of my siblings over the years.

These were the days before McDonalds and Burger King hit Sligo and there were only two restaurants in the town centre, so our café always seemed to be packed. People would come in for breakfast, lunch, dinner – and to fill up after the pubs had shut. Often, we would be open until three in the morning.

Looking back, my parents had an amazing relationship. They weren't soppy or lovey-dovey but I genuinely don't think I ever heard them have a cross word. My dad was mad for music and he would always be playing Jim Reeves and Patsy Cline around the house. He was a pretty good singer himself.

My mum wasn't. She couldn't hit a note.

As clear as anything, I can still hear my dad every morning, in the bathroom as he shaved, singing 'True Love' by Bing Crosby. The other song I remember was Slim Whitman's 'Darling, Happy Anniversary', which he'd always sing to my mum on their wedding anniversary. He'd be hugging her, and she'd be telling him not to be an eejit and trying to fight him off.

What was I like as a kid? My mum used to tell me I was a scourge. I don't doubt she was right. I wasn't a bad kid, but I was

3

this tiny ball of energy, running everywhere, making a racket, always daydreaming and with zero attention span.

Today, I'm sure that experts would say that I had attention deficit disorder. Back then, I was just a pain in the arse.

Being the youngest of seven was pretty cool. With three big brothers and three big sisters to spoil me, I thought I could get away with just about anything. Maybe because I had to fight for attention, I was talkative and I almost never shut up. To be honest, nothing has really changed in that respect.

I loved growing up in Sligo. As a kid it seemed like a fantastic place, and as I grew older, I still felt the same. Because it has a cathedral, it is technically a small city, but really it is a big town – and in its friendliness and its sense of community, it seemed to have the spirit of a close-knit village.

It felt like everything we needed was right at hand. The local shop was a minute away, as were the video store, the church and my school. We were next door to the sweet shop. I guess kids always think that their home is the centre of the world, but I knew it for a fact.

My infant school was called Scoil Fatima and I started there when I was four. My first day was nerve-wracking. The school was run by nuns, and as I held my mum's hand and queued up to enroll, one of the boys ran out of the line and a nun yelled at him and belted him up the arse. It terrified me: was my mum *really* sure she wanted me to go here?

My first few days were traumatic as I tried to fit in. My brother Finbarr was in the school down the road, and one day I saw him with his nose against a classroom window, pulling faces at me. I burst into tears, and it took my teacher an age to calm me down.

Yet I never had any major problems at school. I was only a little dot, but with my three elder brothers around, nobody was ever going to pick on me, and I made friends easily. I'd drive the teachers spare with talking in class and never concentrating, but they knew I would never be any serious trouble.

Like most Irish women of her generation, my mum was very devout and would be praying to St Anthony, the patron saint of lost stuff, if she mislaid anything. She packed all of us kids off to Mass every Sunday. The services lasted an hour. I'm not sure it's the sort of thing any young kid would enjoy, and we got pretty bored, but our going kept Mum happy.

Living over a café was perfect for a boy who loved his food. I would go home at lunchtime or after school and help myself to fishfingers, mash and beans, or grab a few chips and a can of Coke or Fanta and run upstairs. We even had an ice-cream machine.

It was great to have all that stuff on tap, but every night my mum did us a full cooked dinner. My favourite was a real west of Ireland delicacy: bacon and cabbage with parsley sauce. It is hard to think of any way that life over the café could have been any better...

Well, it could have been a bit warmer. My mum never liked central heating – she thought it might give us asthma – so we had little heaters in our rooms and went off to bed in winter in jumpers, clutching hot-water bottles.

Finbarr had the worst of it. His room down the end of the corridor was so cold we all called it The Fridge.

The situation with the heating wasn't Mum's only old-fashioned way. She also had no time for television, thinking it was a waste of time that would get in the way of our studying, so we only had two channels on our telly: RTE1 and RTE2. It meant that I never got to see most of the shows the other kids at school talked about (although for a while I developed an unhealthy fixation with the Australian teatime soap *Home and Away*).

I never minded the lack of TV too much because we had so much else going on. My family had a few horses in a stable right around the corner from our house, and three nights per week or so I'd go straight from school to the yard and saddle up.

We had a grey pony called Jasper and I absolutely loved him. Feeding Jasper after school with Dad or my brother Liam are some of my very happiest childhood memories. And I've got a lot.

Liam and my sister Denise were great riders and Liam took it upon himself to teach me. He was very patient and would take me off on ten-mile trots on Jasper, but he would often complain that I was daydreaming and didn't listen to what he was telling me.

He was dead right. I didn't.

Liam was so mad into the horses that if it was raining and we couldn't get out to ride, he would fix up an equestrian course in the hallways of our house. He would make jumps out of chairs and hurley sticks and he, Denise and I would attempt the course. I was so tiny that I would normally go flying.

Denise and Liam were pretty serious about riding. They entered national tournaments and local jumping shows such as the Sligo Gymkhana and I would go with them. I would get decked out in my jodhpurs and riding hat and trot around on Jasper in the tiny-tots category. I even won a prize once or twice.

More importantly, Sligo Gymkhana was where I met my first girlfriend. Fran and I were both seven, she was very pretty with blonde hair, and she was as tiny as me. We announced that we were boyfriend and girlfriend and took to strolling around hand-in-hand and pecking each other on the cheek. It was a big deal for us. Everybody else thought it was hilarious.

Fox-hunting was big in our part of Ireland and every St Stephen's Day and New Year's Day, my whole family would saddle up and join in with the hunt. Now I am older, I can see what a cruel sport it is, but as a kid it was incredibly exciting and I looked forward to it.

Because we never watched TV, I had loads of hobbies. I had a spell of being mad for Bruce Lee and took up kung fu. I joined a club, the Green Dragon, run by a man called John Sweeney, the dad of one of my school friends, Jonathan.

I worked through to being a green belt before I got bored of kung fu. I entered a couple of competitions, though; when I was proclaimed King of the Spinning Kick and given a trophy, for doing a big roundhouse kick, I could not have been more proud.

I must have had a little thing for exotic violent men, because my favourite toy was a doll of Mr T from *The A Team*. I loved to pull the string in his back and hear his deep, scornful voice: 'I pity the fool!'

Yet while show jumping, first kisses, kung fu and Mr T passed the time, they all faded to nothing next to my love for Michael Jackson.

I had always loved singing as a little kid. As a nipper, I would belt out a song for my uncles and aunties at family parties, and I had a couple of party pieces: 'Uptown Girl' by Billy Joel and 'I Won't Let the Sun Go Down on Me' by Nik Kershaw (I wonder whatever happened to him?). But when I first heard Jacko, it changed everything.

I was eight years old when the *Bad* album came out and it absolutely transfixed me. Michael Jackson! He just seemed so incredible, so brilliant at everything he did. He had this amazing aura, like he had beamed down to Earth from a different planet, and I totally worshipped him.

He took over my little life. For months I played *Bad* to death, over and over, until I knew it by heart. Every inch of the door and walls in my bedroom was covered in Michael pictures. I wrapped my fingers in bandages like him and took to parading around in one white glove.

Even this wasn't enough for me. Seven doors down the road from us was a gentleman's tailor, Horan's, the only place in Sligo that sold hats. I would go in there, try them on and perfect my Michael dance routines, grabbing my crotch and moonwalking for the ladies who worked in the shop. They all laughed their heads off.

My favourite song from *Bad* was the huge ballad 'Man in the Mirror'. I had a video of Michael singing it at a stadium show, in front of thousands of people who were holding up lighters like a city of twinkling lights. I must have watched it a thousand times. In fact, that might be an underestimate.

I studied that video like a set text and sang along with Michael's every note. I had all of his quirky little vocal tics and hiccups down to a tee. I'd make my sisters be my audience and at first they would be falling around laughing, but then they would stop chuckling and tell me: 'Jesus, Shane, you're really good!'

I suppose that what I was doing was basically karaoke, but I had it spot-on and it was note-perfect. I dragged my mum in to watch the 'Man in the Mirror' video and told her, 'That's what I want to do when I grow up – I want to be like him.' She smiled, humoured me and told me that I had to keep studying in case it didn't work out.

In truth, Mum's warning was timely because I wasn't doing great in school. By now I had left Scoil Fatima for St John's National School, then at twelve I went on to the big local all-boys secondary school, Summerhill College. It was fair to say that I was not setting the place alight.

The Filan family had always been academic. All my brothers and sisters had been straight-A and -B students and the older ones were by now leaving for university and doing some serious heavyweight studying. Peter was training to be a doctor; Finbarr was on his way to becoming an engineer. They had all worked hard and sailed through their exams.

I was showing every sign of not following in their footsteps. I wasn't a bad pupil, or particularly disruptive, but I found it impossible to concentrate in class. I would be daydreaming and a million miles away, or else getting told off for talking. The teachers even called my parents in to have a little chat about my shortcomings.

The problem was that none of the subjects really interested me. I was no good at languages, even my own. I didn't mind maths, accountancy and even home economics, but most of the time I would be away in my own little world, imagining being on a stage singing to thousands.

It wasn't like I thought it could seriously happen. I knew that realistically I would never be like Michael Jackson. But in the back of my head there was a different, nervous but insistent voice, nagging away at me with some siren words: 'Look, it happened to him. Why *shouldn't* it happen for you?'

Outside of school, everything was going grand. As I headed towards my teens, like any boy I began to grow interested in girls, although going to all-boys schools made it difficult to meet them. Having broken Fran's heart (or did she break mine? I can't remember…), I would have been about eleven when I decided to try love again.

Her name was Orla and our mums knew each other through taking their kids to Irish dancing. My sister Mairead was big into it. Orla and her mum would come round to visit us, and Orla and I would sneak off to far corners of the house, to hold hands and kiss.

Orla was my 'girlfriend' for about a year. We probably only met four times, because her mum didn't call in all that often, but I liked her and it felt cool to have a girlfriend. She was about eighteen months younger than me, so it was textbook puppy love.

About six months into our relationship, Orla and I decided to try French kissing, like we had seen on *Dallas*. We planned it carefully, but as soon as our open mouths clamped together, we were wide-eyed with horror: 'Euurgh! What was *that*?' We went straight back to kissing on the lips. It just seemed nicer, somehow.

Orla's and my relationship dwindled to a close but I was keen to meet more girls, so I started going with Mum and Mairead to Mairead's Irish dancing championships. The girls there were beautiful, done up to the nines, and I would run around trying to chat them up. I had the gift of the gab so some of them would talk with me, but a lot were put off by the fact that I barely came up to their shoulder.

At home, I was really keen to start working in the café. All of my brothers and sisters had passed through there – Finbarr was a great cook, and Denise was very organized and helped to run the place. I wasn't really old enough to wait tables yet but I would get sent out on errands.

'Shane! Can you get some peas and some curry sauce?' my dad would yell, and I'd be off, grabbing a handful of coins from the till and running between the three local shops to see who had them. I always hoped that Cosgrove's, the grocers over the road, could help me out, as the other two stores were a slog up a steep hill.

I liked doing the errands because it gave me a chance to rob the till. If I was going out to buy a 60p tub of curry sauce, I would take a fiver, and when I came back I'd put £2 back in the till and keep the rest for myself. I never took much and I wouldn't have dared to take notes, but these little infusions of illicit cash came in handy for sweet money.

Because I kept my pilfering small and I was sneaky about it, I fondly imagined I was getting away with it. It wasn't until years later that I learned my parents had known about it all along, and just weren't that bothered.

So by the time I was twelve, life was grand and I could not have been much more content with my lot. The only cloud was my continued mediocre academic performance. I came to dread parents' evenings, when my parents would go to Summerhill College to be told how I never paid attention in class and had a string of demerits to my name because I never shut up.

It was getting to be a pressure on me, because with all of my older siblings being such high achievers, it was starting to look like I was going to be the black sheep of the family – or, more honestly, the runt of the litter.

I felt this even more because I was still so tiny. I longed to be like my brothers, big and strong and playing rugby, but I was a little ferret. I felt people didn't take me seriously because of it. My mum always said a growth spurt would come, but I knew secretly she was worried that I was such a midget.

Thinking back, I guess what I needed was a clue to my direction in life, a confidence boost, a chance to discover something that I was really good at. I got it.

My drama teacher at school was called Mr McEvoy: Dave McEvoy. I didn't get on with a lot of the teachers, who correctly thought I was an annoying little shit who wouldn't keep his mouth shut, but Dave was kind and laid-back and easy to talk to. He also loved music and it didn't take me long to bond with him.

Dave was the person who organized and staged the musical theatre productions at Summerhill College, together with a very posh lady named Mrs Fitzpatrick, and he asked me to get involved and go to rehearsals. To my delight, he said he thought I was somebody who could be really good on the stage.

Unlike English, science or metalwork, singing was something that I knew I was good at (after all, I was definitely Sligo's leading exponent of Michael Jackson karaoke). I got a buzz from hanging out at the after-school theatre classes and for the first time I began to feel I might have found my niche.

I was saying this to Finbarr at home one afternoon and my brother happily agreed: 'Sure, you're a great singer!' But he went further. He had heard that a local theatre group, the Hawks Well Theatre, was auditioning for actors and singers to appear in their musicals. Why didn't I give it a go?

Well, why didn't I? I had nothing to lose.

Hawks Well Theatre was run by a very friendly, driven and formidable woman in her thirties called Mary McDonagh. She was the producer, director, choreographer, and pretty much everything else. I went down to meet her, did a little sketch and a song for her, and she told me that I was in.

I wasn't the only local boy who had gone down to audition for her. There was also a lad named Kian Egan.

Kian was at Summerhill College too, but I didn't know him very well. Although he was a lot taller than me – as were most people – he was in the year below me, so although I had seen him around town and in the school corridors, we hadn't really talked. That all changed as we hung out together at Hawks Well.

Kian wasn't really into school but, unlike me, he was great at English and always won the school poetry competitions. His big thing was rock music. He loved bands like Green Day and Metallica and was in his own metal band named Skrod (anyone who speaks Gaelic will know how rude that is).

This meant he was horrified by my own musical tastes. I had always been about pop, and specifically boy bands: New Kids on the Block and Kris Kross (I even wore my jeans backwards in honour of the latter pair). Take That were just emerging and I loved them from the start.

Kian thought this really wasn't cool at all.

But he and I got on well and bonded over our love of drama and singing. In the run up to Christmas, 1991, Hawks Well was putting on a performance of *Grease*, the John Travolta and Olivia Newton-John musical. It was a full adult production but it had a chorus of teenagers, so Kian and I assumed we would be in that.

It turned out that Mary had other plans for us. She had thought that Kian and I had something about us when we auditioned, so she wrote in a little scene just for us, telling us we were to play Danny and Kenickie's younger brothers. We were quite surprised but it was exciting.

Kian and I had a little scene in the first half where we walked onstage like little mini-Danny Zukos in blue jeans and white T-shirts with slicked-back hair, bumped into two girls and went off with them. It was all very cute.

Right after the interval, I reappeared onstage with one of the girls, Olwyn, who played a character called Cherry. Our dialogue went something like this:

Me: Hey, Cherry, can I carry your books?
Olwyn:    But I don't have any books!
Me: Do you want to go for a walk?
Olwyn:    OK!
Me: Let's go together!

Then the two of us would sing 'We Go Together', the closing song from the movie. Mary explained that on the night we would do it with a live band, with microphones clipped to us, which sounded terrifying but cool. For six weeks, I went down to the Hawks Well after school and rehearsed the arse off that scene.

At rehearsals Kian and I hung out with the kids in the chorus, one of whom was Kian's cousin, a girl named Gillian Walsh. She was two months older than me, had long, curly, strawberry blonde hair and was very pretty and easy to talk to. She stood out to me, and any chance I got, I'd be running over and chatting with her.

On the first night of our week-long run, I felt sick with nerves. The Hawks Well was a proper theatre: it had a double balcony and it held 400 people, and as I stood by the side of the stage waiting to go on, I knew every seat in the house was full. I thought I was going to faint.

When we walked out, the heat of the lights and the noise of the audience hit me and I felt like I couldn't breathe. Somehow I managed to get my lines out, but when the band struck up for the song I hit my stride and we belted out 'We Go Together' pretty well.

We must have looked comical – I was three feet tall and serenading a girl a foot bigger than me – but at the end, there was a roar of applause. The clapping went on for an age. Some people were even standing up! As I stood there, shocked, soaking it all in, one thought was going through my head.

*Yes! This is what I want!* It was the first time I had ever stood on a stage, the first time I had sung in front of a crowd, and I loved it. Afterwards my mum and dad and brothers and sisters took it in turns to tell me how good I was. I lapped up every word.

The applause wasn't the only thing I had liked about the production, though. Gillian had left a mark on my impressionable young mind, and when Kian and I went to see her in another Hawks Well Theatre show, *The Pajama Game*, shortly after my *Grease* triumph, I asked him a favour: 'Can you fix me up with your cousin?'

All credit to Kian, he didn't waste any time. He vanished backstage in the interval to ask Gillian if she would go on a date with me, and re-emerged with the good news that she would. The second half of *The Pajama Game* passed in a blur of excitement for me. It wasn't down to the script.

That weekend, Gillian and I went to a teenage disco called Dino's and had a few soft drinks, a bit of a bop and, at the end, a slow dance and even a bit of a snog. That was it: I was thirteen and I had a new girlfriend. Life was good!

Dave McEvoy from the school drama group had seen me in *Grease* and asked me if I'd be in his next musical. It was to be *Annie Get Your Gun* and because we were an all-boys school, I sang in the chorus and played a girl called Jessie, in a floral dress with a bonnet over my hair, which was tied up in a bun.

That was just a bit of a hoot, but things got more serious when Dave and Mrs Fitzpatrick asked me to audition to be in *Oliver!* and I got the part of the Artful Dodger. It was a proper production, with teachers playing the older roles like Fagin, and I was so excited to get the script. My main thing was still singing, but I loved getting into the acting aspect of it as well.

We did *Oliver!* in front of the whole school and it went great. Naturally, not everybody loved it. Some of the lads in school thought acting in shows was poofy, and enjoyed slagging me off: 'Look at yer fella, dressing up and singing, and being into boy bands!' Oddly enough, it didn't bother me at all.

I was more concerned with what the girls thought. Being the Artful Dodger was the second time I had stood on a stage getting cheered, and I couldn't help noticing just how many girls were into it. Suddenly they were paying me a lot more attention. It was a major confidence boost.

My fling with Gillian had fizzled out after a few weeks and so I started to try to play the field. My role model in this was my eldest brother, Peter, who was still training to be a doctor and was big into his clothes and image. He was always bringing attractive girlfriends home (I used to look forward to them) and I longed to be like him.

I had a simple rule of thumb: I would go after the most attractive girl in the room. I was still a little short-arse so a lot of them didn't want to know, despite my new status as mini-star of the local shows. Rejection never bothered me too much; I would just bounce back, and on to the next one.

Yet I was oddly moral about it all, probably because of how special my mum and dad's relationship was. If I was dating a girl, I would never see somebody else at the same time: it just felt wrong. I would tell my girlfriend, 'It's not working out...' and be snogging the face off her best friend five minutes later.

At home I had started serving tables in the café, which I really enjoyed. I used to like giving liver and onions to the old fellas who came in every day and always sat at the same table. I also got really into cleaning the place when it was closed, for some reason. You could see your face in the floor when I had finished it.

It was like an obsessive compulsive disorder (not that we had heard of the phrase OCD in those days). I would start off cleaning the tables, then have to do the floors, then the pots and finally the walls. By the time I had finished, the whole Carlton would reek of Jif.

Freakish, I know – yet it is something I have carried through to my adult life.

After the success of the Hawks Well Theatre production of *Grease*, my school decided to do the same show. This time I was promoted to Kenickie, and together with Kian and a few other lads we made up the T-Birds.

We wore leather jackets, slicked our hair back and sang all those great songs from *Grease* like some sort of 1950s boy band. It got a lot of attention locally, a few girls screamed at us onstage, and it was a real blast.

It was around that time that a lad called Mark Feehily introduced himself to me.

I knew who Mark was. He was in the year below me at Summerhill College, like Kian, and he had been knocking around the musicals – he had been in *Annie Get Your Gun* and in the chorus of *Grease*. But we hadn't really spoken until he came up and said hi.

Mark was a lot shyer and more self-conscious than Kian and me, but I thought he had balls of steel. I had seen him in school talent shows, which I would never have dared to do, belting out Mariah Carey songs. He had this amazing R&B/soul voice, and he never seemed to miss a note.

Mark and I quickly became great mates and started hanging out at each other's houses. Our new friendship was totally based on singing – we would watch music videos and sing along and harmonize to them. Most people might have thought it was weird but we loved doing it.

He also shared my own musical tastes, which had been disgusting Kian more than ever of late. I was big into Take That by now, and Boyzone; it wasn't that I thought Boyzone were particularly cool, like Take That were, but I loved the fact that they were Irish and they had made it big. It gave me an incentive and made me think, *If they can do it, why can't we? Why can't I?*

Yet my big group at the time was the Backstreet Boys. As soon as they came along, I loved them in a way that I hadn't loved anyone since Michael Jackson.

It's always hard to say exactly why you worship some music, but I thought the Backstreet Boys had everything. Their songs were incredible, they had great melodies and harmonies, and I loved their dress sense. I adored Brian Littrell's voice – plus, of course, they were American, which made them glamorous and untouchable.

Being into boy bands still wasn't hip, but in truth I loved them so much that I didn't really care what anyone else thought. In any case, it wasn't like I lived for them; I was still also doing the things that any normal teenage boy would do. Like chasing girls and drinking.

My first taste of alcohol was cider with some friends in the woods near Sligo one school holiday. After I had drunk it, I was knocked sideways: pretty ropey! I wasn't a big beer drinker, but around the age of sixteen I developed a taste for alcopops like Hooch and Corky's.

I would hang out with my three best mates, Paul, Keith and Brian (who went by the nickname of Brig), in a bar called the Embassy Rooms, which had a snooker hall downstairs. We would always congregate around table seven. We were underage, so I had a fake ID card with my sister's boyfriend's details and my picture.

We would play a few frames of snooker then Mark, Kian and Gillian would join us and we would go into Equinox nightclub up the road. It was only 100 yards away and it was always a nervous walk. I never knew if I would get past the bouncer on the door with my fake ID.

When I did – great! When I didn't, I'd shrug and head for the late-night fast-food place on the same street, the 4 Lights, for their Big 4 Special. All our nights out finished up there. If I woke up in the night hungover, I would sneak down to the café and bury a few cans of Club Orange.

Getting into the clubs got a lot easier when my long-awaited growth spurt finally arrived. I had always loved sports, but now I got big into playing rugby and became a regular for Sligo's under-sixteens and then the under-eighteen team. Then I made it into the Connaught provincial under-eighteen team. I was a number 10 and they told me I had a great left boot.

But even though I enjoyed the craic of a good game of rugby, music was still my first love. Mark and I would spend our downtime hanging out together and singing Backstreet Boys songs, working out all the harmonies. We would talk and fantasize together, and dream of 'doing a Boyzone': becoming pop stars and breaking free of our small-town upbringings to make a career out of doing what we loved.

There was a TV show at that time called *Go for It*, which let members of the public get up and do a song, and Mark used to talk about going on that. And then one day, I just came out with it while I was talking to Mark.

'You know what we should do? We should start a boy band.'

# 2

# THE BOYS IN THE BAND

Mark was into the idea from the start. I knew he would be. We were so much on the same wavelength and on the same page when it came to music. Once we had decided what it was we wanted to do, we set about choosing the other members.

We knew we wanted Kian in the group. He was a great performer and he had the look. We could see only one major setback – he hated boy bands.

As I expected, when I first asked Kian, he couldn't decide whether to be horrified or fall about laughing. By now he had left Skrod behind and was in a different metal band named Pyromania. In fact, I think he was in three bands at the same time. 'Shane,' he asked me frankly, 'are you off your f\*\*king rocker?'

This changed when I played him some Backstreet Boys. Kian is a rocker at heart but so is Max Martin, the songwriting and producing genius behind the Backstreets, and Kian could hear things in their music that he loved.

Plus, like me, he had developed a taste for girls screaming at him in the T-Birds. Yep, he was in.

We quickly recruited three other members. Kian brought in Graham Keighron, a neighbour of his who was two or three years older than us. Graham was a cool lad; he loved singing and idolized the Backstreet Boys, particularly AJ, which endeared him to me straight away.

Michael Garrett was a friend who went by the nickname of Miggles. He was in all the plays with us and was a tall, handsome guy who just oozed confidence. To be honest, Miggles wasn't the best singer out of us, but he looked fantastic and girls loved him.

Derek Lacey was in my year at school and we used to hang around town together. He had been a stagehand when we did *Grease* at school but he could also sing a bit and with his little goatee beard he looked like a model, which worked for us. Even in those days, I think we knew what ticked the boxes.

I can't remember who suggested calling ourselves Six As One. It certainly wasn't me. I think at the time we knew it wasn't the best name in the world, but we went with it. We didn't really have any plans, or any idea what we would do next – until Mary McDonagh took a hand.

It's amazing, thinking back, just what a big part *Grease* played in our lives at that time! Around then, Mary was after staging another production of it at the Hawks Well, and this time I got the big part, the Travolta role: Danny Zuko. Kian played Kenickie and Gillian was Frenchie.

Mary also had an interesting suggestion for us. Why didn't our new band come on and do two songs during the interval at the Hawks Well show?

She didn't need to ask us twice. Six As One vanished off to Graham's house for some fevered practice. We also took to rehearsing in the Carlton Café when it was closed, as the high ceiling and tiles gave it some great acoustics.

To be honest, we put just as much thought into what we were going to wear for the gig. We all used to go to a local clothes shop, EJ Menswear, and the guy who ran it, Eamonn Cunningham, gave us a load of free stuff for the show.

In fact, our entire plan for the gig was basically to be the Irish Backstreet Boys: the Backstreet Boys, Sligo division. Our set consisted of two Backstreets' songs: 'I'll Never Break Your Heart' and 'We've Got It Goin' On'.

So when the *Grease* interval came around, I ran backstage to get out of my Danny Zuko costume and into my Brian Littrell gear, and we all waited in the wings. Mary came onstage and introduced the new local boy band, Six As One... and the screaming started.

It was wild. Word had clearly got around about our previous T-Birds turn, because the Hawks Well was packed out with girls and they were screaming their heads off. Were they taking the piss? Being ironic? They didn't seem to be!

The two songs went down fantastic, and to be honest, Danny Zuko went through the second half of *Grease* in a bit of a daze. After the show, the six of us wandered back out to the front of the theatre to see our parents and the foyer was full of girls, waiting for us, yelling out and even asking for our autographs.

It was the most exciting thing that had ever happened to me. It was like we were proper pop stars: my head was spinning. When we got home that night, all I could think was, 'Jeez – we're famous!' For the first time, suddenly, our dream felt possible. If Sligo liked us this much, maybe other places in Ireland might do as well?

The short gig had been Mary McDonagh's idea, but she had been just as taken aback as us by the hysterical reaction we'd received. She could see that Six As One had got something going on, and she suggested that we should do a full show at the Hawks Well in our own right.

For the next few weeks, the six of us rehearsed every minute we had, learning a whole load of cover versions including Take That's 'Everything Changes' and 'Relight My Fire'. Mary and a guy from the Hawks Well, Stefan, helped us to choreograph a few basic dance routines. We were so serious and intense about the whole thing, and the show went down so well – we were basically singing into a wall of screams.

It was amazing. Deep down, I know we were all thinking: *Is this really happening? Is it a dream?*

My romantic life had also been looking up. By now I was sixteen, and I had actually managed to stay with one girlfriend for more than a few days. Her name was Helena, and she was a lovely girl; she even came home to meet my parents. She was one of Gillian's best friends, and still is.

Yet after a good few months together, Helena and I split up and suddenly there I was: young, free and single again. With my new-found local fame I could probably have enjoyed a few flings, but it didn't work out that way. Instead, I was finding myself more and more drawn to Gillian.

I had always really liked Kian's cousin, and increasingly I was noticing how well she dressed, what a good dancer she was, how pretty she looked. We were still going to Equinox regularly with Kian, Mark and the gang, and often I would spend the whole evening chatting with Gillian. We would always look for each other.

Nothing happened between us, partly because at the time I still thought she was just a really good friend, but largely due to the fact that Gillian had a boyfriend on the other side of Sligo. Sometimes she would vanish halfway through the evening to go to see him. When she had gone, I would really miss her.

I guess sometimes things are so close at hand that you can't see them. One Friday night at Equinox, Gillian and I spent all night talking, messing around and drinking Sex on the Beach cocktails. Lying in my bed that night above the café, my head was so full of her that I couldn't fall asleep. It was five in the morning and I was still lying there awake, with my eyes like saucers, thinking about Gillian.

The next day I was walking through town with a friend and by chance we bumped into her. I can still picture what she was wearing: maroon corduroy trousers and a pair of runners. As I went over to say hello, I started sweating; my heart was pounding, and I could hardly speak.

*What was happening here?*

Easy: I was falling in love. Suddenly, I was totally besotted with Gillian. We had been great mates for five years, but now I didn't want to be mates any more – I wanted far, far more than that. But I didn't dare say anything to her. After all, she had a boyfriend.

After the success of our full gig at the Hawks Well, Mary had a few ideas to take Six As One forward. One was that she thought we shouldn't be called Six As One. Mary suggested we become IOYOU (pronounced 'I owe you'). I wasn't sure this was an improvement – in fact, I thought it was shite – but I had no better ideas, so IOYOU it was.

Mary also asked us to go into a local recording studio and make a CD single. F\*\*k, yeah! Even a few weeks ago, the idea of being in a band and playing gigs had seemed like walking on the moon – now, here we were making a record!

It seemed important that we didn't just do cover versions so Mark and I started trying to write our first song. It was called 'Together Girl Forever' and it was a love song. Well, actually, it was a song about Gillian.

After I fell in love, I hadn't dared to say a word to Gillian about how I felt, but I hadn't stopped going on about her to the other lads in the band, particularly poor Mark. He and I sat on a bench in Peace Park, by Sligo Cathedral, writing lyrics for 'Together Girl Forever'.

Mark shoved the pen and paper at me. 'You write it!' he told me. 'You're the one that likes her!'

'Dreams are for believing and some day they will come true,' I wrote. 'That we would be together, no one else but me and you…' It felt good and cathartic to write it all down.

We recorded it in a poky little home studio in Sligo and it was such an adventure as the six of us crammed in there. It was the first time we had worn headphones and sung into mics, and we all kept basically asking each other the same thing: 'Do I *really* sound like that? Jesus!'

We did 'Together Girl Forever', 'Everlasting Love', which Mark had written, and a song with Graham doing a rap. Mary arranged a photo session for the sleeve picture in The Mall, the local art centre, and we all got special boy band haircuts. EJs fitted us out with some black suits.

When we got the CD a couple of weeks later – 'Together Girl

Forever' by IOYOU – I couldn't stop looking at it, and played it to death. In truth, it was pretty simple, basic music, but it seemed such a big deal. I remember thinking, *If we don't get any further, at least we've done this.* The single went on sale in The Record Room, the local record shop, and about 100 people bought it in the first few days, the vast majority of whom were related to us. We dared to dream that it might make the Irish chart but in the end it sold about 1,000 copies, nearly all in Sligo.

We did a couple of little gigs around Sligo. At the same time, I was still playing rugby and even got invited to trials to play for Ireland at youth level. However, it clashed with an IOYOU gig. There was only going to be one winner, and it wasn't rugby.

Mary managed to get IOYOU on the telly. That Christmas we went to the local hospital and sang a cappella Backstreet Boys' songs to sick kids to try to cheer them up. An evening news programme, *Nationwide*, filmed us, so we got twenty seconds on national TV.

This was all grand and pretty exciting but at the same time I knew I had decisions to make about my future. Coming up to my seventeenth birthday in 1996, I left school. In line with my usual academic mediocrity, I had to retake my leaving certificate.

Maths and computer studies were the only subjects I was any good at, and my sister Yvonne, who was by now a fully qualified teacher, took me in hand and gave me extra grinds. She worked me hard and the night before my maths exam we were up until the early hours.

I went into the exam after only three or four hours' sleep and did great: I got an A, which was rare for me and totally down to Yvonne. At least it meant that I had a couple more options as I tried to work out what to do with my life.

My mum and dad had always been supportive of my music and acting but I knew they'd like me to get a trade under my belt. IOYOU was fun but small-scale and we were making no money out of it. I knew that a boy band was what I wanted to do more than anything, but in my heart I also knew it was a fantasy.

I had to study or get a job.

I decided that if I was going to college, I should spread my wings and leave Sligo. I applied to, and got accepted by, the Limerick Institute of Technology, 140 miles away, to study business and accountancy.

In truth, I was going reluctantly. I still longed to make a go of music, and I was totally hung up on Gillian. But she was with her boyfriend and seemed completely oblivious to how I felt, so I just figured it was not to be: I'd go off to college and meet somebody else.

Brig, my best mate from school, was also going to Limerick IT and at first it was quite exciting moving down there together. We shared a room in a house that we rented with some older students from Cork, and set out to see what Limerick had to offer.

It didn't have a lot. Or rather, it probably did, but I didn't want it. I thought my course was boring and I didn't like the lectures, so I stopped going to them. Instead, I stuck posters of the Backstreet Boys up in our room and dreamed about making the band work.

I made a few friends and Brig and I played a lot of pool in the student union but I never felt at home in Limerick. I didn't meet any nice girls, I was homesick and, in truth, I was still missing Gillian like mad. It felt like a mistake – I didn't want to be an accountant – and after six months, I dropped out.

I moved back home and promised my mum that I would get a job and also enroll in Sligo to do a different course. I signed up at a local college to start a business and computing degree the following autumn and a great mate of mine, Paul Keaveney, got me a job in a business supplies store called Buckley's.

Buckley's was OK, in fact I quite liked it, and I spent my time moving boxes of nails, sweeping up and inputting orders on the computer. Yet it always felt like a stopgap, and I couldn't help telling my colleagues all about how I was in a band that, you never knew, might make it one day.

Life fell into a routine, but one bit of excitement came with the news that the Backstreet Boys were touring and were coming to Dublin. When the tickets went on sale, Kian and I queued outside Star Records from five in the morning to buy them.

It was six months away, but it was something to look forward to.

We definitely needed a boost to our spirits because IOYOU had slipped into a hiatus. After the excitement of the gigs, the single and the TV appearance, nothing was happening. Mary had done a lot for us but we weren't sure where the band was going next.

Mary had given us a formal management contract to sign but we weren't sure about it. Because we were so young, we had shown it to our parents. Some of them liked it, some of them didn't. My mum thought we should get legal advice.

What we really wanted, of course, was to be managed by a proper music-industry big-hitter, a major name like that guy in Dublin, Louis Walsh, who had created Boyzone and built them up from nowhere. Obviously, we knew that was too much to hope for; it wouldn't happen in a million years.

I was in the pub with the other lads one night, bemoaning the fact the band was going nowhere, when Derek said that Gillian had broken up with her boyfriend.

Derek dropped it into the conversation as casually as if he had made an offhand comment about the weather, but as soon as he said it, I was in shock. I felt jittery, nervous: the butterflies in my stomach were in danger of being burnt by the fireworks that were going off next to them.

My mouth had gone dry and I felt as if I couldn't speak, but I gave it a go: 'Really? Is that right?'

'For sure,' nodded Derek. 'They're properly over.'

Wow! It was the best news that I could have heard, and yet a part of me was thinking, *Oh God, here we go again*. Over the past six months I had been trying to get over Gillian, accepting that I had no chance. Now, suddenly, I was in turmoil again.

As it happened, I didn't bump into her around town for the next few weeks. Instead, I knuckled down to my day job at Buckley's and hanging out with Kian and Mark. Mary's contract was still sitting around, unsigned.

My sister Mairead was by now in college in Dublin and every few weeks I would go up and stay with her in her apartment. One weekend at the start of 1998, Kian came with me. We were sitting around, mildly hungover, in the morning, when Mairead's phone rang.

It was my mum – for me.

'Shane, listen,' she began. 'I've been on the phone with that Louis Walsh, who manages Boyzone, and...'

*What? Why was she taking the piss like this?*

I wasn't in the habit of putting the phone down on my mum, but that was what I did. She rang straight back.

'Shane, I'm not joking. I've been trying to get him for months and last night I finally talked to him about your band. You're meeting him in Dublin tonight!'

Again – *what*? I had a meeting with Boyzone manager Louis Walsh, one of the most important men in the whole Irish pop business – and my mum had fixed it up? I listened as she filled me in.

Like any mother, Mum wanted the best for her son. She had misgivings about the management contract Mary McDonagh had offered IOYOU, and she had taken them right to the top. She had made it her mission to talk to Louis Walsh – and she was armed with a very special weapon.

She came from the same village as Louis. The MacNicholases and the Walshes were both from Kiltimagh in County Mayo. She had never met him, but apparently that hadn't stopped her from calling his office daily for weeks and weeks.

He had never got back to her but my mum is nothing if not persistent. When he finally picked up, she had introduced herself as Mae MacNicholas from Kiltimagh, and explained that her son was in a Sligo boy band named IOYOU.

'Oh, I've heard of them,' Louis had told her. He had seen our twenty-second TV appearance on *Nationwide*!

As my mum rattled through this bizarre tale, my heart was racing. I would never even have dared try to get in touch with Louis Walsh and my mum had just gone and done it, as casual as you like. He had told her he was way too busy with Boyzone to manage another band, but he was happy to have a chat with us.

But it was her last line that was the killer: 'You're meeting him tonight in some place called the Pod!'

When I put the phone down for the second time, I felt as if I was going through a bizarre out-of-body experience. Kian was just as shocked. We spent the day running around Dublin trying to buy the right clothes to meet Boyzone's manager. (We bought jackets and polo necks – exactly what Boyzone would wear!) The Pod was Dublin's trendiest nightclub, where bands like U2 and hip DJs such as Gerry Ryan and Dave Fanning would hang out. Kian and I rocked up trying to look cool but feeling shit-scared. We gave our names and were asked to wait.

I had never seen so much as a photo of Louis Walsh before and had no idea what he looked like. I was imagining a guy like Michael Jackson's manager: very cool, tanned, long hair tied in a ponytail and wearing a leather jacket.

So I was incredibly surprised when this ordinary-looking little fella popped up in front of us, all skinny and chirpy in a checked shirt and jeans, grinning away, holding out his hand to be shaken and talking at us nineteen-to-the-dozen.

As we followed him upstairs to the Chocolate Bar, the Pod's VIP area, Kian and I arched our eyebrows behind his back and silently mouthed the same question: 'Is *this* Louis Walsh? *Really?*'

Yet as Louis sat us down and got us a beer, he could not have been easier to talk to – except that he spoke so fast, we could hardly tell a word he was saying.

Louis told us he had seen us on the telly and had heard that we were good singers. We had brought a copy of the IOYOU CD along, and he straight away put his finger over one of the boys on the cover and said, 'Ah, six is too many – five is a lot better.'

Shit! We were sitting with the most important – actually, the only – music-industry person we had ever met, he was giving us advice, and it was the last thing we wanted to hear. But Kian and I felt lucky to be there, and when Shane Lynch and Keith Duffy from Boyzone wandered into the bar and Louis introduced us, our eyes were on stalks.

*Had we crossed a line into a magic kingdom? Was this really happening?*

Louis talked to us, or at us, for about an hour then headed off, telling us to enjoy the rest of the night in the Pod and to keep in touch. Kian and I were buzzing from meeting him and had a few beers. In fact, the pair of us got bullets, as we say in Sligo.

Louis had said that he would give us any help he could, and Kian and I went back home and told the other lads what he had said about having six in the band. We weren't sure if we would hear from him again, which was why I was amazed a week later when he phoned to invite me to Ronan Keating's twenty-first-birthday party.

Naturally I was mad excited about this. Ronan was like pop royalty in Ireland – and Britain – at the time. Louis said there were one or two people he'd like me to meet and I could take a friend. Kian couldn't make it so I asked Miggles, because I knew he was a good talker.

The Pod was definitely the place to be in Dublin at the time and that was where Ronan's party was. My mum and dad gave me a bit of money and, like the fashion victim I was, I spent the day before in Grafton Street buying my outfit: a grey jacket, polo neck, combat trousers and ankle boots.

There was a weird trend in Dublin for hipsters to wear specs with clear lenses. I knew Ronan had some so I thought that I had better wear some to his bash, too. God knows what I was thinking of.

Well, actually, I do know. I was thinking, *I might be a bag of nerves, but at least I can look cool.*

The party was crazy. Ronan and his fiancée Yvonne made an entrance on a Harley-Davidson, dressed as Danny and Sandy from *Grease* (*Grease* again!). Louis introduced Miggles and me to a mate of his, Brian, who had managed bands, and we tried to make a good impression on him just in case – you never knew – he wanted to manage us.

Admittedly, my bar was set low – Equinox in Sligo – but it was the most glamorous night I had ever seen. A lot of the Irish football team were there, and I got to talk to Ronan for about a minute. At one point I went to the toilet and Ken Doherty, the snooker player, was there, having a slash.

I stood at the next urinal to him and was pissing away when I heard a Geordie guy on the other side of me say, 'Hello, Ken, how are you doing?' I glanced over at him. It was Alan Shearer.

At the end of the night, Louis told me he would be in touch. I could only hope that he meant it.

It turned out that he did.

A week later, I was hanging out with Kian, Mark and the lads in a bar named MJ Carr's on the outskirts of Sligo. My phone rang.

'Shane, Shane, hi, this is Louis! How you doing? Look, the thing is this...'

It was Louis, talking even faster than usual, and in the noisy bar I couldn't hear a word he was saying. I jumped up from my seat and ran out to the corridor. 'Sorry, Louis, can you say that again?'

'I was saying, can you get to Dublin next weekend?'

'Yes. Why?'

'You're supporting the Backstreet Boys.'

# 3

# LOUIS, LOUIS

When somebody gives you the thing that you want, that you need, more than anything else in the world... what do you do? How do you react?

I managed to hold it together, just about, while Louis told me all about it. He had managed to swing us two – two! – nights opening for the Backstreet Boys at the Royal Dublin Society (RDS) venue in Ireland's capital the next weekend: the same shows that Kian and I had got up in the middle of the night to queue to buy tickets for.

When we finished the call, I lost it. The other IOYOU lads had all run into the corridor and gathered around me when they'd heard me say Louis's name. We were screaming, cheering and hugging each other, unable to take it in. I found myself down on my knees, sobbing my heart out for joy.

*We were supporting the Backstreet Boys. We were supporting the Backstreet Boys.*

I said the words over and over to myself. I still didn't believe them.

I also knew exactly who I most wanted to tell. Gillian had a part-time job waitressing in the upstairs restaurant at MJ Carr's.

I sought her out and broke the amazing news. She was as lost for words as I was.

Gillian was due to be working on the night of the first gig and didn't know if she'd be able to get it off. I found her manager and begged her to give Gillian the night off. The boss could see how excited we were and happily agreed.

The next week went by in a blur of intensive, delirious, wild-eyed rehearsals. Kian was by now working in EJ's, as did I occasionally, and Eamonn came through with a load of free Sonnetti and Firetrap gear for us to wear onstage. IOYOU travelled up to Dublin fuelled by equal parts exhilaration and panic.

The first gig was on 17 March, St Patrick's Day, and the night before we all went to the RDS to hang around outside. We looked in a window. The Backstreet Boys had loaded up their gear and were messing about playing basketball in the arena on a portable court.

There they were! That was them! Brian Littrell! Nick Carter, with his floppy blond fringe! I was as excited to see them in the flesh as I was to support them.

Well, that's not quite true. As we stood in the wings the next night, about to run the gauntlet of 8,000 people, I could have heaved my guts. I felt sick with nerves. An American guy, some kind of MC, appeared onstage and yelled, 'Hey, let's all give it up for IOYOU!' There was no way out now.

We did three songs: 'Together Girl Forever', 'Everlasting Love' and 'Pinball Wizard' by The Who, which was our big rock number. We sang them all into a blizzard of screaming. Hardly anybody in the place would have heard of us, but they knew we were Irish lads and they loved us for it.

It was so exhilarating. In the dressing room afterwards I felt like I was glowing with happiness, yet I was also a little scared. I was thinking, *That was so brilliant! I never want this to end – please don't say tomorrow night is the last time we will ever do this...* I tried to put my worries to the back of my mind and enjoy it. It honestly felt like life couldn't get any better. I was wrong. When we arrived the next afternoon to sound-check for the second show, the Backstreet Boys were playing basketball again and invited us to shoot a few hoops with them. It was by far the coolest thing that had ever happened in my young life.

The second night's show was just as thrilling, and afterwards the Backstreet Boys invited us to go to the Pod with them. We went on their tour bus, got ushered past the waiting queues into the club and then headed straight for the VIP room, where Brian, AJ and Kevin hung out and chatted with us.

They say you should never meet your heroes. Well, bollocks to that! The Backstreet Boys were great. On the way back to our B & B that night, I remember thinking, *This sort of thing just doesn't happen. If IOYOU never do anything else, at least we have had these two incredible nights.*

And then Louis told us he wanted to manage us.

He phoned Kian and broke the news as we were on the train back to Sligo after the second Backstreet Boys gig. He explained that the gigs had effectively been an audition for us, and we had passed. When Kian told me, I couldn't believe my ears – or our luck. Jesus! I knew how massive this was.

*Boyzone's manager wants to manage us!*

But there was a catch. Louis told Kian that he still hadn't altered his opinion from what he had said in our very first meeting. Six was too many for the group. He didn't think Derek fitted in, or that he was up to it. He had to go.

Shit. I went from elation to despair in one second. Derek was such a great guy. He was one of my best mates in the band, if not my best.

'No,' I said to Kian. 'We can't do it. Let's try to talk Louis out of it.'

We sat on our hands for a few days in the hope that Louis might change his mind. He phoned Kian again and asked if we had sacked Derek yet. Kian admitted that we hadn't.

'Look,' Louis told him. 'I'm serious about managing you. But you have to do this.'

We were torn. Derek was our friend and we felt like we were betraying him. At the same time, Louis Walsh – LOUIS WALSH! – wanted to manage us and turn us into the next Boyzone. This was our chance of a lifetime; we weren't about to blow it. Kian and I called a band meeting in the sitting room at my house.

Once we were all there, I just came out with it. 'Derek, Louis wants five in the band, and he thinks you're not suited to the group.'

It was horrible. Derek hadn't seen it coming and was just so upset. He started crying, and that set me off too. He didn't say much: what could he say? He got up and walked out of the room. Our friendship finished right there, and I didn't blame him. It was just too much to take.

I had lost somebody who was hugely important in my life. But it wasn't all bad news; I was about to gain a soul mate.

Gillian and I had started seeing each other around Sligo again a few weeks after she and her boyfriend had split. We were hanging out, but we were also both wary. I was nervous and didn't know what to say to her; she was just coming out of a long-term relationship.

I think we both knew how we felt by then, but neither of us dared say. If I plucked up the courage to make an awkward move, Gillian drew back, maybe fearful that she was on the rebound. She still didn't know that I had written 'Together Girl Forever' about her.

A week after the Backstreet Boys gigs, I walked her home from her part-time job at MJ Carr's. She was staying at Helena's, and I went in for a couple of minutes and then said that I would be off and headed back out the front door.

As I turned to say goodbye, Gillian was right behind me, on the step above. She leaned down and kissed me.

My knees buckled beneath me. I honestly don't know how I didn't faint. It was the first time we had kissed since we were twelve and it made me feel like I had never felt before. *Wow!* When we pulled apart, I didn't know what to do.

'I'll call you tomorrow,' I said, trying to play it cool. Cool was the last thing I was feeling. As soon as Gillian closed the door, I virtually exploded with joy.

I ran all the way back to the Carlton, laughing and roaring like a madman. My head was a jumble of wild, euphoric thoughts: *This is it! She is my girlfriend! I've finally got her!*

And I had.

I could not have been more ecstatic at getting together with Gillian – but it almost led to me getting kicked out of the band.

Now Louis was our full-time manager, he was hard at work arranging meetings for us with record labels. He told us the first one was to be with a man from Sony BMG Records, who was flying over from London so that we could audition for him on a Saturday lunchtime at the Westbury Hotel in Dublin.

The guy's name was Simon Cowell.

The night before the audition, I was out in Sligo with Gillian. We were in Equinox drinking Sex on the Beach, as usual. I knew I should really get an early night, but we were having a great time, I didn't want the evening to end, I could sleep it off on the train in the morning... I fell into bed at 2 a.m.

The next morning on the train up to Dublin with the band I was bleary-eyed and thickheaded. I felt like shit. Louis met us at the Westbury and asked why I looked so f\*\*ked. I said I'd had a late night. Louis, understandably, didn't look best pleased.

We had never heard of Simon Cowell. He wasn't famous in those days: he was just a record-label A & R man. But Louis told us that he had turned down the chance to sign Boyzone in their early days, and was now masterminding the career of 5ive, so we knew he was a big deal.

Simon had hired a suite at the Westbury and we introduced ourselves as we filed in. He looked exactly like I imagined a record executive would look: immaculately turned out, very confident, super posh. (I can't claim that I noticed at our first meeting how high he wore his trousers.)

We sang the Backstreet Boys' 'Quit Playing Games (with My Heart)' for him. The cocktails and my lack of sleep caught up with me and I struggled through the song. Simon hardly looked at me. We finished, left, and Louis stayed behind to talk to Simon.

He reappeared a few minutes later. We hardly needed to ask what Simon had thought. Louis had a face like thunder. He stormed up to me... and slapped me in the face.

'What the f\*\*k was that, Shane?' he yelled at me. 'I'll tell you what it was – it was shite! He didn't like you!'

I had never seen Louis like this; never seen him so furious. He was raging at me. Simon had only liked two of us: Kian and Mark. He said he didn't think I was a star. 'I was counting on you!' Louis yelled. 'You had to deliver – and you f\*\*ked it up!'

It was too much. I couldn't cope with this attack. I felt like in three minutes, with one hangover, I had messed up the band; my career; my whole life. I burst into tears.

My crying seemed to abate Louis's anger. It was like a storm had passed over as he looked at me and shook his head.

'Don't panic,' he said. 'I know what to do. Simon has said if I get rid of you and find somebody else, he will come back and see the band again in a few weeks. You can grow your hair long, dye it blond and audition great next time. He will never recognize you. Trust me!'

As plans went, this stupid scheme sounded to me like something that Mr Bean might have dreamed up, but I nodded eagerly. I would give it a go. At least I was still in the band. I had a lifeline.

Far from being put off by this setback, Louis was a man on a mission. He wanted to get some decent material to send to the record labels, and fixed up for us to spend a few days in London recording with a hip new songwriter and producer named Steve Mac.

I sat next to Mark on the flight over. It was the first time either of us had been to London and we were super-excited. We flew in by night, and I remember punching Mark on the shoulder as we gawped out of the window at the metropolis: 'Oh my God, will you look at that! Big Ben!'

Steve Mac had worked with Damage and Boyzone and was a cool guy in a New York Yankees baseball cap who was only a few years older than us. His writing partner, Wayne Hector, was a hip Londoner with a great singing voice. They looked the business and we wanted to impress them.

It was intimidating being in a proper professional studio that made the place in Sligo look like a broom cupboard, but we got into the session. Steve and Wayne listened to us all sing one by one, and then we recorded three songs that they had written: 'Everybody Knows', 'The Good Thing' and 'Forever'.

Steve was giving me at least half of the lead vocals on every song and also handed Mark a lot of leads. He seemed to like our two voices. This was a big confidence boost for me. After the Simon Cowell fiasco, I needed it.

Louis had apparently asked Steve Mac to report back to him with his thoughts on us. I suppose it was another audition that we didn't know about – and once again, we didn't all pass it. When we got back to Sligo, Louis phoned Kian and said he wanted Graham out of the band.

F**k. Not again! This was getting to be a habit, and not one that we liked. Kian was the closest to Graham, and pleaded with Louis to think again. We even put on a gig in Sligo and videoed it to send to Louis, to show him how good Graham was. It was no good: Louis was adamant.

Thankfully, I didn't have to break the news this time. Louis volunteered to do it and phoned Graham, who was half-expecting it. Louis did a very cool thing. He told Graham he thought he wasn't right for the group, but he liked him and he wanted him to be our tour manager (whatever that was).

Graham did an even cooler thing. He agreed. We were all relieved: at least Graham would still be part of the gang and he stayed with us for a bit, unlike poor Derek, who had been totally dumped.

So now Louis had cut two members from the band, were we good to go? Not at all. Our manager had been convinced that six was too many for a boy band; he was equally sure that four was too few. Louis declared that we needed one more member, and arranged auditions to find him.

It may seem odd just how ruthlessly Louis was imposing his vision on the band, and how we all went along with it. But we were wide-eyed kids, culchies from the west of Ireland, and he managed the biggest boy band in Europe. As far as we were concerned, Louis Walsh was God.

We weren't really looking for another lead singer, because we knew by then that Mark's voice and mine gelled well together and sounded special. We just needed someone who sang and danced well and looked great.

The auditions were at The Red Box, a small performance space inside the Pod (in Dublin, in those days, all roads led to the Pod). Louis and the four remaining members of IOYOU sat behind a desk to assess the nervous hopefuls singing for us. The funny thing was, we saw scores of people, but we ended up choosing the first two.

The first guy up was a tall, floppy-haired blond lad named Brian McFadden. He was in a flowery blue short-sleeve shirt, which he made a point of telling us was his dad's. It certainly looked like a dad shirt. He was the image of Nick Carter, and I remember thinking, *Brilliant! He looks like a Backstreet Boy!*

Brian seemed a bit of a headcase, talking non-stop in a thick Dublin accent, but when he stopped yakking and got around to singing, he had a fantastic voice and picked out harmonies with forensic precision, which nobody else in the band could do.

Next was another Dubliner called Nicky Byrne, a sharp fella who had hair like Ronan Keating and carried himself well in his brown corduroy jacket and blue polo-neck sweater. Nicky looked the business and had a cool vibe about him. He sang us Boyzone's 'Father and Son' and his voice was great too.

We saw a load of other people as the day went on, but no one else was as good and all our conversations kept going back to Brian and Nicky. At the end of the auditions, we asked the best four or five people to stay behind so we could interview them to see if we'd get on.

Brian came back in talking 500 words per minute and was a proper up-for-the-craic Dublin lad. He said that he had seen us supporting the Backstreet Boys, and explained that he wanted to leave the boy band he was in and join us to work with Louis Walsh. I thought he was great.

Nicky seemed more laid-back and mature and told us he had been a football goalkeeper who signed to Leeds United and then played for Shelbourne and Cobh Ramblers. He said he was dating Georgina Ahern, the daughter of the Irish Taoiseach, Bertie Ahern.

For some reason Kian decided to give him the third degree.

'If we said you had to give her up for the band, would you?' he demanded.

'No, I wouldn't!' said Nicky, looking like he thought it was as daft a question as I did.

We couldn't decide between Nicky and Brian and we asked them both to come back for a second audition. They sang a few Backstreet Boys' songs with us and were both brilliant again. Kian wasn't sure about Brian. He thought he was mad, but he could see what a great voice he had and how much fun he could be.

We were still going around in circles, trying to choose, when Louis suddenly said: 'Why don't we have both of them?'

Eh? We pointed out that this would take us back to six members – which Louis had thought was too many.

'Yes,' said Louis. 'We'll include them both and then take a vote on the final five.'

This was very clever by Louis. We had an inkling that he wanted Michael out of the band. He didn't always like his attitude, and Steve Mac had not been as keen on Miggles's voice in the studio as he was on the rest of us. But Louis was smart. He let us decide for ourselves.

Brian and Nicky agreed to move to Sligo for a few weeks. Brian came to stay with me. Nicky was staying with Michael, but he could see how things were going and felt awkward, so we made up some excuse why he should crash over the café, too.

The final nail in Miggles's coffin was an IOYOU audition for Virgin Records in Dublin. Michael missed the train and was late, which infuriated Louis, and when he finally arrived he went on and on about the Spice Girls, who were Virgin's big act at the time.

Michael knew the way the wind was blowing and was desperate to hang in there, but as he gabbled on and on, it came over as trying too hard. Louis was rolling his eyes, and although we sang five a cappella songs really well, Virgin passed on us.

It all had to come to a head, and we had the decisive band meeting a few days later at the Pod. Louis said the vote was between Nicky, Brian and Michael and then handed over to Graham – who, let's face it, knew all about being cut from the band.

'Everybody wants Brian to be in the band,' said Graham. 'It's down to Nicky or Michael. We'll have a secret ballot in the toilet.'

It seemed a strange place to vote to me, but Graham went off to the loo and we all filed in one by one to write a name on a piece of paper. Democracy in action! Graham re-emerged and stood by the pub table.

'The members of IOYOU are Shane Filan, Kian Egan, Mark Feehily, Brian McFadden and Nicky Byrne,' he said.

Miggles could not have been more gutted. His head dropped and he slumped forward in his seat as if the life had been sucked out of him. His phone rang and he picked it up and hurled it across the bar.

'Oh, OK,' he said. 'Well, that's fine.' It clearly wasn't. Nobody knew what to do, or to say. It felt like things couldn't possibly get any more tense or difficult. We were wrong.

Louis had booked us all tickets to see *Grease* (yep, *Grease* again...) at the Point that night and Michael decided that he was still coming. Before that, he and I had to go to the airport: he was now dating Gillian's best friend (and my old girlfriend) Helena; she and Gillian had been on holiday to America for two weeks, and we were picking them up.

To make matters worse, Nicky – who had just taken Miggles's place in the band – drove our silent car to the airport. In the arrivals terminal, I hugged Gillian as Michael told Helena, 'I'm not in the band,' and cried. Then we all got back in the car to go to *Grease*. It could not have been more awkward.

Michael was a great guy and he had been with us right from the early days as Six As One. We all felt bad, and we all felt for him. I hoped we'd stay friends, but he vanished off the radar. Had it been me, I would probably have done the same.

Now that we had our final line-up, the pace really picked up. Louis fixed us an audition with a fella named Colin Barlow, who had signed Boyzone at Polydor Records. After weeks of rehearsal we were getting pretty slick; we knew it had gone well and they made us an offer, which was exciting.

Before Louis could accept it, though, there was one very important date in our diary: the return match with Simon Cowell.

Simon had been true to his word and agreed to come back to Dublin to see IOYOU re-audition with the new members. Louis had told him he had got rid of the deadwood from the band – which, as far as Simon was concerned, included me.

In the three months following my hangover fiasco I had been busy turning into a master of disguise. I had gone on a few sunbeds to get a tan; my hair was well over my shoulders and peroxide blond. Oddly enough, I quite liked that look.

Waiting outside the audition room at the Pod, I was shitting myself. The other lads tried to encourage me, saying I looked so different now there was no way Simon would recognize me, but I was sure I would be rumbled. I took a deep breath, walked in and sang my heart out.

What a difference being sober makes! It was totally unlike our first audition. Simon was smiling and nodding, and Louis told me afterwards that a few bars into 'Everybody Knows', our first song, Simon leaned over and asked him, 'Who's the new guy? I love his voice! He's so much better than that other chap.'

'Yeah,' agreed Louis. 'I got rid of him.'

'I'll sign them,' said Simon.

We sang about six songs, a mix of Boyzone, Boyz II Men and Backstreet Boys – B bands clearly worked for us! After we were done, Simon came and sat down with us.

'I really like you guys,' he told us. 'You've got good looks and harmonies and there is something unique about you. You're a genuine male vocal pop group.'

This worldly, super-sophisticated London music executive was talking about putting us to work with Steve Mac again, and with Max Martin, the Swede who wrote and produced for the Backstreet Boys. We loved what he was saying and how he was focusing on our voices.

One thing that Simon didn't like was our name (and, to be fair, it *was* bollocks). 'I think IOYOU is absolutely horrible,' he said, and suggested something that reflected our west of Ireland roots. We settled on Westside.

'We're signing with him,' a beaming Louis told us, as soon as Simon had gone. 'He was the one I wanted all along.'

A couple of years later, I asked Simon if he had realized I was the same guy from our failed audition at our second meeting. 'Of course I knew, kiddo,' he smirked (Cowell always called us 'kiddo'). I didn't believe a word he was saying.

We had a major-label record deal! It was such a mad buzz to tell Gillian and my family about it, and for the first time I felt like the crazy dream I had had for years, as a little culchie kid worshipping Michael Jackson and the Backstreet

Boys, might even come true. Jesus – I had a chance of being a pop star!

We hadn't yet signed a contract, but now Louis went into overdrive. The first thing he did was to move us to Dublin for a few weeks. Mark and I stayed with Nicky, Kian stayed with Brian, and Louis told us to hang out 24/7, get to know each other inside out and basically become a gang; a proper band.

He fixed it up for us to appear on The Beat on the Street, a music roadshow-cum-mobile festival run by the 2FM radio station. That summer we travelled around Ireland playing ten-minute lunchtime slots on the back of a trailer to a few hundred people in places like Cork, Limerick and Ballina in County Mayo.

We were all in denim and wore head mics, even though we were miming. Our dance routines weren't great. Nicky had never danced – he had only just stopped being a footballer – and he was always going right when the rest of us were going left. We'd come offstage, or, rather, off the trailer, going, 'Jesus, that was awful!'

I suppose we were paying our dues. Our Beat on the Street shows were a bit of a shambles, but they went down OK with the crowds. But I am very glad there were no camera phones and YouTube in those days.

In any case, we had some rather more serious dates to plan for. Louis had given us the support slot on the forthcoming Boyzone tour.

So that hectic summer of '98 we split our time between hanging out and rehearsing in Dublin, weekends in Sligo, and trips out to do roadshows. Louis's plan to help us bond worked. The five of us spent so much time together – working, playing cards, getting drunk – that we became like brothers.

We didn't find too much we didn't like about each other, apart from the brief spell when the rest of the band decided that I was sometimes a bit slow to get the joke, or the point of things, and started calling me Trigger out of *Only Fools and Horses*! I soon knocked that one on the head.

Louis pulled a couple of real masterstrokes for us. The first was to get us on the Boyzone tour, which was such exciting news we could hardly take it in. The other was to get Ronan Keating involved with the band.

Louis announced that Ronan was going to be co-managing us. This was fine by us – after all, he was a superstar! Ronan was great, and he didn't have to do too much except occasionally hang out with us and give us bits of friendly advice. But the buzz around us started to get even bigger once his name was attached to the band.

After Ronan got involved, he invited us up to his house to chill and get to know him. Gillian and I drove up there with Mark and Kian. We were so awkward that we didn't know what to take as a present, so we got him a bottle of whiskey and a bottle of Baileys – like he wouldn't have those already!

Ronan gave us a tour of his house and showed us his pool. There were a few of his mates there as well, and after dinner we all got to drinking.

We were up half of the night and it got messy. Ronan and his mates were enjoying winding up their wet-behind-the-ears young guests, and at one point gave us shots to drink. They had vinegar in them. It was revolting.

In the early hours, Gillian and I staggered up to bed – and broke the bed. It just fell to pieces beneath us. We were so embarrassed and mortified... oh my good God! We have broken Ronan Keating's bed!

The next morning we were the last ones down to breakfast because we were dreading telling Ronan what we had done. He just laughed and wound us up something rotten, and we got a lot of funny looks and smirks (obviously, like any fella, I was secretly quite proud).

Louis's idea of getting Ronan involved was brilliant, because it got thousands and thousands of Boyzone fans as well as the media interested in us. The story was that Ronan had helped to form us, and so many people heard our name for the first time (even if that name was Westside).

The Boyzone tour was the big one we were looking forward to, but while we were waiting for it to begin, Simon and Louis sent us back to Steve Mac and Wayne Hector's studio. They played us some tracks they had written, like 'Swear It Again' and 'If I Let You Go', but one song stood out a mile.

It was called 'Flying Without Wings'.

# 4

# 'EVERYBODY'S LOOKING FOR THAT SOMETHING...'

There is so much music in the world and you hear so many songs every day that it is incredibly rare for a song to stop you in your tracks and make you think, *Holy God*. The first time we heard 'Flying Without Wings' was like that.

We were all standing around Steve Mac's plush studio as he told us that he and Wayne Hector had written this new song and Wayne had sung the vocal on the demo. He pressed play on his console.

'Everybody's looking for that something, one thing that makes it all complete...'

As soon as the song came flooding out of the speakers, I was completely overwhelmed. Jesus, what a tune this was! I can't think of a time I have ever been so amazed at a song on first listen – not before, not since. It may be a cliché, but it's true: the hairs on the back of my neck were standing on end.

'You'll find it in the strangest places, places you never knew it could be...'

Why did the song blow me away so totally? It was talking to me. It was a love song, sure, but it was also about chasing a dream, and it felt to me like it could be about us, right now, looking to make it as a band and conquer the world and become the next Backstreet Boys.

Listening to it, it felt like I was thinking aloud.

It wasn't just me who felt that way. I glanced around and saw my shock reflected in everybody else's faces. When it finished there was a stunned silence, then we all said a variant on the same thing: 'Jesus! Can you just imagine if we had a song like that?'

But it wasn't that simple. Steve Mac said that he was in the process of probably giving it to Stephen Gately from Boyzone to sing. Stephen loved it, he had already recorded a version, and it was possibly going on the soundtrack of a movie.

Ah, shite! It was so disappointing, but at the same time we understood. Stephen was in Boyzone, he was a big name and a proper star, and who were we? Five gawky kids in some new band that nobody had heard of... Of course Steve and Wayne would give it to Stephen first.

Yet we couldn't stop talking about 'Flying Without Wings'. The next time we spoke to Louis we were gabbling on about this unbelievable song and how it would have been ideal for us but we were too late. Louis must have said something to Simon, because he went down to Steve's studio to hear it.

And suddenly... we had the song. Simon clearly agreed that it was perfect for us. I don't know what Simon said to Steve or what kind of deal he did, but out of the blue Louis told Mark and me to head back to London and record 'Flying Without Wings'.

We were only doing what they call a guide vocal, without the rest of the band, so that Simon and Louis could hear it, but the session was still amazing. I put a little croak in my voice as I sang that brilliant first line, and Mark completely nailed all the difficult high notes.

Our two voices were totally different but they came together so magically on that song. It made us do a double take. What were the odds on voices as complementary as ours both coming out of a tiny little town like Sligo?

'Flying Without Wings' was a major step up for us. Without being too cocky, we felt it showed we were a proper male vocal group, not 'just' a boy band for girls to scream at. Simon and Louis both felt the same when they heard it, and said the same thing: 'Wow! We have got some serious singers here...'

The weird thing was that on the day that Mark and I recorded it, Ronan knew we were in town and invited us to dinner at a posh Japanese restaurant called Benihana. With him were his wife Yvonne, Irish singer Brian Kennedy... and Stephen Gately.

Mark and I felt cool about having dinner with Ronan and Stephen, but we were also a little uneasy. Stephen had no idea we had just recorded the song that had been meant for him, and as Mark and I got quietly pissed, we thought, *F\*\*k! He is going to hit the roof about this – and we're about to go on tour with Boyzone!* The days and weeks leading up to the tour passed in a blur of hyperactivity. There was a lot of singing; a lot of dancing; a lot of rehearsals. We were doing a twenty-minute slot to open up their *Where We Belong* tour and it felt like the biggest thing we had done to date – by far.

Simon got involved in choosing the set list and in styling us. This time, we were nothing like the Backstreet Boys in their baggy jeans and hoodies; Simon got us dressed up in smart jackets and woolly polo necks. Come to think of it, we looked like mini-Simon Cowells.

Boyzone were so massive that it meant we were playing our very first tour in venues like aircraft hangers. The opening show was at the Bournemouth Centre, and I was so nervous as I stood twitchily by the side of the stage that I felt as if my life was flashing before my eyes. *This was it! Could we do it?*

The adrenaline buzz as we ran out onstage was amazing. The set Simon had chosen for us was all ballads, no upbeat songs, but the harsh lights and our heavy Savile Row clothes had us sweating like pigs. What carried us through was the sheer excitement... and the screaming.

The noise was incredible. These girls had hardly heard of us before, but they thought we were Ronan's protégés and they seemed to like us, and they yelled their hearts out. Being screamed at by 4,000 fans... *really*? It was beyond our wildest dreams. Backstage afterwards, we were all too dizzy and disoriented to think clearly.

Not that there was any danger of getting carried away. Louis wanted to milk this tour to the max. When Boyzone had first started out, he had made them hang around outside Take That's Dublin gigs introducing themselves to the fans going in, and he did the same to us.

So before every Boyzone show, Louis sent us out to greet the fans. It could have been embarrassing but luckily the girls were cool with us. We sang a cappella versions of 'Swear It Again', signed autographs, and handed out photos with a cheesy message on the back (I would like to stress we did *not* write this):

Westside are five gorgeous Irish boys and they're going to take the world by storm! If you like angelic voices, smooth moves and beautiful songs, then clear some space on your bedroom walls and in your record collection 'cos Westside are coming...

Kian, Brian, Nicky, Mark and Shane have the looks and the talent, and they're gonna be absolutely huge. Who says so? None other than Ronan Keating, who loves them so much he's decided to co-manage them! He'll be there with tons of top pop advice and the boys hope that you'll be there with your support too.

To be part of the Westside story, fill this form in, pop it in the post (you don't need a stamp), and we'll get a whole bunch of Westside info out to you...

We loved doing the Boyzone shows but offstage the tour wasn't glamorous. Not for us, anyway. We travelled on a poky little bus, with Graham getting used to being our tour manager, and stayed in B & Bs and dirt-cheap hotels two to a room (except for Mark, who liked to have his own room).

Boyzone were cool. They could have resented us as we were coming right onto their turf: we had the same manager and Louis was pushing us hard as 'the new Boyzone'. But if they did, they hid it well. Stephen must have been pissed off about 'Flying Without Wings', but he was nice to us too.

It was an insanely full-on tour for a new band that had never put out a single, let alone played live. We even did two nights at Wembley! The arenas were still filling up when we played but it was still incredibly exciting.

Fans already had their favourite members. Louis told us to introduce ourselves onstage every night – 'Hi, I'm Shane' or 'Hi, I'm Kian', no second names – and while we all got a good scream, Brian's was always the loudest. Well, to be fair, he *did* look like Nick Carter!

We would come offstage so giddy and high each night that there was no way we could just toddle off to bed. We wanted to party but could hardly afford a beer. Occasionally, Boyzone took pity on us and invited us back to their hotel bar.

Ronan hung out with us a bit and travelled on our tour bus a few times. He would give us friendly advice – and some of it was about girls.

The Boyzone tour was the first time that we met girls who wanted to get with us for what we represented, not for who we were. It was quite low-level because we were still unknown, but even so girls would be flirting with us outside the venues or tracking us down to our hotels.

Ronan didn't give a lecture, just a few wise words: 'Be careful. If you get famous, you'll get a lot of attention from girls and it will often be for the wrong reasons. You'll be tempted and it's up to you what you do. But be careful.'

It was good advice. Some of the band listened to it closely, and some totally ignored it – because, of course, we were all in very different situations.

For my part, I wouldn't do anything that would endanger my relationship with Gillian. I was finally with the girl I loved and it had taken me a long time, a lot of courage and a few false starts to get there. There was no way that I was going to risk all that for a quick shag on the road.

Nicky was the same, as he had been dating Georgina since he was twelve, so he and I shared a room. Mark always had his own room but he didn't really go off with girls. We just figured he was quiet and a bit shy.

Kian and Brian were a different story. They were both single and happily so, and when Ronan had warned us some girls would target us because we were getting famous, Brian had let loose a big grin that clearly said, 'I don't give a shit what their reasons are! Bring them on!'

We never talked about it, that wasn't how we were, but Kian and Brian shared a room and I am pretty sure they reacted to girls throwing themselves at us in the early days in the way most red-blooded single fellas would do. Why not? It didn't bother me. It was none of my business; and, in any case, if not for Gillian...

The Boyzone tour had been a mental experience, and seeing Ronan and the others every night opened our eyes to what being in a mega boy band was all about. We didn't dare to dream that we'd ever be as big as them, but what an adventure!

After the tour, we went down to London to sign our record contract with Sony BMG at long last. We also learned we would be getting a new name. It turned out there were a few other bands knocking around called Westside or West Side. We would have to change it.

The two options seemed to be West High or Westlife, and Simon settled it: 'Let's go with Westlife.' So, there we were. Westlife it was.

Simon was in the BMG boardroom for the signing, as was his right-hand man, Sonny Takhar, a straight-talking London guy who was to do a lot of the day-to-day work with us. We were signing a five-album deal that would pay us about £4m if Westside, sorry, Westlife took off.

Lately, my life was often starting to feel like a dream. It happened again right there and then. I scribbled my name, and as we sipped champagne and had our photos taken, I thought, *Well, this is it! We're going to be pop stars! I'm going to be a millionaire! I can buy a f\*\*k-off car!*

I was nineteen years old.

After the Boyzone dates we went on a *Smash Hits* roadshow tour. It featured some big stars, like 5ive, Steps and Billie Piper, but we mostly kept ourselves to ourselves. It was just shyness. At heart we still felt like five Irish lads who could get found out any minute. But *Smash Hits* gave us an award for Best New Tour Act, which we loved.

Gillian had visited me in London or Dublin a few times but I had hardly been to Sligo or seen my family in months. When I got a few days at home after the *Smash Hits* tour, it happily coincided with a long-awaited payday.

For although we might have been signing multi-millionpound contracts, the truth was we were all broke. We hadn't seen a penny so far and had been living off hand-outs from Louis. That all changed when we each received a £25,000 advance on a publishing deal (not that I knew what publishing was).

I had never seen so much money in my life and, naturally, I did the only sensible thing I could. I went out and spent £20,000 on a car.

I had always been mad for cars but I had never been able to afford one. This was a beauty, a 1993 silver BMW. I can remember exactly what it cost: £16,750. The insurance was

£4,000; not unreasonably as I was a wide-eyed teenage wannabe pop star.

That car became my pride and joy. I used to love picking up Gillian from her house in it, and when she wasn't around, I would carefully do laps of the town with four or five mates squeezed in with me. I'd hand-wash it in the car park over the road, and at night I'd park it outside the café and pray that nobody scratched or vandalized it.

Some people probably thought it was a bit cocky for me to buy myself a swanky car as soon as I got money. I figured, I'd made my first few quid, I didn't have any other expenses – why *shouldn't* I get a cool car? In any case, it was a six-year-old BMW. It wasn't *that* flash.

I only got a few days to chill out in Sligo with Gillian. Now the real work was set to begin. We had to make an album.

Simon Cowell being Simon Cowell, Westlife were starting at the very top. As winter fell, Louis told us that we were to fly straight out to Sweden to work with the shit-hot producers at Max Martin's Cheiron Studios, who had helped to turn the Backstreet Boys into global superstars.

The Backstreet Boys' producers! This was another of our 'Holy God' moments. They were starting to come thick and fast.

I had never been outside of the UK and Ireland before and Stockholm sounded as glamorous as going to New York. I had no idea what to expect. Scandinavia! It just seemed so exotic... I distinctly remember packing earmuffs.

I didn't use them much, but even so we landed in Sweden in the thickest snow I had ever seen. There were fans waiting for us at the airport; they had heard of us from the Boyzone tour. We're not talking The Beatles here, there were literally ten girls, but it still felt very cool.

These same girls would wait for us every morning outside our hotel and walk to Cherion with us. And the studio was something else. Everywhere we looked there were platinum discs for the Backstreet Boys, for 1 million, 5 million, *10 million* sales. All that we could think was, *What are* we *doing here?*

Per Magnusson, David Kreuger, Rami Yacoub, Jörgen Elofsson, Jake Schulze, Andreas Carlsson and the other Swedish guys were very professional and efficient, and they were also fun to work with. They played us loads of songs like 'If I Let You Go', 'Fool Again' and 'Miss You'. This was all new to us: we were overwhelmed and very impressed.

We would go into the studio at midday and record track after track. The producers gave me, Mark and Brian nearly all the lead vocals and had me starting off virtually every song. It was all full-on: we got pizza and lasagna delivered in the evenings and worked till midnight.

A couple of times the producers took us to snazzy local bars and clubs where a beer cost about twenty times what it did in Sligo, but mostly we were too knackered from singing all day to go out in the evenings. After a couple of weeks, we flew home for Christmas.

That Christmas in Sligo gave me a chance to reflect on what had been a crazy, life-changing year. I had started 1998 as a failed accountancy student; I closed it as a dreamer, with dreams that were coming true in HD.

What a year... We had lost three members, found two more, supported the Backstreet Boys, gained a famous manager, changed our name (twice), toured with Boyzone, signed a record deal and made an album. I enjoyed a great, happy Christmas that had the feel of a calm before a storm.

How true that was.

In the New Year we were back in Sweden to wrap up the album, which was to be called, simply, *Westlife*. It sounded great to us, just the mix of powerful ballads and pop tunes that we wanted. Now, I think that it is too long and could have lost a few songs; then, we loved it.

Simon and Louis had a master plan. We would put the album out at the end of the year, in November, release three singles leading up to it, and in the meantime do non-stop interviews and promotion to get our name about.

There was talk of playing our trump card, 'Flying Without Wings', at the start, but Simon wanted to hold that back until right before the album came out. Instead, he decided to put out 'Swear It Again' as our debut single and sent us off to make a video for it.

This was yet another new experience for us. We were at Pinewood, the famous London studio. They were filming a James Bond movie there at the same time. We didn't dare speak to Pierce Brosnan, but we waved as he drove past us in a tuxedo on a golf buggy.

The video concept was the band standing all in black on a big glossy stage, miming our singing in front of a sixty-piece string orchestra. It reminded me of acting in plays at the Hawks Well, but the cameras were a new factor, and it was nerve-wracking working out when to look at them and when to look away.

We spent a few days filming this vid and apparently it cost something crazy like £100,000. We thought it looked grand but then Simon hated it, and made us reshoot it in a theatre with plush red seats. As normal, we went along with it.

Everything then became focused on the release of the single in April and the Sony BMG publicity machine took over. We all pretty much moved into a hotel in London full-time as we did weeks and weeks of TV, radio and magazine interviews.

Doing TV shows was a new thing for us, but after our initial nerves we took to it quite quickly. We soon became regulars on *CD:UK*, the Saturday morning kids/music show, and got friendly with hosts Ant and Dec and Cat Deeley, who weren't much older than us. We always had good craic with them.

As a kid, I had always dreamed of what it would be like to do interviews, and now we were talking to newspapers and magazines every day. We were amazed they were so interested in us, but they had heard of us from the Boyzone tour and winning the award from *Smash Hits*.

The interviews were OK as we are all Irish lads with the gift of the gab. Mark was always the quietest, but I could rattle on and Brian normally came out with some entertaining free-form bollocks. In my head, I would be waiting for the inevitable question that came in every – and I mean every – single interview:

'Shane, do you have a girlfriend?'

And every single time I would lie. 'No,' I would tell them. 'I don't.'

Why did I do this? Firstly, Louis and the record label had quietly advised us to play down the girlfriend angle. Fans love to think that the guys in boy bands are available, and it didn't make sense to shoot ourselves in the foot this early by saying we weren't.

Nicky didn't have this option. Georgina was the Taoiseach's daughter, so his relationship was high-profile and widely known. It was different for me, with Gillian. I could get away with it.

Yet it was also for Gillian's sake – and she agreed with the subterfuge. She was starting college in Sligo, studying business, and she wanted her life there to be as normal as possible. We had no idea if Westlife was going to take off or not, but if it did, she hated the idea of being known as just 'that pop star's girlfriend'.

Even so, I felt guilty every time I said it and saw the resulting feature claim that 'Westlife's Shane is young, free and single and on the lookout!' It was a white lie, and a harmless one – but, ideally, I would have preferred to be honest.

The interviews kept coming and got bigger and bigger. We were getting front covers; *Smash Hits* put us on their cover before we even had a single out, the first time they had ever done that. Radio 1 was playing our single to death. We could sense that things were snowballing even though we could hardly believe it.

'Swear It Again' was coming out in Ireland two days before the British release, so we also did a load of promo there – and it was in our homeland that we first got a clue as to just how crazy things were about to get.

We were to sign copies of the single at the Blanchardstown Centre, a big shopping mall in Dublin. We knew people were getting to know of us in Ireland, due to the Boyzone link and to Ronan plugging us, but we had no idea how many people would turn up.

As our people carrier drove through Dublin's busy streets, we speculated nervously. Five hundred? Could there be a thousand? Although we didn't admit it, at the back of our minds was the *Spinal Tap* scenario where we arrived to find nobody there.

We got to the Blanchardstown to be met by what looked like a football crowd, if football crowds were made up only of crying, screaming teenage girls. Security men met us and hustled us through corridors to a waiting desk. On the way, they said there were at least 5,000 people there.

Five thousand! Jesus – that could fill the Point Depot! The next four hours were a blur. We calmed down the fans who were too excited to speak; posed for photos; signed singles, photos and scrapbooks; dispensed kisses. We hadn't met even a fifth of the people waiting for us.

We had to leave for another signing in Cork and hated to let the other fans down, so we went onto the roof of the shopping centre to wave at the thousands below who had not even got into the mall. As we peeked over the edge, the shrill screech of the screams was like a jet taking off.

Suddenly we knew what it felt like to be in the Backstreet Boys, in Take That, in Boyzone, even in The Beatles. *How in the love of God was this happening?* We got a police escort away from Blanchardstown and, heart pounding, I stared across the car at Louis. He was grinning like a cat in a lake of cream.

It wasn't just a 'Holy God' moment. This one was 'Holy f\*\*k!' Despite all we had done to that point – the album, the video, the TV, the interviews – our fame had been theoretical. This was the first time we had seen it – *felt* it – at first hand. We were in shock.

What it did show us was that our single was going to do well in Ireland. When 'Swear It Again' came out the next week, it went straight in at number one. It was such a proud moment. Ireland is a tiny country, sure, and we maybe only sold 10,000 copies (half of them at the Blanchardstown Centre...) but it meant a lot. It was our home; our land.

The big test lay across the water. We knew how very much it mattered how well our first single did in Britain. It could make or break a band. In a way, all of our efforts up to that point had been leading up to *this*.

What did we hope for? We didn't dare say. We knew things had been going well, but who knew how well? We just hoped to get into the top ten. That would be a brilliant start.

We found out our fate on a Sunday – of course. Sunday is always chart day. It was Sunday 25 April 1999. We were recording a track in Pete Waterman's studio in London, killing time until the chart show later that afternoon, when Kian's phone rang.

It was Louis.

'Lads, I have some news for you.'

We all held our breath.

'You're going to be number one.'

# 5

# 'SHANE, I LOVE YOU!'

It had been just over a year since I had dropped to my knees and sobbed with joy at MJ Carr's when Louis had phoned to tell me that IOYOU were supporting the Backstreet Boys. Now we were top of the charts.

We had never in a million years remotely imagined anything like this happening, and happening so quickly. It would be easy to say that it felt like a dream, but as I scrabbled for my phone to tell Gillian and my parents the news, I thought that I would never even have dared to *dream* this.

Being number one brings with it its own special ritual, of course. Two days later, we were at Elstree Studios in London to perform on *Top of the Pops*, a show I had watched religiously every week for as long as I could remember (at friends' houses; it wasn't on either of the two channels that Mum let us have at home).

Beforehand, I was very nervous about our performance. A lot of artists mimed on *Top of the Pops*, but Simon decreed that we should sing 'Swear It Again' live, which meant that I had to lead off and sing the first verse on my own in front of 5 million people. Nice one, Simon!

Simon saw that I was worried, and had a brainwave. 'Why don't you sit down to sing?' he suggested. 'It will help you to concentrate.' He had the idea of us all sitting in a line along the front of the stage on bar stools.

Westlife didn't particularly have any up-tempo songs then and we weren't really a dancing band anyway, so it made sense. Of course, we weren't to know that over the years those stools would become our gimmick and the thing that millions of people associated us with!

(As well as, incidentally, gaining us a reputation as the laziest band in pop. What can you do?)

*Top of the Pops* was filmed right next door to the *EastEnders* set so we had a quick goose at that. I was overawed at being on *TOTP*, especially when I bumped into Shania Twain, a beautiful, tiny woman in thigh-length boots, backstage. 'Howdy,' she trilled at me as I gawped, starstruck.

There were only about 100 people in the studio audience but there were a few Westlife fans there yelling for us, which helped. My mouth felt dry as Jamie Theakston introduced us, lined up on our stools behind him. I took a deep breath and hit the opening note, and it went fine.

'Swear It Again' was still number one the next week so we took our stools back to *Top of the Pops*... and then began one of the most insane and intense periods in the band's history. If we thought we had been busy before, now we had a number one, it *really* went crazy.

'Swear It Again' was also a decent-sized hit in a few European countries, so we did short follow-up trips to play PAs (personal appearances) or do interviews. Each trip away was the first time that we had been to whichever country it was, and it was an incredibly exciting and exotic time.

Or rather, it would have been if we had actually got to see any of the countries we were in. We soon learned our tight schedules didn't allow for any of that. What we saw of most countries consisted of this: airport-car-record label-car-radio station-car-hotel-car-radio station-car-airport.

On a flying visit back to Stockholm, we got to meet a new, upcoming US rapper called Eminem. He was following us onstage to do a song at a radio station roadshow, and as we crossed paths, he sneered at us: 'Wow! You're the new f\*\*king Backstreet Boys, huh?'

We were taken aback, and a bit gutted, and I held forth to the rest of the band afterwards: 'He's a bit of a bollocks, isn't he? What a dickhead! What the f\*\*k does he know? In any case, a white guy trying to be a rapper – shit, he's never going to get anywhere…'

At a radio station in Madrid we met Britney Spears, who had just had a massive hit with '… Baby One More Time'. She was nice but just sitting quietly in the corner, with short hair, and I was a bit disappointed.

I guess I was hoping that she would be in pigtails and a school uniform.

We saw a bit more of Spain when we went to Tenerife for three days. Our second single was to be 'If I Let You Go' and we flew out to the Mediterranean to make a video for it.

It was the first time I'd been to a sunny holiday destination and I had no idea how to dress. On the first day, I appeared by the hotel pool in flip-flops, white socks, shorts, a vest with a shirt over it and a bum bag.

The rest of the lads fell off their sun loungers laughing and sent me back up to change. Truth be told, as a vain boy, I was mortified.

For the video we had to stride down a beach in vests looking mean and moody as a pair of horsemen galloped through the surf behind us. It was hard to keep a straight face but it was our second vid, we were getting used to the cameras and we were on the way to becoming professional poseurs.

Being in Tenerife and soaking up the sun was great, but it was the first time we realized how knackering making videos can be. We would start at eight in the morning and end at two at night: an eighteen-hour day to make – what? Three minutes of film?

It was all about 'Hurry up and wait': hours and hours sitting around a Winnebago eating sweets, drinking Coke and talking shite. Normally, Brian would regale us with stories of his adventures in Dublin, tell jokes or just ramble on. He was definitely the band entertainment.

Everything was new, and fresh, and it was such a huge buzz for Westlife to be getting successful in Britain, Ireland and even Europe. It was even more amazing to realize that our new-found success had spread to countries that some of us had hardly heard of.

Sony BMG said that 'Swear It Again' had gone down great in Southeast Asia and so Simon packed us off over there in the early summer of 1999 for a short promo tour. We didn't have the first idea what to expect; as I remember it, we were all just excited about going on our first long-haul flight.

We landed in Indonesia and as we got off the plane the heat and the humidity hit us. It was like we were on a different planet.

We were expecting to be met by a driver and maybe a local record-label person, but as we rode an escalator into baggage reclaim, we heard a mad noise.

*Thunk!*

*Thunk!*

*Thunk!*

There was a big window alongside the reclaim area, and all we could see were a thousand or more girls packed against it, faces squashed against the glass, banging on the window as if they wanted to smash it. We thought they might just do it.

As we cleared customs into Arrivals, the whole hall was crammed with excited fans, aged between about twelve and eighteen, screaming, crying, waving and holding up signs:

'SHANE, I LOVE YOU!'

'KIAN, YOU ARE MINE!'

There were ten security guards waiting and they had to take us out one by one with the fans fighting them to get to us.

It was the same in Malaysia and the Philippines. We sped around in vans with security and girls would jump into taxis and tell them to follow us. They'd pull alongside at speed, the girls yelling, 'Hello! We love you!' and the taxi driver grinning, giving us a thumbs-up and totally ignoring the chaotic road in front of him.

How do you start to make sense of that? How do you process it? It was bizarre, exhilarating, surreal and a bit scary. We giggled nervously as we were pursued through Manila or Kuala Lumpur: we felt a long, long way from home and at the centre of a whole lot of madness.

Louis had seen it all before with Boyzone, of course, and he tried to keep our feet on the ground. However, what really brought home to us how insane things were becoming was going back to Sligo.

That summer of 1999, when we were not on the road, we had largely been staying in London. The record label put us up at the K West hotel in Shepherd's Bush. I was living off room-service meals of steak and mash every night. Gillian would often fly over at weekends.

It seemed like we had done a signing session in pretty much every city going except for Sligo, and we were desperate to put that right. Maybe we figured our hometown would give us a welcome dose of normality. The reality was exactly the opposite.

We did a signing for 'If I Let You Go' at The Record Room. The police had closed off part of the city, the thousands of fans were delirious and our hometown was the scene of the same pandemonium we experienced everywhere else we went. Even here, the rules had changed.

The next week, 'If I Let You Go' became our second single to go straight to number one. It knocked Ronan Keating's solo record 'When You Say Nothing At All' off the top, which was weird: just a year ago, he'd been like a god to us.

Simon and Louis were working us into the ground. They put us back on the *Smash Hits* roadshow. In contrast to the first year, when we were wide-eyed newcomers, now we were headlining over Steps, B*Witched, Billie Piper... and a new girl band from Liverpool called Atomic Kitten.

Atomic Kitten hadn't yet had a big hit with 'Whole Again'. They were starting out and were pretty unknown, just like we had been the year before. They were a lot of fun and we had a good laugh hanging out with them at the shows.

They were all proper funny, quick-witted Liverpool girls and the most over-the-top was Kerry Katona. Kerry was lovely, a very pretty blonde girl and a bubbly, sunny person, a real motormouth who was always laughing, swearing and talking flat out. She seemed like the Kittens' version of Brian.

Brian certainly noticed her. They were like two sides of the same coin and they clicked straight away. After we met the Kittens for the first time, he couldn't shut up about her in the dressing room afterwards: 'Ah, that Kerry, she's amazing, isn't she? She's class, that one!'

We could see Brian fancied Kerry and they were doing some pretty serious flirting all throughout the tour, but we didn't think too much of it: we figured it was just Brian being Brian. There was so much else going on that it wasn't a big deal for us.

It seemed like in a flash we were becoming the biggest boy band in Britain. Suddenly, we were hardly off magazine front covers and the radio. Our nearest rivals were 5ive, who were a couple of albums ahead of us and seemed to be on *CD:UK* every week, the same as we were.

We were probably a bit in awe of 5ive, because they had had a lot of hits, but there was definitely a rivalry between us, and a couple of them would never acknowledge us when we met. But they had a very different image to us.

5ive were the new East 17-type bad boys of pop, whereas Westlife were squeaky clean. Or, at least, that was how we were seen. Simon and Louis were adamant that we had to set an example and be role models, because we were going to have a lot of very young fans, some of them not yet even teenagers, looking up to us.

Simon was also in charge of 5ive, of course, but for whatever reason he wanted to cast us as the clean-cut, well-dressed, polite young lads that girls could take home to meet their mums. He liked us being in the pop papers but he didn't want us getting snapped falling out of nightclubs drunk.

We were just normal young lads, but we went along with all of this. We liked a drink but none of us were alcoholics, and we certainly never went near drugs. We had seen Robbie Williams going off the rails and leaving Take That: it was the last thing that we wanted to happen to us.

In any case, we didn't need to get high. We were flying every day – quite literally in October '99, when 'Flying Without Wings' was finally released as a single. We had known from the second we were given it that it was our secret weapon, and without being cocky, we weren't at all surprised when it went to number one. It was a song that deserved to.

In fact, with our first three singles having all gone straight in at number one, I think we were beginning to feel invincible. When the *Westlife* album was released the following month, we sat back and waited for it to do the same.

It didn't. *Westlife* went into the chart at number two – pipped to the top by just a thousand sales by Steps' *Steptacular* album.

I could pretend that we weren't gutted by this – but I would be lying. It was a bit of a shocker. We knew Steps from the *Smash Hits* tours and bumping into them at TV studios and we liked them, so it was nothing personal. But we had also liked our image as the band that always got to number one.

So we brooded for a few days, but it didn't last. We might have lost our unbeaten record but *Westlife* was still flying out of the shops and in no time went platinum: 300,000 sales. This was seriously major.

In fact, what could be bigger than that? Well, maybe the chance to play for the Queen of England.

Four weeks after the album came out, we appeared at the Royal Variety Performance. It was at the Hippodrome in Birmingham and, to say the least, featured quite a range of talent: Steps, Charlotte Church, LeAnn Rimes, Joe Pasquale, Barry Manilow and Ken Dodd. Lucky Her Majesty!

Sony BMG told us that we should promote our upcoming Christmas single, a cover of Abba's 'I Have a Dream'. The label had suggested we cover it, and Louis had agreed, and said we should do it as a double A-side with an old 1970s ballad called 'Seasons in the Sun', which, if I am honest, I had never heard of.

It was pretty nerve-wracking singing Abba in front of the Queen, and even more so when we queued up to meet her afterwards. Her courtiers briefed us in advance on the protocol. We were to call her 'Your Majesty' or 'Ma'am'; we didn't speak to her unless she spoke to us; we didn't put out a hand to shake unless she extended hers to us.

The Queen was surprisingly small and proceeded down the line of artistes fairly slowly, not speaking to many of them. She was wearing a brightly coloured dress that looked like a Quality Street wrapper.

When she came to me, she stopped and looked me up and down.

*Jesus! I'm about to talk to the Queen!*

'That was a lovely song you sang,' she told me, in that world-famous cut-glass accent. (I suppose you'd call it the Queen's English.) 'Did you write it yourselves?'

'No, Ma'am,' I told her. 'It is by Abba.'

She smiled and moved on down the line of band members – including Brian, who had clearly forgotten every word of the advance protocol briefing we had been given.

'Ah, Ma'am, that's a lovely dress you have there!' he greeted her, extending his hand with a beaming smile. An invisible thought bubble formed over the heads of the other four band members: 'Brian, shut the f**k up!'

Meeting the Queen was one more highlight in an amazing year that ended on yet another high. In a TV ceremony voted by viewers, we won the Record of the Year award for 'Flying Without Wings', beating Ricky Martin's 'Livin' La Vida Loca', Britney Spears's '… Baby One More Time', and even Ronan's 'When You Say Nothing At All'. When they read out our name as the winners I jumped up from the table, punched the air, and my shirt burst open to the waist – but I didn't care. Yet again, I had to wonder, *Is this really happening?*

But our incredible year hadn't quite finished with us yet. I don't know whether the Queen bought a copy, but 'I Have a Dream' followed our first three singles straight to the top of the chart.

As Westlife headed back to Ireland for a much-needed holiday, we were Britain's Christmas number one.

Our lives had changed beyond recognition. At Christmas in Sligo that winter of 1999, it showed. For one thing, fans from all over the world had started undertaking pilgrimages to my home at the Carlton Café.

I had given my mum and dad a few gold discs for our singles and they had dotted them around the café's walls. Some girls would fly in from Italy or Japan and nurse a glass of Coke in the Carlton for five hours.

Mum loved chatting to them. If I were ever home, wandered in and said, 'Good morning' to those girls, they just froze.

Mostly people in Sligo were cool with us. That was a relief. As I walked around town, everybody wanted a word or a chat, and I was determined to give it to them. I didn't want anyone saying that yer man had gone off, got famous and turned into a bigheaded bollock.

Naturally, not everybody in Ireland loved Westlife from the off. There are always begrudgers and a few people would throw us nasty comments if they had a few drinks in them. It never really bothered us. I'd just think, *Mate, check the charts!*

We occasionally got abuse in Dublin. I'll never forget around that time being in a minibus and passing a kid of about twelve on a mountain bike. He clocked us and set off in pursuit, his legs whirling like a windmill. He caught up with us at traffic lights, stared in the open van window and let us have it: 'WESTLIFE! ARSE BANDITS!'

Luckily, we were laughing too much to be offended.

In Sligo, though, we were hometown heroes and most people seemed proud of us. The biggest danger was that I would go out for a drink with Gillian and never get a chance to speak to her because of everyone coming up wanting to talk. After all, there was a lot to talk about.

It had been such a mad year. In 1999, Westlife had had four number-one singles, a number-two album, got massive in Asia and even started to get big in South America. It was all the more weird as we hadn't even properly been on tour yet.

That Christmas in Sligo, Kian, Mark and I calculated that we had worked 103 days non-stop. It was great to fall back into the routine of local pubs, vodka and Red Bull, table seven at the Embassy, and Equinox.

On Millennium Eve, me and the Sligo lads hired out a local club called the Penthouse for a big party for our friends and family. It was such an exciting night. A new era was dawning – and we all sensed we had some incredible times ahead.

As Westlife reconvened early in 2000, we learned some wild news. Brian had started dating Kerry Katona and had spent Christmas in Dublin with her. That wasn't all he had done. He had asked her to marry him.

It was crazy sudden, but that was Brian for you, and after the initial shock we were all pleased for them – they clearly loved each other. Kerry moved to Ireland pretty quickly and started getting really friendly with Gillian.

At this point, thinking back, I was living the life of Riley. I had money coming in by now, and as well as loving my cars, I got well used to going out with our stylist and splashing three or four grand on designer clothes.

Yet I was also determined to plan for the future. I knew my family couldn't go on living above the Carlton forever, and I set about building a home that my parents, brothers and sisters, and Gillian's family could call home for years to come.

My dad had bought a farm at a place called Carraroe on the outskirts of Sligo a few years earlier and gave me a piece of land as a present. Gillian and I hired a local architect, and we talked him through exactly what we wanted in our dream home for both of our families.

We had a very specific vision for it. I saw it as almost like a stately home; I knew I wanted it to be made with Irish-cut stone and to have a tower, plus a top floor with a bar and a cinema and a games room. Gillian designed the décor, which was all classy French château.

Gillian and I got totally into the house and it became our pet project. We knew the Carraroe house would take a long time to build. Mind you, we never imagined it would take anywhere near as long as it did…

I was still keeping up the silly pretence in interviews that I didn't have a girlfriend, and people certainly bought it. That Valentine's Day I received not hundreds but thousands of cards, as did the rest of the band. I suppose it was lucky that Gillian was not the jealous type.

Westlife ramped up again when we headed off to Mexico to film a vid for 'Fool Again', which was to be the fourth single from our debut album. Even by our standards, this was to prove an incredible trip.

We were getting pretty big in South America and we had to have armed security everywhere we went. We filmed the video on top of a skyscraper with a helicopter launch pad. Brian was so scared of heights that he freaked out if any of us went near the edge to wave to the crowds below.

The only bummer from the trip was getting robbed. Our hotel advised us to put our valuable stuff in just one safe, and when we got back it had all gone. I was really pissed off as my mum had bought me a Gucci watch that got nicked. Kian lost a ring that he really liked and our cameraman had lots of gear taken. It was shite.

Although our first album had been massive, we didn't tour it in Britain because Simon and Sony BMG were keen on trying to break us around the world. In the May of 2000, we did a short *East Meets Westlife* series of gigs back in Asia. If possible, the reaction was even more hysterical than on our first visit.

I'd have loved Gillian to come with me but she was doing exams in Sligo at that time. One funny thing was that if I had done the course at her college I had signed up for before Westlife got massive, I would have been in one of her classes.

Gillian told me that my name was still on one or two lists of students, and one day a new tutor took a register at the start of a class and asked, 'Is Shane Filan here?' One lad in the class shot back, 'Nah, that fella is flying without wings.'

In any case, there would have been no point in Gillian coming out to Asia with me. We spent all our time holed up in hotels, doing interviews or being screamed at by fans at gigs or signings. In Indonesia and the Philippines, fans rushed the stage and ripped the clothes from our backs.

A return trip to South America shortly afterwards was just as mental, including getting trapped in our tour bus by crowds on our way to a TV station in Buenos Aires. The TV crew had to improvise by interviewing us on top of the besieged bus as the fans chanted our name.

You never, ever forget experiences like that – and they seemed to be happening every day.

Yet there was one country in particular that Simon and Louis had their eyes on us breaking. It was the Holy Grail of show business: America.

The first time you see New York is amazing. As our yellow cabs weaved through the skyscrapers and the steam puffed up from the grilles on the street, it made me think of every US drama and cop show I had seen as a kid. It was as if we had leapt onto the other side of the screen.

We thought we had a good chance to break the States. Simon and Louis had told us all about our label boss there, Clive Davis, a music-industry legend who had signed Janis Joplin, Bruce Springsteen and Whitney Houston. If I am honest, I think at this point, we thought everything was possible.

We were ready to work to make it happen and that was just as well because America was a slog. It was nothing like home, where we put out a single, went on TV a few times and it all went mental. To break America, you had to work – hard.

For a few weeks in that summer of 2000, the five of us lived on planes and highways. We would do early-morning calls from our hotel to breakfast radio shows, fly off to do a lunchtime gig or PA in a shopping mall, and then play early-evening gigs, performing support slots to half-empty arenas, before moving on to a new town. The next day, it would start all over again.

We didn't just see New York and Los Angeles, we pinballed around the whole country, visiting Sligo-sized towns in the Midwest or the South. America blurred into one crazy, giddy haze. Most days, if you had asked us to name the city we were in, we couldn't have told you.

It was fun, sometimes, and it was exciting – *shit, we are in America!* – but mostly it felt like we were banging our heads against a brick wall. It seemed that the era of the boy band had passed in the States, and it was all about hip-hop and R&B. Still, what the hell? It was a fantastic adventure.

We returned home with America firmly unbroken but Asia still loved us and we headed back out there for yet another short promo tour. Talk about contrast! We left a land that was indifferent to us and arrived in a place where our every move led to hysteria.

Once again, Indonesia and the Philippines were unhinged. We would show up for what we thought was a low-key PA singing a few songs to find 10,000 people waiting for us. You may think: How can you ever get used to madness like that? It's a good question. But, in a strange way, we did.

We played one huge show in Indonesia and when it finished the crowd just all milled around outside the arena waiting for us. The police went to try to clear them away and the venue's security men promptly attacked the cops. There was this huge ruck – police against security.

Everything seemed bizarre, exaggerated, larger than life, and the surprises just kept coming. While we were in Indonesia, Louis called Kian with some extraordinary news: we were to do a duet with Mariah Carey.

Mariah is still a huge star but back then she was one of the biggest superstars in the world; it would be like being told now that you were going to sing with Rihanna or Katy Perry. We were all excited, and Mark was completely blown away: Mariah is his all-time idol.

We were to sing a cover of Phil Collins's 'Against All Odds' and we had to record the song and make the video in just two days in Capri, Italy. We flew straight there from Asia – or, rather, four of us did; poor Kian had managed to lose his passport.

Capri was beautiful and we met Mariah for dinner the night we flew in. We were all dead nervous and she was a regal presence as she wafted into the restaurant, all flowing chiffon gown and air kisses. What do you say to someone like that? But as we ate, she turned out to be surprisingly normal.

We were used to doing recording sessions during the day and knocking off at six, like a normal job, but Mariah is more nocturnal. Her people – and there were lots of them – told us to meet her in a clifftop studio the following evening at about 10 o'clock.

We were in the studio until four in the morning. Mariah cradled a glass of wine and while she was pretty un-diva-like again as she chatted to us, we were still in awe. When she put the headphones on, her voice was phenomenal; it was hard not to laugh with delight as we listened.

The funny thing that happened with Mariah was that the following day, after we had shot the video, a photographer took some snaps of us all to promote the single. Mariah sat at a desk and the photographer told us to gather around her, as if we were reading lyrics off the desk.

Mariah is a very sexy woman, she has got some outstanding natural assets, and she was wearing a very low-cut top that day. It was hard not to stare down her cleavage as we leaned over her, but we all tried to control our lustful urges – except for Brian.

A couple of days later, Sony BMG phoned Louis and told him that the photos were great except that Brian was ogling Mariah's tits in every shot! There wasn't one that they could use; in the end, they had to repaint his eyes digitally onto the final image. Brian thought this was hilarious. To be fair, he was right.

We knew 'Against All Odds' would be the first single from our second album, but now the time had come to record the rest of the record. We decided that we would like it to have one big difference from our debut.

*Westlife* had been a massive album for us and it had helped to make our name. We were totally proud of it and we had thrown ourselves into performing its songs – but at the same time, we hadn't written any of them.

We had exploded into the pop world like a volcano, but not everybody liked us. Not writing any of our own material just gave ammunition to those critics – and there were already plenty of them – who proclaimed Westlife to be mere pop puppets: all-singing, all-dancing pretty-boys without a shred of originality.

If I'm honest, I never really cared what people like that said. They were never going to like a boy band, and my instinctive response was: 'Just have a look who's top of the charts, mate!' Some of the lads were more bothered, and Brian said he'd like us to have a go at writing a song or two.

This was intimidating, given that whatever we did would be judged against people like Steve Mac and Wayne Hector and Max Martin's team, who were the very best in the business.

How could we hope to equal that? Talk about being the underdogs. Still, Brian, Kian and I put our heads together and wrote a number called 'Fragile Heart'. It didn't come easy, and if I ever listen to it now – which I don't often do – it is OK, but not great. Probably we should have asked for outside help with it, rather than just doing it between us.

Even so, Simon said it was 'quite a nice song' and let us put it on the album – we knew he wouldn't do that if it were a load of shite. It was beginning to seem like everything we touched turned to gold and we started getting a bit cocky.

It's impossible to have the kind of sudden success that we had had without it going to your head a little bit, and making the second album, we definitely began to believe a bit of our own publicity.

The first sessions for the album, in Steve Mac's studio, had gone well. Steve and Wayne had been playing us great new songs like 'What Makes a Man' and it was clear the record was going to be as strong as our first one, if not better. We were not the same people making it, though.

Whereas Steve and Wayne had dealt with timid little culchies before, now we were getting messy. We thought nothing of going out and getting bananas at night and turning up at the studio hungover. Or we would slouch in one by one, hours late.

I guess we were figuring, *Why the f\*\*k shouldn't we? We're Westlife!*

It wasn't exactly Ozzy Osbourne biting the heads off bats or throwing TVs out of hotel windows, but we would get chips from the chippy and leave the papers and rubbish strewn all around Steve's studio. After a few days he had had enough and put a phone call in to Louis and Simon.

'The little shits are coming in here thinking they're Mariah Carey!' he told them. 'They're leaving my studio like a right f\*\*king tip!' Louis phoned and had a word with us, and we apologized to Steve, saying we hadn't meant any harm.

The penny didn't drop, though, because a couple of weeks later we were back in Sweden, recording songs like 'I Lay My

Love on You' and 'When You're Looking Like That', and we were behaving exactly the same. We'd go in late for sessions saying that we were tired (i.e. still drunk); a couple of times, we didn't turn up at all.

The Swedish producers got just as pissed off and they also put a complaining phone call in to London. The first thing we knew about it was when Louis showed up in Stockholm. He wasn't mincing his words.

'I'm f\*\*king done with you lot,' he told us. 'You're a f\*\*king nightmare. Simon is getting calls at the label and he thinks you are turning into arrogant little shits. He's really annoyed and isn't sure you're worth the hassle. To be honest, neither am I. I'm washing my hands of ye.'

Louis stormed out of the studio. We looked at each other, ashen-faced. *Did he mean it?* A couple of us followed him outside, where he was waiting for his car.

He was still livid. 'I f\*\*king mean it!' he said. 'You're doing everything I told you not to. I don't even know why I bothered coming out here – you're not worth it. I'm flying back to Dublin.'

His car pulled up. He got in and left without a backwards glance.

*Shit. This was major.*

It scared the hell out of us, and later Kian phoned him at his hotel and begged him to give us a second chance. We promised that we would clean up our act and toe the line. Louis relented.

He knew exactly what he was doing, of course, and his shock tactics worked. Westlife had just become one of the biggest pop bands in Europe, but at the same time we were still gullible young lads who could not believe our luck and thought it could all vanish as quickly as it had appeared.

We knuckled down and finished the album, which we called *Coast to Coast* after the first line from 'My Love'. We had had our ups and downs making the record, but when it was done we thought it was fantastic. That September, the Mariah Carey duet came out as a single. It became our sixth consecutive number one.

The album was to follow six weeks later, and we had some serious doubts about Sony BMG's release strategy. They had scheduled it up against the Spice Girls.

Geri had just left the Spices but they were still massive and their comeback album, *Forever*, was going to be enormous. After losing out to Steps first time around, we could all see it happening again, even when people at our label were telling us, 'No – we think you can beat them!'

I have to give the label this: they put their money where their mouth was. As a publicity stunt, they hired us a jet, and for two days prior to the album's release, they flew us from city to city to do record signings.

That forty-eight hours was totally insane. Having not toured Britain yet, it was the first time we had come properly face to face with the people who were buying our records, and it was all totally overwhelming. Everywhere we went it was in cars with blacked-out windows, with police escorts and total mayhem.

We started out in Glasgow where 2,000 people had been queuing up since dawn. Birmingham was the same, as was Manchester. Whenever we got out of a car, there would be fans in our faces, screaming, crying, roaring, even more overcome than we were.

What did we feel at the heart of it? The usual: amazement, exhilaration, fear, but most of all this… 'Jesus, this is great craic!' Yet at the same time we were looking at each other, grinning, blinking hard, and asking: 'What's so special about us? What do they see in us? Why is this happening?'

We signed everything we could, but there was no way that we could meet all the people who had come. We couldn't have done it if we'd had ten doppelgängers each. In between signings, we'd try to catch a couple of hours' kip – then it was back on the jet and off to the next official riot.

The jamboree ended up with a launch party at London's preposterously posh St Martin's Lane hotel. It had been two days of sheer madness… but it had been worth it. In that week's album chart, the Spice Girls were a speck in our rear-view mirror. *Coast to Coast* had sold nearly a quarter of a million copies. We had our first number-one album.

It felt like we literally couldn't be any bigger.

How little we knew. We were about to enter our world-domination period.

# 6

# NO SLEEP TILL DUBLIN

*Coast to Coast* was flying out of the shops at an insane rate and suddenly we were realizing that Westlife weren't just pop stars: we were becoming a phenomenon. It seemed like every day brought yet another reason to pinch ourselves. *Is this for real? Are you sure?* When you're living in a hall of mirrors, the bizarre becomes normality. 'My Love' went to number one, and we got loads of attention because we were the first artists in chart history to get to number one with our first seven singles. Not even The Beatles had done that. We couldn't believe it.

Another major thing had changed. With two multi-platinum albums behind us, suddenly we were earning serious money. The only problem was finding time to spend it; rather than wallowing in the success of *Coast to Coast*, we went straight out on another *Smash Hits* roadshow mini-tour with Atomic Kitten and A1.

When we got a few days off in Sligo, I indulged my one fetish again: cars. Nicky had turned up to the video shoot for 'My Love' in a brand-new navy BMW with cream leather and I loved it. I wanted to get one exactly the same, but in black.

Kian wanted to do exactly the same too, but I thought we would look a pair of nobs driving the exact same car around Sligo, so maybe I would get the 5 series. I went to see the town's main BMW dealer, a local character named Martin Riley.

Martin had a smile as wide as one of his windscreens when he saw me walking across the forecourt. I think he knew he had a good day coming up. I asked him if he had a 5-series BMW in black.

'No, I don't, but I've got a lovely car here,' he said, directing me towards a gorgeous blue-velvet BMW with a champagne leather interior. 'Let's take it for a test drive!'

It wasn't black, but the second I sat in the car, I knew I was going to buy it. I paid for it feeling like a kid buying a sweet shop. It was £56,000. I didn't even bother to haggle.

Looking back, we could have become unbearable right about now, but Louis was very good at keeping us grounded. He would tell us, 'You're very lucky boys, but it could all be over in the morning'; if any of us had a hissy fit, he'd be saying, 'Look, you can easily be replaced.'

Really, it was brilliant management. Louis was pretty laid-back and never interfered unless we started behaving like maggots, but he knew exactly how to control us. Without him, we would have f\*\*ked things up a thousand times.

In any case, somebody was about to give Westlife a short, sharp reality check – a three-inch-tall clay workman in blue dungarees with an irritating catchphrase.

Simon had chosen 'What Makes a Man' from *Coast to Coast* for our Christmas single for 2000 and I guess we all blithely assumed it would waft to number one exactly the same as its seven predecessors had done. It sounds bigheaded, but we had got used to winning the league every season.

Louis normally called us halfway through the week when we had a single out to tell us our midweek chart position. It was always good news. Well, not this time.

My mum and dad had let me do out a space at the top of our house as my own little apartment, and I was lying on my black leather couch in the afternoon watching TV (I even had more than two channels to choose from) when Louis came on the line.

'Shane, it's not good news,' he began. 'You're number two.'

'Number two?'

'You're miles behind Bob the Builder.'

Yes: 'What Makes a Man' might be a gorgeous power ballad but it was no match for 'Can We Fix It?', the theme tune to the BBC kids' cartoon series about a hard-hatted, pint-sized handyman. We had sold 270,000 singles, our most ever in a week; Bob had shifted half as many again. That little f**ker had fixed us.

It sounds stupid now, but we took this setback seriously and felt shit for days about losing our 100-per-cent record. It seemed like everywhere we went, shop windows were full of little Bob toys, laughing at us. It nearly ruined our Christmas.

Gillian and I fancied a break so I booked us a skiing holiday in Switzerland for over New Year. It was a total fiasco.

When it came time to fly out, there was two feet of snow in Sligo, the roads were blocked and we had to get a train to Dublin airport. I had not been on public transport since Westlife got famous, and I sat in a corner with a hat pulled down low, desperate not to be recognized and cause a crowd scene.

Gillian and I had imagined a romantic break in a log cabin, but when we got to Switzerland, we were booked into a Ritz-Carlton city-centre hotel a five-hour round trip from the nearest skiing – and there was no snow! What was the point? The next morning, we flew straight home.

We got to Dublin airport to be greeted by a big new display: 'Welcome to Ireland – the home of Westlife!' Ireland was still snowed in and it took us six hours to drive home, but we had a great New Year's Eve in Sligo.

I never used that travel agent again.

The New Year brought an exciting new challenge. Westlife were about to go out on our first full, proper tour.

It was weird that we had got this far and sold millions of records without touring. Mainly it was because we hadn't toured the first album, as Simon had been so keen on trying to break America. However, it did mean that an incredible desire had built up to see us perform live.

In some ways, it was ridiculous. We were about to go on the road with our own show for the very first time and we were booking venues that bands normally take ten years to get to. When we first set eyes on our itinerary, we were all shitting ourselves.

As fast as we announced dates, they sold out in minutes. Literally minutes. Then the promoter would add more. As we went into rehearsals at Dublin's Factory Studios, we knew we had to play fifty-two nights in vast British and Irish arenas… including ten nights at Wembley Arena and thirteen at the Point Depot.

Great. No pressure, then!

The rehearsals were intensive to say the least. We knew we had to put on an amazing show visually as well as musically to reach the back of those huge arenas, so Simon and Louis drafted in a shit-hot choreographer called Priscilla Samuels.

We liked Priscilla straight away. She was a really cool London woman; and my God she could dance! She reminded us of the Backstreet Boys' choreographer, whom we'd met when we'd supported them back in the day, which obviously endeared her to us as well.

I'm not sure her first impressions of us were quite so positive.

Priscilla knew she would have her work cut out with us. We were a band known not for dancing but for sitting on stools. I had danced in plays and Brian had been to dance school, but Kian and Mark weren't big dancers. Nicky had only stopped being a footballer a year ago and had never danced in his life.

On her first morning, Priscilla put some music on in a big rehearsal room and said, 'Just dance what you feel when you hear this – express yourselves!' Some serious free-form madness went down. Nicky was doing some sort of weird rave dancing and running on the spot.

Priscilla took a deep breath and set about whipping us into line. Within a couple of weeks she had us jumping about in sync like the Backstreet Boys. My feet were OK but I couldn't help waving my arms about and she was always shouting at me. I got let off a few arm routines by claiming I needed my hands to hold my mic.

We wanted our vocals to be perfect on tour – that was what Westlife were all about – so a gospel singer named Laurence sat at a grand piano and taught us harmonies. We also had to wear in-ear monitors, which had us yelling our heads off until we got used to them.

Yes, we needed total focus as we prepared for a tour that would see us play to more than half a million people – so that was when Brian decided to tell us that he was going to be a dad.

Actually, it wasn't Brian who told us. It was Nicky. He had gone out with Brian, and Brian had said to him, 'Oh, I need to buy a house.' Nicky had asked him, 'What do you need to buy a house for?' And Brian had said, 'Because I'm going to be a dad.'

It's weird now to think how we reacted to this news when Nicky told us. We acted like a bomb had gone off. We all felt as if it could be the end of everything. I raced into the toilet in the studio, looked in the mirror, puffed out my cheeks and went, 'Whew!' Why was this? I suppose we thought: would it change the way people saw the band? Would it make our fans see us differently? Would Simon give up on us?

How could we still be young, available, supposedly sexy pop stars if one of us was a... *dad*?

I remembered that Keith Duffy had had a baby halfway through Boyzone and it hadn't done them any harm, but it still felt scary. When Brian came in and we all congratulated him, it was clear he was scared as well. Sure, he loved Kerry, but he was only twenty years old.

Looking back, it's odd how badly we took the news – it wasn't like Brian had gone and got a fan pregnant, or something – but as ever, Louis talked us down. 'It's not going to change anything,' he told us. 'Anyway, what can we do?

95

'It is what it is.'

After the initial shock, we didn't dwell on it for too long. That was how it was in Westlife back then – you couldn't chew on anything for long because some other mad adventure would be along to distract you. And the next one was a good one.

The BBC asked us to record a single for Comic Relief. We were going to do a cover of Billy Joel's 'Uptown Girl', which was a buzz for me because I had loved it ever since I used to sing it to my mum and dad when I was five years old, and I still knew it off by heart.

But that wasn't the mad bit. The mad bit was that we were going to make a video for the song... with Claudia Schiffer. Claudia Schiffer! The world's most famous supermodel, and I was going to be serenading her in a diner!

Naturally we were shitting ourselves, but come the day it was Mariah Carey all over again. Claudia was as drop-dead gorgeous as we'd expected but she was also super-friendly, nice and, well, *normal*.

That was the weird thing with us. We'd meet celebrities and feel overwhelmed, while never realizing that that was what we were ourselves now too. Sure, we knew that we had sold a lot of records and we were in a famous band, but we never felt like we were special, or we were *stars*.

I guess this was partly down to our backgrounds, and partly down to Louis doing a damn good job of keeping us humble and nervous. But when we met real A-list celebrities, we felt like... *competition winners*. For better or worse, that feeling never really went away.

Then again, if you do want to feel famous or special, a pretty good way is to have half a million people screaming their adoration at you. And our first tour had sold half a million tickets.

The *Where Dreams Come True* tour kicked off in Newcastle on 9 February 2001. Like every date on the tour, it was in a stupidly big enormodome. The Telewest Arena was a sea of 13,000 screaming up-for-it party animals, a lot of whom had decided to come in deely-boppers (remember them? Those crazy headbands with two pronged, bouncing embellishments.).

We hadn't just sold the place out once: we were doing six nights there.

The show began with us all swinging down onto the stage on harnesses, and as we waited, hidden high up in the gods, and heard 13,000 impatient Geordies chanting the band's name – 'WEST-LIFE! WEST-LIFE!' – I suddenly felt like I couldn't remember even one minute of the show. Clearly, the last month's intense rehearsals had been a complete f\*\*king waste of time.

'WEST-LIFE! WEST-LIFE!'

It was our first live show, it was a massive production, and as I balanced on my harness, the set list, harmonies, dance moves and costume changes that we had obsessively honed melted to mulch in my head. I didn't even know what my name was. I looked over at Kian and saw the same terror all over his face.

'WEST-LIFE! WEST-LIFE!'

The lights went down and the shrill chants became a mass roar of anticipation. *Shit! This was it!* Five trembling souls zip-wired down into the cauldron; the arena; the bear pit. It was the closest I had ever been in my life to a panic attack.

We started with 'Dreams Come True' – well, obviously – and to this day I can't remember a thing about it. I was on autopilot, lost in the heat, the deafening screams, the fear, the out-of-body feeling. I felt like I couldn't breathe.

We had a pretty high-energy – for us – start to the show, and had put on way too much hairspray. In seconds, it was rolling into our eyes so we couldn't see. A few songs in, we sprinted offstage for our first costume change and looked at each other. We were all sweating like we could be wrung out.

'That's the hard bit done,' one of us said (it might even have been me). 'Now let's go and finish the show!'

From that point on, we loved it. We felt as if we were surfing neat adrenaline. The wild crowd were singing every word with us, not just of massive hits like 'Swear It Again' and 'Flying Without Wings' but of every single song; in between tracks, all we could hear were thousands of voices yelling, 'We love you!'

What kind of eejit would *not* enjoy that? That gig in Newcastle was the night I discovered that I loved playing live best of everything in Westlife; best of everything I had ever done. It was, and it still is, the best feeling in the world.

There is no way, after experiencing euphoria like that, that a band could meekly file backstage, have a glass of milk and a chat, and toddle quietly off to bed. So we didn't.

The tour should have been sponsored by Red Bull because we were drinking lakes of the stuff. Our favourite tipple at the time was vodka and Red Bull, and every night, after we came offstage, we got completely and totally trashed on it.

Something had to give. We had been in a pressure cooker for two years, working non-stop doing interviews and promo with hardly a day off, criss-crossing the globe, playing up to this image we had of squeaky-clean, butter-wouldn't-melt-in-their-mouths robots. We had gone from anonymity to international fame beyond our wildest imaginings.

Jesus, we were still only twenty years old!

Onstage, we were slick, professional and family-friendly; off, it was total party time. As I said, we were never a drug band, and girls were out of bounds for me, but we drank... and drank... and drank. Sailors on shore leave would have given Westlife a wide berth on that tour.

Work hard and play hard? You could say that again!

We were limited in where we could go. Pubs were out of the question: we'd have got torn limb from limb. Once or twice we hired out VIP rooms in local clubs. Mostly, we did the easiest thing: holed up in our hotel bar, where our two very harassed, overworked security guys could keep an eye on us.

Vodka and Red Bull is an incredible drink. The vodka sends you bananas while the Red Bull convinces you that you are fine and keeps your energy levels sky-high. Some nights I'd get through half a bottle of vodka on my own, easy.

Nicky was more of a beer man but Brian and Mark would cane the vodka as well, and Kian and I were like a tag team. It became an unspoken contest between the two of us: anything you can drink, I can drink more. See, we are typical Irish lads in more ways than one.

We were probably still drunk when we had a surprise high-level encounter on that tour in Glasgow. We were doing five nights at the SECC, and next door the British Labour Party were having their annual conference.

We got a message that the Prime Minister, Tony Blair, was keen to meet us. Wow! Really? We were taken to his private room, where he got his guitar out, talked about bands he loved and got our autographs for his kids and their friends. Mr Blair seemed a very nice guy who was really into music.

What a crazy experience! It was just one more thing to laugh about after the show that night as we got steaming drunk in the hotel bar yet again.

We had no shortage of things to drink to. Two weeks into the tour, the 'Uptown Girl' Comic Relief single came out and went straight to number one.

Normal service had been resumed. We felt we were back where we belonged.

On the road, we would lie in our beds in an alcoholic haze every day until early afternoon, then get taken to the venue to sound-check and the whole shebang would kick off again. Gillian flew out to join the tour at weekends but I didn't even slow down the partying then; she just joined in with us.

Kian and I went out and got bananas twenty-four nights in a row. The shows were still grand because our adrenaline and youthful energy was carrying us through them, but it couldn't go on forever – and our new drunken lifestyle caught up with me in Sheffield.

We were doing three nights at the Sheffield Arena, and after the second one we stayed up literally all night necking vodka. Normally we called it a day around 3 a.m., but on this night we had gone clean through. Back at the venue the next afternoon, I wasn't just half-drunk: I was still pissed.

We were doing interviews about the release of 'Uptown Girl' for Comic Relief and Sky News were there, but as our tour manager rounded us up, I made an informed, and accurate, decision: 'No, I can't do it!' Instead, I spent my time running up and down the corridors in my boxer shorts, giggling, before being found curled up asleep in the dressing room in a pair of deely-boppers.

It was hilarious… and then the hangover hit. The crippling, evil, all-crushing hangover; the worst I had ever had by a million miles, as twenty-four days of drinking caught up with me. I was sick as a dog and puking non-stop: sunk into a desperate, depressed gloom, I was talking of pulling the show.

We were never really going to do that, but as I was virtually carried to the stage to be strapped into my harness, I puked into one of the buckets that Karen from our production team had strategically placed by the side of the stage. Nice!

*If I can get through this*, I told myself, *I will never drink again*. The lights went up, the harnesses sailed down…

'Hello, Sheffield!'

I got through it. The old cliché is true: the show must go on. The crowd's energy lifted me and I told myself that out there were 10,000 fans who adored Westlife and who had never seen us live before; I couldn't let them down. As my alcohol poisoning lifted, I even started to enjoy the show.

Even so, enough was enough. That night, as Kian called at my room to start the partying, I told him I had different plans.

'Nah, you're all right. I'm gonna have a quiet night in, get some sleep, and try to hit the gym in the morning.'

Kian stared at me in incomprehension and slight disgust and then headed off down to the bar.

Of course, I was back on the sauce the next night – and stayed there, as we romped through the nuclear-hysteria levels of shows in London, Belfast and Dublin. Our first night at Wembley felt pretty special… but then so did the other nine.

Everybody likes to be appreciated in their own country and our thirteen nights at the Point Depot, with all of our friends and families caught up in the screaming throng, were the highlights of the whole amazing tour. Most nights after the Dublin shows we headed down to Lillie's Bordello, which had taken over from the Pod as the city's hip nightspot where local celebs like Bono hung out.

Now that Brian was with Kerry, Kian was the last member standing who was flying the flag for Westlife with the girls. Kian was very selective, but he sure had a good selection to pick from and he enjoyed himself.

There again, Ronan's warning proved astute when a girl did a kiss-and-tell on Kian all over a Sunday tabloid front page. She was quite complimentary and said what a stud he was. Kian wasn't cheating on anyone so he hadn't done anything wrong, but he was still mortified: he hated the thought of his mum reading it.

I felt sorry for Kian – and more relieved than ever that my policy was to look, but not touch. Gillian was my life and you don't throw your life away.

After six weeks of UK dates, we got a one-day break before the tour swung through Europe, including five shows in Germany, then a few dates in the Middle East and South Africa, where we were doing really well. The last fortnight, in Southeast Asia, was reliably berserk.

We developed a routine to try to help us hold on to at least a little bit of our sanity. As we sat in a tour bus in Kuala Lumpur as screaming girls launched themselves at the vehicle like weapons, or we were pursued through the crazy traffic of Phnom Penh, Mark, Kian and I would adopt comedically thick, exaggerated west-of-Ireland accents to remind each other who we were.

'You're from Colga, Calry, County Sligo.'

'You're from Lynn Dale, County Sligo.'

'You're from the Carlton Café in Castle Street, Sligo.'

'Look at the state of us. What the hell are we doing here?'

Yet this primitive reality check stood no chance of working when everyday life was so mind-boggling. Just when you thought things couldn't get any madder, they did. Like when Louis asked us: would you like £500,000 to play a private show for the Sultan of Brunei?

I've never been big into politics, haven't got a political bone in my body, but the wealth we saw in Brunei was obscene. The Sultan sent a private jet to fly us out there, and a Rolls-Royce to pick us up from the airport. His palace made the Taj Mahal look like a Portakabin.

As a car freak, the trip did my head in. The Sultan had about 3,000 cars, including just about every Ferrari and Porsche and Lamborghini ever made, in every colour you can think of. We were even allowed to test-drive a couple.

We played a free (to them) 5,000-people show in the Sultan's grounds on a stage he had built for his previous guest, a few months before – Michael Jackson. We never saw the Sultan, I don't know if he even came to the show, but we met his two wives and their ten children. Even his five-year-old was dripping in more diamonds than I had ever seen in my life before.

*I am from the Carlton Café, in Castle Street...* We returned to Sligo exhausted but elated. The *Where Dreams Come True* tour had lasted four months, been to twenty-two different countries, entertained 600,000 people and made £12m.

OK, we had drunk our body weight in vodka and Red Bull and trashed our livers along the way, but it could hardly have gone better. Westlife were on top of the world.

So naturally, as it came time to begin recording our third album, we did the most sensible thing that we could do.

We started falling out with each other.

# 7

# 'MUM, THIS IS THE POPE...'

What Louis Walsh had done right at the start of Westlife had been brilliant. Once we had settled on our final line-up, it had been a fantastic idea to pack us all off to live together to get to know each other inside out, and it had worked like a dream.

That intensive bonding period had turned the five of us into brothers, especially when the madness exploded around us and we had to cope with the head-spinning insanity of fame. On tour we were together 24/7, a gang whether we were working, playing, chatting, eating, scheming or just falling-down drunk.

As Louis had wanted, it was us against the world. We loved each other.

Having said that, it is impossible to spend all of your time in each other's pockets without rows and arguments breaking out. Tensions and bickering would creep in, and occasionally we would have niggling fallings-out on the road that would drag on for days.

It would always be about something dumb, like one of us joking that somebody was putting on weight or not looking too good, but then we would get offended and give each other the silent treatment. It was stupid, really, but life in a band can make you stupid.

Brian and I might fall out and not talk for days. We would meet each other in a hotel corridor or at the side of the stage and look away as if the other person wasn't there. Or I would not be talking to Kian, except via Nicky or Brian.

Eventually, Mark or somebody would say, 'Look, will you two f\*\*king eejits talk to each other! You're arguing over nothing!'

It was always petty, it was never a big deal and once it was over, it was over; we didn't bear grudges. For the most part, we got on grand, but these tensions did come up now and then, especially as our fame and success made us all more confident in our opinions.

It was time to record our third album, and figuring that if it's not broke, you don't fix it, Simon wanted to pack us off to London and Sweden as usual. We agreed to a few trips, but at the same time, we had been away from home a long time and we were all for spending some time in Ireland.

The record label saw our point and put us into Windmill Lane Studios in Dublin, where U2 had made so many of their records. I stayed with Brian and Kerry in Dublin during the week and went back to Sligo at weekends. For a couple of months, it was almost like a normal life.

It was great to hang out with Gillian and see my family again so regularly; and there was plenty for me to keep an eye on. The building work was well underway on the big house at Carraroe, and while there was still a long way to go, it was exciting to see it going up.

It was just when everything was sunny in the garden and everything was going great that some pressures opened up in the band – over songwriting.

After writing a couple of our own songs on *Coast to Coast*, we were keen to do more. Our lawyers had just negotiated us a massive contract extension with Sony BMG, worth about £10m, and people around us were in our ears telling us that we could earn even more if we wrote songs, and that we were missing out on a lot of potential royalties.

Brian and I were getting pretty close at this point. I was staying at his place during that spring and summer of 2001, we had both got into golf, and Gillian and Kerry hung out and saw a lot of each other. It made sense for Brian and me to start writing a few songs with professional songwriters.

We mentioned this to Mark, Kian and Nicky, and in no time at all, the three of them had formed into a separate team doing the same thing. I suppose they felt threatened and wanted to make the point that they could write as well as we could, but it divided the band into two camps.

It wasn't as if we were short of great material for the new record, which was going to be called *World of Our Own*. Steve Mac and Wayne Hector had given us the title track and 'Queen of My Heart', and the Swedes had written songs such as 'Evergreen'.

We knew we needed those guys, they had helped to make us to an extraordinary degree, and we were incredibly grateful for their help. It wasn't like Brian and I thought we were Lennon and McCartney – but at the same time, we wanted our songs on there.

The final decision, as ever, came down to Simon. I'm sure he knew all about our little split. We had all been giving Louis earache, and I'm sure he was talking to Simon: 'Jesus, they're going on about songwriting again!'

Louis probably advised Simon to humour us and that's what they did. When Simon chose the final album track listing, there were three McFadden/Filan songs, three from the Byrne, Egan and Feehily camp – and 'I Wanna Grow Old with You', written by myself, Brian and Kian.

At the time, it kept everybody happy. Looking back, I am not sure at least four of our songs should have made the album. But I guess it is the kind of thing that labels have to do when they are dealing with pushy little boy bands who are developing pop-star egos.

Brian had to record some of his vocals for *World of Our Own* separately because he had more important things to worry about than how many songwriting credits he got on a pop album. At the end of August 2001, Kerry gave birth to little Molly.

Like most young blokes, Brian had been scared when he learned his girlfriend was pregnant, but he was proud and glowing to be a dad. We could see it in him. He did admit, however, that he was worried about going on tour a few months down the line and having to leave Kerry and Molly behind.

I was also about to experience a change in my own personal life – and I was delighted with it.

Three years into Westlife, I was still telling interviewers that I didn't have a girlfriend. The joke was wearing thin. As the band got bigger it was getting harder and harder to keep Gillian a secret, and in any case I didn't want to. I had had enough of sneaking around.

The pantomime came to an end when Gillian and I spent a weekend at a nice hotel in Dublin. Somebody at the hotel must have tipped off the papers, because a photographer got a long-range shot of us leaving and getting into a taxi.

We didn't know a thing about it until the following weekend, when the picture appeared in the *News of the World*. It was a world exclusive, apparently:

QUEEN OF HIS HEART!

The story reported that 'Heart-throb Shane has dated Gillian Walsh for more than a year' (well, try nearly four years...) and quoted 'a source' as saying, 'The couple are in constant touch with each other wherever Shane is in the world. His phone bill is massive but he doesn't care – he really loves Gillian.'

I had to wonder who this 'source' was. My guess was some hack in the office making the quote up, as they always did.

Still, now the truth was out, it was a huge relief. It made day-to-day life more honest. Gillian was also OK with it by now but hated that the photo of us they used was a bit shite, so the next time we went to a function all dressed-up, we let the press get some shots of us together.

It felt good to stop sneaking around and as 2001 neared its end, life as a whole felt pretty grand. 'Queen of My Heart' was released as the lead single from *World of Our Own* in November and went straight to number one, and the album followed it there a week later.

Ha! So where are you now, Bob the Builder?

Then, just when I thought life couldn't get any better, we got invited to meet the Pope, John Paul II.

The invitation was to sing at a special festive performance that the Vatican held every Christmas. I was so excited – but nothing compared to how my mum was when I asked her and Dad to come with me. It was like she was going to meet Jesus.

We flew over to Rome in a private jet, only to find that we had somehow managed to leave the band's suits behind. We could have bought new ones there, but instead we panicked and sent the jet back to pick them up. No expense spared, huh?

The performance was nearly a disaster. The Vatican had asked – well, told – us to sing 'Little Drummer Boy', but at the rehearsal the 100-piece orchestra were playing it three keys above our range. Mark might just be able to get there; I had no chance.

Luckily, Kian saw Dolores O'Riordan from The Cranberries, who were also performing, hanging around at the rehearsal. When he asked her, she happily agreed to guest on 'Little Drummer Boy' with us, meaning we could sing the backing vocals. She was our angel of the Vatican, no question!

After the show, we got to meet the Pope, who was very old and frail. I was nervous and awkward, but it was wonderful to see how happy it made my mum as she bent forward and kissed the ring on his hand. She looked like she had... well, gone to Heaven.

Back in Ireland, Brian and Kerry had bought a lovely house in Wicklow, and Gillian and I went out to visit them and see baby Molly. They all seemed so happy, and I remember Gillian and I looking at each other and saying, 'Wow – what if we had a life like this?'

I was a groomsman two weeks later in January 2002 when Brian and Kerry got married with a huge reception at Slane Castle. They sold their wedding pictures to *Hello!* and it was a full-on celebrity bash with paparazzi outside. They just seemed a really happy couple.

Mind you, I was a very happy young man shortly afterwards, when I bought myself a Ferrari. As ever, part of me thought, *Should I do this? Are people in Sligo going to think I'm a f\*\*king prick?* But then I thought, *Look, I can afford it and I want it. Why shouldn't I? The people who slag me would probably do the same if they could!*

Brian, Nicky and I went to a Ferrari dealership in Surrey. Brian bought a canary yellow Ferrari that looked a bit like a spaceship and Nicky bought a red one. I loved the red one as well but was a bit afraid of looking like a cliché, so I test-drove a black Ferrari 550 Maranello. It was amazing.

It cost £94,500. I phoned my accountant. 'Can you transfer the funds into my account?' I asked him. 'Can I buy it?'

'You're f\*\*king mad,' he told me. 'But you can do whatever you want.' I did.

Brian, Nicky and I walked out of that showroom as three young lads who had just spent a quarter of a million pounds on cars. My insurance came to £13,000 a year. I honestly think cars then were like a drug to me.

Then again, it was better than actually spending my money on drugs, I suppose. People ask if I often got offered drugs in Westlife but it only ever happened three times – once in Sligo, when I got offered a line of coke in a toilet nightclub. I remember thinking, *Jesus, of all the places...* I wasn't even tempted by it. In fact, I was terrified. My mum and Louis had both drilled into me the dangers of drugs and where they can lead you and leave you. In that respect, at least, our squeaky-clean reputation *was* justified.

In any case, I wasn't just wasting all of my hard-earned cash on premium vehicles. I decided it was time for Gillian and me to get onto a more secure footing.

For months, she had been renting a flat in the middle of Sligo and when I was in town I would spend half of my time there and half at my parents' house. We had freedom and it felt a bit like the best of both worlds, but seeing Brian and Kerry's domestic bliss had also made us hanker for more.

My mum was never interfering or judgmental, but one day even she asked why Gillian and I were dossing down in a poky one-bedroom pad when I could afford to buy a much nicer place. It was a very good question and when I gave it some thought, I wasn't sure what the answer was.

So Gillian and I bought a house in Carraroe, near to where my family mansion was still being built. It felt a big move, and it was… but at the same time, I was lucky enough to be able to buy it outright, for cash.

Early in 2002, 'World of Our Own' came out as a single and went to number one. I was very proud of that because when I had sung it, I was absolutely bollocksed.

We had recorded it during the Dublin album sessions. Steve Mac's initial plan was for Brian or Mark to sing lead but he hadn't been totally happy with the result. I had arrived in the studio still steaming from the night before and he had asked me to have a go.

'Ah, shite, man,' I had told him. 'I can't do it. I'm hungover and my voice is f**ked.'

'No, give it a go, and make it nice and raspy,' Steve had said. I did, and to my surprise, it came out great. In fact, of all the producers we worked with, it was Steve Mac who helped me to find parts of my voice I didn't even know were there.

The *World of Our Own* tour kicked off in Europe in April and would take us through the next few months. It was pretty cool – it had a loose space theme, and we all got to enter out of planet-like globes at the start of the set. A world of our own, see?

The tour was in the round, and we ticked off another of the big London venues when we played five nights at Earls Court. We were still partying, but nothing like the insanity of the *Where Dreams Come True* tour. In Dublin, we did another thirteen gigs at the Point, and we rounded off with our first headline stadium show, in Killarney.

The tour was on at the same time as the World Cup in Japan and it seemed like the whole country was watching the football. Ireland did well, drawing with Germany in the group stages before being knocked out on penalties by Spain, and it made our Irish gigs fantastic craic.

As the tour came to an end, we put out 'Bop Bop Baby' as a single. It was a song that Brian and I had co-written, so really I should have been chuffed, but in all honesty I was in two minds about doing it.

I was surprised when Simon had phoned me to say that he was releasing it as a single because I didn't think it was all that good. Maybe I was right, because it only got to number five, our worst chart performance by far.

Simon is very canny and I suspect he may have done it to teach us a lesson: so we would learn which side our bread was buttered on and go on singing the songs that Steve Mac and the Swedes gave us, and stop bothering our pretty little heads about songwriting.

We had a laugh making the 'Bop Bop Baby' video, though. We were all got up in medieval garb in a dungeon on the film set where they made *Harry Potter*. Vinnie Jones was in the video playing the baddie and was great to hang out with. Naomi Campbell was supposed to be in it, but she cancelled the day before and Leah Wood stepped in.

Simon still had his eye on the biggest prize of all – America. We had got nowhere at all on our first attempt, a couple of years earlier, but he still thought we might be able to crack it and sent us back over there for a month that summer.

He thought we might be able to break big with 'World of Our Own', which he felt could work over there. We even made a new video for it, just for America. We stayed in Los Angeles, got some Californian sunshine, gazed at the Hollywood sign and worked like mad.

Yet on that second American trip, some tensions that had been bubbling beneath the surface of the band came to a head – and led to our worst argument yet.

In recent months, there had been a definite trend in our photo shoots. We were doing shoots for the record label, for newspapers, for magazines, and each time photographers had the same request: 'Can Shane stand in the middle?'

It didn't seem like a big deal, but it was starting to rankle with the other lads. We had always wanted Westlife to be a band of equals and not like Boyzone, where Ronan Keating was the standout star, but they thought things were heading that way.

Before we flew to the States, the other lads complained to each other and then raised it with me. This made me feel like they had been talking behind my back, so I argued with them: 'What does it matter? So I'm in the middle – what's the big deal?'

Out in LA, we did a two-hour photo shoot for the US label and the photographer must have taken 1,000 photos. I was in the middle in every single one. Even I had to admit it was a bit weird.

After the shoot, the band went to a diner, and we ended up having a huge fight. It started off the same as usual, with the lads saying it wasn't fair and I was being raised above them; like Justin Timberlake had been in 'N Sync. I was pissed off, and I let them all have it with both barrels.

'Look, what the f\*\*k is your problem? I'm a lead singer. We are a band. We're all pop stars; we're being paid the same; we're having a good laugh. Am I supposed to ask to be on the edge of the pictures? I just stand where I'm asked to stand. Get over yourselves!'

By the end we were shouting and Nicky and I had a stand-up row that ended with him storming out of the diner. 'If you've got a problem, talk to Louis about it!' I yelled after him. The lads got on the phone and did exactly that.

In the context of our trip, it was an even more ridiculous thing to be arguing about – because Westlife's second American 'invasion' was the same story as our first. We went to loads of local record-company launch parties and tried to charm the arse off the media, but our timing was shite.

Boy bands were dead in America. 'N Sync and the Backstreet Boys had split up and we had missed the boat: radio stations weren't playing anything like us. Well, once bitten, twice shy, and Simon and Louis had to accept that we would never happen in America.

It disappointed us, but we weren't gutted. We had so much going on in Europe, Asia and everywhere else that it was hard to be too downcast: it just wasn't meant to be. We figured that at least we could always go on holiday to America, chill out and be anonymous.

We certainly couldn't do that in Indonesia or the Philippines!

When we got back to Ireland from the States, Louis phoned me up and told me some unexpected, and seriously major, news – I had been offered a solo record deal.

The offer had come from Universal Records, whom we had turned down to sign with Simon, but who had signed Boyzone. They had seen Ronan launch a solo career outside of Boyzone, and were wondering if I wanted to do the same.

It was a good offer, about two or three million quid, but I wasn't tempted in the slightest. It wasn't about the money. I had loads of money in Westlife. I loved being in the band and I didn't want to leave it for the world. Plus, if I am honest, the very idea of going solo terrified me.

So my decision was easy: thanks, but no thanks. Louis was relieved that I felt that way: he didn't want me pissing off the others and maybe breaking up the band. In fact, he saw that this news was the perfect way to reunite us.

Louis called a band meeting and the other lads started giving out again about me being in the middle of the photos. I was fed up of this by now and let loose with another of my 'Get over it!' rants. Louis heard us out, picked his moment, and then dropped his bombshell.

'Listen, lads. Shane has been offered a solo contract!'

The room went silent. I could see one thought on four faces: *This is it. F\*\*k. He's leaving the band.*

'But he's said, "No",' Louis continued.

Everyone looked relieved and started throwing questions at me at the same time: 'Really?' 'What's the story?' 'Are you sure you're staying?'

'Yes,' I explained. 'I don't want to go solo. I want to be in Westlife. So stop worrying about f**king photos!'

It was another management masterclass from Louis, and a brilliant way to kill that particular issue stone dead. Having said that, we did try to mix up our photo-compositions a bit more after that.

We also cleared the air about a few other niggles we had in the band. Some of us were a bit pissed off as we felt that Brian's partying meant he wasn't always on top form, and Mark had kept us waiting a few too many times.

Louis patiently explained to us the common sense that we had all got too pig-headed to see. We were one of the biggest bands in the world, none of us was perfect, and we were going to fall out sometimes. The key was being big enough to talk the problems through.

As usual, we quickly had something else to think about. The time arrives in every band's life when they have to think about Greatest Hits albums, and ours had come very quickly. We had put out three albums in three years, and Sony BMG were keen to strike while the iron was hot and put out a singles compilation.

We were excited about this but also a bit worried. We talked it over: would a Greatest Hits send out a signal that it was all over for the band? Would it be hard to follow up?

Were we nearing the end of the shelf life for a boy band?

We went back and forth, but in the end we just figured: shit, Simon and Louis know what they are doing here. Everything they have touched has turned to gold so far. So, as usual, we fell into line and agreed to record a few new songs for the album, then do a big Greatest Hits tour the following year.

We recorded a new single called 'Unbreakable' and gave the Greatest Hits album the same title. They both went straight to number one in November 2002, and the album stayed on the chart for more than a year.

Yes, maybe the record label did know what they were doing.

Somehow word had got out about my offer to go solo – but not that I had turned it down – so in all the interviews at the time of *Unbreakable* we were being asked if Westlife were splitting up. At least we could honestly say no.

By now, we had done so many interviews since we started that they could be a real slog. Journalists all tend to ask the same questions as though they are the first person to think of them. It all gets a bit Groundhog Day.

The European and Asian promo trips were the hardest. The local record companies would squeeze in radio slots, TV shows and interviews from eight in the morning to eight at night. In truth, the novelty of jetting around the world to talk to people about the band had now definitely worn off.

We started asking the local PRs to cut a few things out of our schedules. We didn't want to be difficult or diva-ish but at the same time we knew if we slaved away 24/7, it would kill the band – or we would kill each other.

Far more enjoyable was a holiday to Dubai that Gillian and I had just before Christmas 2002 – when I asked her to marry me.

I had not actually planned to propose on that trip – in fact, I bought the engagement ring at a jewellers in the hotel – but I had never felt more certain about anything in my life. After a candlelit dinner, Gillian and I went for a night-time walk along the beach next to the warm Gulf waters. We lay side-by-side on recliners then I got up, fetched the ring from my pocket and held it over her head. As she gasped, I got down on one knee. 'Will you marry me?'

When she accepted, I was the happiest man in the world.

Our families were delighted when we told them the news and we had a very happy Christmas in Sligo. We decided to keep the Christmas theme going and get married right at the end of the following year.

Westlife might have been having a few ups and downs, but the *Unbreakable* tour through Europe and Britain in the spring and summer of 2003 was fantastic. We had a brilliant stage set, with weird sci-fi and Las Vegas-style neon lights, and played a few stadiums as well as our usual arenas.

It seemed like we had finally graduated out of the Point and we did two gigs at the Lansdowne Road rugby ground in Dublin, which was pretty amazing. I was even more proud of being hometown heroes when we played at Markievicz Park in Sligo.

Yet we felt as if Westlife were at a crossroads. The Greatest Hits album represented a full stop to the first, hugely successful part of our career. We had already been around for far longer than most boy bands managed. For the first time, we felt as if we didn't know what was coming next.

It was a weird, uncertain time, and looking back, we started making some bad decisions. Maybe we had an identity crisis. Maybe we were tired of getting criticized for only ever singing ballads, because we started thinking about maybe reinventing Westlife and doing rockier numbers.

Kian was a bit of a mover for this. He was really getting into the business side of the band and liaising between us, Simon,

Louis and Sonny. He enjoyed that organizing part of the job, and was almost becoming Louis's assistant manager. It was fine by me: I could never be arsed to do stuff like that.

Kian came into Steve Mac's studio raving about a song called 'Rainbow Zephyr' by a rock band from Northern Ireland called Relish. It had been a hit in Ireland and he wondered if we could rework it. Well, why not? We rejigged it into a soulful, up-tempo number that we renamed 'Hey Whatever'.

We were all dead pleased and thought it could be the start of something new for Westlife, and Kian went and pushed for it to be released as a single in September 2003. Simon thought it was OK, no more than that, but we had nothing better, so he agreed.

We might have liked our new direction – but that didn't guarantee that our fans would. The first single from a new Westlife album had always, *always* gone straight in at number one.

Not this time. When Louis phoned Kian, the news was not good. Kian was pretty down when he called me. '"Hey Whatever" is only number four,' he said. 'And Simon has called us in for a meeting in his office tomorrow morning at eleven.'

This was a meeting at which Mr Cowell did not mince his words.

'Sit down, kiddos,' he told us, as we all filed into an executive office the size of a football field. 'We need to have a talk.'

'I think you're losing your way. You're falling into a trap and you're losing sight of what you are. And quite frankly, if you carry on the way you are...

'This band is over.'

# 8

# THE STRIFE OF BRIAN

There is one thing I should say here. The Simon Cowell who had just said those fearful words to us, from the other side of his enormous desk, was not the same Simon Cowell who had signed us.

Actually, that's not true. Simon hadn't really altered – he was still the same person; he still thought he knew everything; he still called everybody 'kiddo'. But his circumstances had changed dramatically.

When Simon had signed us five years earlier, he had been a big player in the music industry, sure, but effectively he was just another record-business executive. Then, in 2001, he had become a judge on ITV's *Pop Idol* on Saturday nights. The following year, he did the same in the States on *American Idol*.

His fame had rocketed. Simon was the same on those shows as he was in meetings with us, very opinionated and telling it straight the way he saw it, but the media and the public had really latched onto him. The A & R man working behind the scenes to make stars had become a star himself.

He had taken to it like a duck to water. Seriously, if Simon had walked down the street with one of Westlife now, it would have been hard to say who would be recognized more. He had become a proper celebrity, all over TV, magazine front covers and gossip columns – and he loved it.

We had found it hilarious watching Simon become a bona fide superstar, especially as he'd essentially done it just by being himself. Sitting in our crisis meeting now, the music mogul, with his immaculate shiny hair, glowing tan and perfect white teeth, looked like he was turning into Tom Cruise. Every inch of him looked famous.

Yes, we loved what Simon had become – but we didn't love what he was telling us.

'I think you're losing the plot,' he repeated. 'You're forgetting what you are and you could be finished very, very soon.'

*Shit.* His words hit me like a punch in the face. I felt sick to my stomach. Here was the man who had signed us, named us and made us, telling us that we were as good as over. Had it come to this?

I snuck a glance around the table: at Louis, at Kian, at Mark, at Nicky, at Brian. They all looked like they were at a funeral. Was that what this meeting was?

Simon let his words resonate, as he wanted them to, took in our reactions – and then produced his miracle cure.

'But I'm not going to let that happen, kiddos,' he grinned. 'I am going to save you from ruining your careers. Your fans love you singing love songs, and *this* should be your next single.'

Without even looking behind him, Simon leaned back in his big black leather executive chair and pushed a button on his gleaming sound system. Some gentle piano chords filled the air, and then a soft, yearning vocal. 'I remember all my life, raining down as cold as ice...'

Hang on. I knew this. We all did. This was... 'Mandy' by Barry Manilow? Everybody looked aghast. Everybody except Simon, who sat back smiling, smoking and nodding along as the song built to its big, schmaltzy chorus. 'Oh Mandy! Well you came and you gave without taking, but I sent you away...'

All the time the song was going on, Simon was working his meeting magic. Simon was amazing in meetings. He just had the knack of always getting exactly what he wanted from people. I always said he should have been Prime Minister.

What Simon would do was scan the room for the people who seemed most opposed to what he was suggesting. Right now, that was everybody, although Mark and Brian were the two who tended to least like Westlife doing cover versions. Simon would catch that person's eye... and give them a sly wink.

It was incredibly powerful. It was like Simon was sharing a secret, drawing you into his confidence: 'It's you and me, kiddo.' You always found yourself smiling back, wanting to agree, seduced by his charm and charisma. 'Well,' you'd think, 'maybe he *has* got a point...'

That trick had worked well when he was just Simon our A & R man, and it was irresistible now that he was one of the biggest TV personalities in the country. Right now, in this meeting, Simon was doing a lot of surreptitious winking.

Barry Manilow's power ballad wafted to its epic close. There was an uneasy silence. I think most of us were still thinking, *Are you taking the piss?* But nobody said anything. Who would break the silence?

It was Nicky: 'Ah, that's me mam's favourite song!'

Simon gave Nicky a particularly big wink for that one, and then he gave it to us straight.

We had to think of what our fans wanted. We might want to be cool, and edgy, and mix things up a bit, but they didn't need that from us. Our millions of fans had no desire for us to try to be hip, or to change.

They just loved us singing love songs and ballads, Simon concluded – and they didn't care if they were covers or not.

It was a powerful argument from a master politician and it was hard to argue with. Mark and Brian raised some token objections in the meeting, but the problem was... we knew that he was right.

In a way, though it was a hard thing to take, that was a massive landmark meeting for Westlife. Kian had pushed for 'Hey Whatever', and got some of the blame when it didn't work; he could have felt crushed, but afterwards he summarized things brilliantly.

'OK, so we may not always like doing covers, but what is cool, exactly?' he asked. 'Is it cool to change and to be getting to number five or number twenty in the charts? Or is it cool to go on for ten years yet and still be having number ones? Simon's right!'

When we went back into the studio to finish off our fourth album, to be called *Turnaround*, there was no more talk of us writing songs or covering indie tunes. Instead, it was a record of smart, slick ballads and pop songs, the majority of them by Steve Mac and Wayne Hector. Classic Westlife.

And, what do you know? As we were doing our usual non-stop round of media interviews, 'Mandy' went straight in at number one in November 2003. *Turnaround* did exactly the same a week or two later. It was almost like that cocky Mr Cowell knew what he was doing.

It was such a relief. Up until our Greatest Hits, Westlife had had a perfect, faultless career (apart from the upset caused by that little bastard Bob the Builder). We had certainly had a blip this year, our worst to date, but now we all felt back on course and on top of the world again.

Right at that point, it felt like... could things get any better? And for me the answer was yes, a thousand times better, because I was about to marry Gillian.

It was a Christmas wedding. We both loved Christmas so it seemed the natural choice to get married then. We settled on 28 December, in that lull that always happens before the New Year celebrations kick in.

People always say that a wedding is the bride's big day and the groom just shows up, but in our case we were both keen to make the day unforgettable. We had always dreamed of getting married in a castle, so we chose Ballintubber Abbey for the service, in Mayo, with a reception at nearby Ashford Castle.

Joanne Byrne of Presence PR, who had been Westlife's PR in Ireland from the very start, volunteered to organize the wedding. She had her work cut out. The media were desperate to gain access, and she had celebrity magazines like *Hello!* and *OK!* in her ear trying to weasel their way in.

Gillian and I had never shown the slightest interest in selling our big day to a magazine but a bidding war somehow broke out regardless. The day before the wedding, Joanne called me to say that a celebrity magazine had offered us €1m for exclusive coverage.

Even then we said no. I felt like the day should be private and not for sale and the thought of the world gawping at our wedding photos seemed weird. Over the years, all the other Westlife lads have sold their wedding days, and good luck to them; it's entirely their business. But it wasn't for us.

Before the wedding, I was dead nervous. This was a different kind of nerves to before a Westlife show, when it was all about anxiety and adrenaline and hoping that nothing would go wrong. This was a nervous elation. As I stood at the top of the aisle, a single, simple thought echoed around my head, *I'm getting married! I'm getting married!* There were a couple of thousand fans alongside paparazzi behind the security barriers outside the abbey. Gillian was arriving in a traditional horse-drawn carriage, and I knew she must have got there when screaming broke out. When she appeared at the top of the aisle, she looked perfect.

Father Gilhooley, whom I had listened to at Mass every Sunday as a kid, took the service. It was beautiful. Afterwards Gillian and I went out for a few minutes to wave at fans and let the press get some shots. It kept them happy, and it meant that they left us in peace when we went off to enjoy the party.

Louis had loaned Gillian and me his black Bentley to use as our wedding car and we were driven in it to the castle for the reception. At the castle gates, we switched into the horse-drawn carriage for our big entrance.

Every groom worries about his reception speech. I was no exception. I knew what I wanted to say – that I loved Gillian, and I always had – but I didn't want to sound cheesy. I hit on an audacious plan: I would sing to her.

I wasn't totally sure about doing it – was it even more corny? – but my groomsmen, my old school friends Keith and Brig, had urged me on and said I had to do it. Even so, all through my speech, I was wondering: *Is this stupid? Is it going to fall on its arse?*

It was too late to back out now, so at the end of my speech, I serenaded Gillian with an a cappella version of our favourite song, 'our tune', I suppose: 'Amazed' by Lonestar.

'I don't know how you do what you do / I'm so in love with you / It just keeps getting better / I want to spend the rest of my life with you by my side / Forever and ever…'

Singing it felt good, truthful and righteous. I looked at my new wife as I sang to her, and she was crying. When I looked around the room, virtually everybody seemed to be clapping and wiping something from their eye.

Well, if you can't cry at a wedding, when can you? It was one of the many high points of a day that was a fairy tale from start to finish. We could not have been happier.

Gillian and I both stayed sober all through our big day so the next evening we were gagging for a party. We pushed the boat out and hired a helicopter to fly us back to Sligo, where Gillian's best friend Helena had arranged a big bash for us at McHugh's pub.

It was a fantastic mad party that went on all night, and at 7 a.m. Gillian and I left to find the town white all over. We walked home hand in hand through the snow. When we got up, my dad asked me what time we had got in.

'Oh, about 3 o'clock,' I lied.

'That's odd,' said Dad. 'You left a trail of footprints in the snow, and it didn't start snowing till 7!' Even now I was a married man, he was still keeping an eye on me.

Gillian and I took off to the Maldives for our honeymoon. For the first week, we stayed at a Hilton hotel in a glass-floored suite that was set on stilts in the sea. There were two of them close to each other, reached by a wooden jetty from the beach, and as the porter drove us over on a buggy, he confided, 'You have a famous neighbour for your stay.'

'Who's that?' I asked him.

'Sir Paul McCartney.'

Paul McCartney? F**k! I was incredibly excited and my eyes were on stalks as I gazed out of our window trying to spot him. Gillian is rarely starstruck, and she had a word with me: 'We're on our honeymoon, Shane! Forget about The Beatles.'

It was hard to forget about Sir Paul the next morning when he sent us a bottle of champagne and a breakfast of strawberries with a congratulatory note. For the rest of the day, I was in a daydream: *I'm on my honeymoon; we're in paradise in the Indian Ocean; a Beatle is sending me breakfast...* Gillian and I still have the champagne. We treasured it too much to drink it.

I didn't bump into Paul, though... until a couple of days later, when I was walking along a little leafy walkway to get a massage in the hotel spa. Suddenly there he was, right in front of me. He gave me a thumbs-up, opened his mouth and started singing:

'Oh, Mandy! You came and you gave without taking, and I sent you away!'

He sang a few more lines, congratulated me again and walked on. I have had my fair share of surreal moments in my life, but being serenaded by Sir Paul McCartney in the Maldives is up there with them. When I sing 'Mandy' live now, even today, Macca pops into my head.

We spent the second week of our honeymoon on an absurdly idyllic neighbouring island. Our villa was right on the beach and even if we walked 500 yards into the turquoise ocean, it only came up to our waists.

We were in paradise. Life was perfect.

When Gillian and I got back to Ireland, we moved into our house in Carraroe. It was a great place to supervise the work on the big family mansion. The roof had gone on now but we were still looking at a few more months before we could all move in. It was wonderful to see it finally come together.

In fact, I made a little move into the property market. The Irish economy was booming, everybody was talking about the Celtic Tiger, and I decided to buy five houses in Sligo and rent them out. I only had to put down a 10 per cent deposit. It seemed like a good investment and a pretty foolproof plan, and was a nice sideline from the band.

After the wedding and the honeymoon, I felt like I had had a great break from Westlife for a few weeks and when we got back together I was raring to go. The *Turnaround* tour was due to kick off at the end of March 2004 and was to be the usual full-on arena jaunt around Britain and Europe.

Three weeks before the first date, we all went to the Meteor Awards in Dublin. They gave us Best Irish Pop Act, which if I am honest was not a total surprise – it was the third year in a row that we had won it! Even so, it was always grand to win and the Meteors were a great night out.

Brian was there with Kerry. I had last seen them at our wedding and they had been on great form. They had had their second daughter, Lilly-Sue, in the February of the year before, and they should have been on top of the world.

But Brian was not a happy man at the Meteors. It seemed like he was in a sulk and just didn't want to be there. When we won our award, he reluctantly came up to the stage with us to get it, but then he wouldn't come to the press room afterwards so the photographers could take a winners' snap.

It didn't seem like a big deal. Louis stood in on the photos to bring the number up to five and we covered for Brian, saying he and Kerry had had to get home for family reasons. It sounded reasonable and no journalists questioned it. Why would they?

We figured it was just Brian being Brian. We had seen him plenty of times before being in a strop and acting the maggot, and then suddenly snapping out of it and being his usual happy-go-lucky self. A couple of days later we all met up again at the Factory Studios in Dublin to start rehearsals for the *Turnaround* tour.

First days of rehearsals, when you are all rusty and out of practice, can be a bit dodgy, but we all nailed it that day, both with the singing and dancing. We were all congratulating each other afterwards and saying how good it was looking when Brian suddenly asked, 'Can we meet up tonight, lads? I want to have a chat.'

Kian, Mark and I had rented an apartment in Dublin for the length of the rehearsal period so we all agreed to meet there that evening. As we waited for Brian to arrive, the rest of us idly speculated on what he wanted to talk about.

We hadn't got a clue. We guessed that it might be about songwriting again: Brian had been the band member who was the most into writing our own material, and he had been the most pissed off when Simon called us in, gave us his talking-to and asked us to cover 'Mandy'. We figured he might want to let off a bit more steam about that.

In any case, we didn't imagine it was anything serious; he had seemed happy as could be that day in rehearsals, and we were looking forward to clearing the air before sitting back and all having a beer and a laugh.

Brian arrived, looking a bit awkward. Any time that he was embarrassed, he always had a weird little smirk on his face, and he had it now. We did our usual hugs and handshakes, sat down and waited to be enlightened.

'Well, what's happening?' asked Nicky. 'What's up?'

'I'm hanging up my boots, lads,' said Brian.

*What? What the f\*\*k?* We were all dumbfounded... then we started grinning. We were being *Punk'd*! Brian was doing a wind-up on us for Ashton Kutcher's new MTV show. Ah, good one!

'You f\*\*king joker, Brian!' Nicky told him. 'You're having a laugh, right? There are cameras in here!' He even patted him down for microphone wires.

'There are no cameras, lads, and I'm not messing,' Brian said. 'I'm serious. I'm hanging up my boots.'

There was a stunned silence in the room. Then we all spoke at once.

'Eh? What do you mean?' 'Hanging up what boots?' 'You mean walk away?' '*What*?'

'I want to leave the band,' Brian said. He was still smirking unhappily. 'I don't want to be in Westlife any more.'

We all gazed at each other as the penny dropped. Shit. He really meant it. We all reacted in different ways. Mark sat quietly

(I found out later that Brian had already confided in him, but Mark hadn't thought he would go through with it). Kian and I went into shock. Nicky shot Brian three questions at once.

'What's the problem – is it one of us that you don't like? Are you sick? Is it Kerry or the kids, are they OK?'

Brian didn't really give any details. He just said that he was not enjoying it any more and hadn't been content in the band for a while. 'It's not you,' he said. 'You're my best friends. I'm just not happy.'

I was flabbergasted. Westlife was the best job in the world. 'Brian,' I asked, 'how can you not enjoy being in this band?'

For the next hour, the conversation went in circles. Nicky was finding it the hardest to accept what Brian was saying. 'Ah, c'mon man, whatever it is, we can fix it,' he was telling him. 'That's what we're here for. We're a band. Shall we get counselling? Yeah, let's all get band counselling!'

Eh? Steady on, Nicky! Brian looked awkward, like he hated being there, but he just kept saying the same things. It wasn't any of us; it wasn't anything to do with Kerry; he just wanted out. It became clear that this wasn't Brian's usual messing. He wasn't going to change his mind.

Shite. We had a massive tour starting in nineteen days... what the hell were we going to do?

And another thought began to form in my mind. Jesus. I had just got married, I had built a huge mansion, I had five rented properties and a massive mortgage... but this could be the end of the band. This could be it, where it all ends, right here. The terrible scenario played out in my head. Pop bands just don't go on when a member leaves. Look at the Spice Girls after Geri left,

'Darling, Happy Anniversary': My parents, Peter and Mae, on their honeymoon, August 1967.

Family portrait for my brother Finbarr's confirmation: *Back row, left to right*: Dad, Finbarr, Yvonne, me in my mum's arms (that's a lampshade on the wall behind her – not a funny hat!) *Front row*: Peter, Denise, Mairead and Liam. Easter, 1980.

LEFT: Me, aged 3.

BELOW: Lord and Lady Grantham of Sligo: Even at an early age, I loved getting into character.

LEFT: '*And the tiny tots winner is …*': Me on Jasper at the Sligo Show aged 5, 1984.

BELOW: My first appearance in Croke Park, as a mascot for my brothers' big hurling win for Sligo, 1986.

ABOVE: The Bruce Lee years: King of the spinning kick!

LEFT: '*I pity the fool*': Me and my beloved Mr T doll.

OPPOSITE: My first holy communion: Thanks for the haircut, Mum!

My front yard: Castle Street, Sligo, where I grew up.

First year in Summerhill College, Sligo. As you can see, I wasn't exactly the tallest in my class.

LEFT: IOYOU with Mary McDonagh: *Left to right*: me, Michael, Derek, Mark, Graham and Kian. Classic nineties haircuts all round!

ABOVE: One of our first ever photo shoots with the final line-up. Check out my blonde hair!

LEFT: Performing at the 2FM Beat on the Street in Ballina, Co. Mayo, July 1998.

LEFT AND BELOW: At Pinewood Studios filming our first ever video for 'Swear it Again'. *PA images*

Learning how
to pose …
*PA images*

LEFT: 'The making of a boy band': An article from the *Irish Independent*, April, 1999. Picture includes Sonny Takhar (*bottom right*), Ronan (*bottom left*), Louis, (*top right*), and Simon, (*centre*). *Irish Independent*

Walking into star records on our return to Sligo, 1999.

Meeting the Queen for the first time, Christmas 1999. *PA Images*

With Denise van Outen after winning Record of the Year, 1999 for 'Flying Without Wings'. *PA Images*

LEFT: My 21st birthday: Opening the Harrods summer sale. *PA Images*

BELOW: Me and the boys in Time Square, New York, summer 2000. *Corbis*

The boys with my mum. Thank God she made that phone call to Louis!

On location with Mariah Carey (in that famous pink top) for the 'Against All Odds' video shoot.

ABOVE: Winning record of the year for the second time for 'My Love'. *PA Images*

LEFT: Being presented with the key to the city of Sligo, by then mayor, Rosaleen O'Grady. A very proud day for me.

Me and Mum meeting Pope John Paul II. It was a very special moment for both of us.

LEFT: On set with Claudia Schiffer shooting the video for 'Uptown Girl'.

ABOVE: What a car: Behind the wheel of my black Ferrari 550 Maranello.

or Take That after Robbie quit… they were all over. Why should Westlife be any different?

We could not have been more stunned. Brian couldn't wait to get out of the room. As he left, we all hugged him and said, 'Look, have a think about it, let's talk tomorrow.'

'We can chat tomorrow, lads,' said Brian. 'But I've made up my mind.'

And he was gone.

As the door closed behind him, we all stared at each other. Nicky just looked devastated. Kian was in tears. Mark was silent, apart from occasionally mouthing, 'Jesus Christ.' I felt hollow, helpless… then suddenly I felt very angry.

There was a big fireplace on one side of the room, and I leapt up and started pacing up and down in front of it. Pacing, and shouting.

'What the f**k is that about?' I asked the others. 'What does he think he's doing, leaving us? Well, you know what, f**k him! If he wants to f**king leave, good luck to him! We can go on without him!'

The other lads looked doubtful, and I wasn't even sure if I believed what I was saying. But that didn't stop me carrying on.

'We can do the band with four of us. Mark and I are still here and we do all the lead vocals. We can still do the show… we *are* the show! We've got f**king thousands of fans waiting for us and he's not going to end this band and ruin our lives!'

I wasn't even angry at Brian while I was ranting. He had to do what he had to do. I was angry at the thought of Westlife, of our lives, being snatched away from us. We couldn't let that happen.

Kian phoned Louis and kept it simple: 'Louis, Brian's after leaving the band.'

Louis kept it simpler: 'What the f\*\*k? I'm on my way now!'

He made it from south of the Liffey in fifteen minutes flat. He must have jumped every red light in Dublin.

Louis was great. He came into the room going, 'What the f\*\*k happened?' but quickly saw that we were in a state. He sat and listened carefully as we relayed what Brian had told us, and nodded when we said it didn't look like Brian was going to change his mind. And then he started to lift us.

'Look, you can go on with four of you,' he said. 'Nicky and Kian can pick up all of Brian's singing parts. You can just split everything four ways. Don't forget, there were only four in The Beatles!'

'Ah, come on, Louis,' we told him. 'Don't go comparing us to The Beatles. We're no Beatles.'

'OK, then. You can only fit four in a taxi!'

We looked at each other and we all cracked up. And I think then, at that moment, we knew that we were going to try to make a go of it.

We were all too much in shock to rehearse for the tour the next day, so instead we reconvened at Nicky's house. Louis had phoned Simon, who simply said, 'OK. Do we replace him? It's your call.'

Louis put it to us, and for a split-second we wondered about bringing somebody else in, but... no. There wasn't even a conversation to be had. Now it was all about the four of us, and it was down to us to make it work.

We had loads of fears, though. What about the *Turnaround* tour? Fans had bought tickets expecting to see Brian there –

would they still come? Our booking agent, John Giddings, came to Nicky's house to discuss it with us. He explained that the whole tour was sold out, but anybody who was disappointed that Brian wasn't there could get a refund.

Then we saw Brian again. He came out to Nicky's house for a meeting to decide how we were going to announce that he was leaving the band. As you might expect, the atmosphere was fairly tense.

It was a bit weird. Brian offered to do the *Turnaround* tour with us. I suppose he was just trying to soften the blow. He suggested that he did the whole tour and we didn't tell anybody that he was leaving. We could put out a statement at the end instead.

Brian was trying to help, but his idea made us angry. None of us liked the thought of touring what would basically be a lie. We wanted to be upfront with the fans – we didn't want to end the tour, make an announcement and have them all saying to us, 'Why didn't you tell us earlier?'

We also figured that we would need this tour to see if we could make Westlife work as a four-piece. It was time for a fresh start.

'No,' we told Brian. 'If you're going to leave, leave now.'

He agreed. In fact, he looked pretty relieved.

We decided to hold a press conference to announce that Brian was quitting. It was Kian's idea. Looking back, I'm not sure we should have done it given the emotionally fraught nature of the whole thing, but it felt like we had had a death in the band, and we wanted some sort of ritual, or funeral, to mark it.

Our press agent, Joanne Byrne, set up the press conference at the Four Seasons hotel in Dublin. She had her work cut out.

The day before, word leaked out that Brian was leaving, and all the papers started writing about how much money we had all made from the band, and asking if it was all over for Westlife.

The day itself was bizarre. It just felt like a really weird, f\*\*ked-up day. It was certainly big news, and we all filed into the room to face an arsenal of cameras and microphones. The hotel suite was packed with journalists; *Sky News* even flew Kay Burley out to cover it live.

Brian spoke first and confirmed that he was leaving. He didn't really say anything he hadn't told us already; just repeated that he hadn't been happy in the band for a while, and he wanted to be able to spend more time with his family, especially his two young daughters.

Kian had written a letter to Brian from the rest of the band and planned to read it aloud. Some of us weren't so sure about this and thought it would be better given to Brian in private, but Kian felt strongly that we had all been through a lot together and he really wanted to do it.

He stood up at the press conference and read it out, thanking Brian for everything we had all been through together.

'We have shared some unbelievable times throughout the years and will always hold them, and you, very close to our hearts,' he said. 'We have shared laughter, tears, success, weddings and babies, but most of all we've shared our dreams.'

Kian is a very emotional guy and he couldn't get through the letter without tearing up. By the end, he was almost bawling. It was awkward, and Brian sat at the end of the table, looking down, with that smirk back on his face.

I think afterwards Kian really wished that he hadn't done it. He was pissed off because he felt Brian had been laughing at him for crying on national TV. That wasn't true; it was just the face that Brian always unknowingly pulled when he was embarrassed. But the whole day was a grim ordeal.

In the middle of this crazy media storm, of course, we had the little matter of the *Turnaround* tour to prepare for.

By now we were on a mission with this. We had something to prove. As well as relearning all of Brian's vocal parts, we also asked Priscilla to give us harder dance moves than usual. We had to prove – to ourselves, as well as to the fans – that we could be f**king brilliant without Brian.

We were going to be wearing pinstripe gangster suits and white hats, and Priscilla came up with a routine where we opened the show by each doing individual dances one by one, caught in a spotlight. It looked amazing, really cool.

Fuelled by adrenaline, anger and panic, I don't think Westlife had ever worked harder than in those rehearsals for *Turnaround*. Shit, we were going to give it our best shot – and if we were going to go down, we were going down fighting! By the first date, we were a well-oiled machine.

The tour kicked off at the Odyssey Arena in Belfast, which was always a great city for Westlife. I have to say, we were fantastic that night. We were fighting fit, it was a chance to shed all the fear and frustration we had carried for weeks, and I genuinely think that it was one of the best shows we had ever played.

We were in great voice, it was slick, and everything we had painstakingly rehearsed, all the adjustments we had had to make to cope with losing a member, went like a dream. We kept catching each other's eye onstage, and grinning. *Yes! We can do this!*

The crowd's screams nearly took the roof off, and in our dressing room afterwards, Louis, Sonny, John Giddings, our families and friends all fell over themselves to inform us how great we had been and tell us that we were better as a four-piece. We knew they weren't just saying it, and it was great to hear.

The whole tour was amazing. The fans were just brilliant. Everywhere we went, they told us: 'We love you – if Brian wanted to leave, that's his business, but we love you forever.' Before the tour, we had been braced for thousands of fans demanding their money back. John Giddings told Louis that not one person had returned their ticket.

Brian came to the third Belfast show and came backstage to see us afterwards. By then, the anger had mostly passed; I just felt he had made a really daft decision, and he would regret it in years to come. We hugged, said goodbye, and went our separate ways.

We had come through the darkest period in the band's life by far – and we had survived. The *Turnaround* tour showed that Westlife could not just carry on as a four-piece; we could go from strength to strength. The world could see that we weren't about to call it a day.

Even so, Brian quitting had shaken a lot of the certainty and security I had always felt in the band. It made me think that at some point in the future, things *would* come to an end. Most boy bands don't last as long as we had; even Westlife couldn't go on forever.

What would I do then? How would I provide for my family, and pay the mortgage on the house we were building, and all my other bills? I decided that I needed to have a back-up plan for when it was all over.

Maybe I should get more heavily into this property thing.

# 9

# IT'S A RAT PACK – AND WE'VE BEEN CAUGHT!

Early in 2004, my brother Finbarr got offered an engineering job as an operations director of a medical device company in Belgium. It was a good career opportunity but he wasn't sure about moving his family away from Ireland, and we didn't want him to go. I had a better idea.

My low-level property-investment sideline, buying houses in Sligo to rent out, was going well, but being busy or away all the time with Westlife, I didn't really have time to focus on it. I asked Finbarr if he would like to stay in Ireland and help to look after my investments full-time.

They were looking pretty good so far. The Celtic Tiger Irish economy was booming and the five houses that I had bought to rent out eighteen months earlier were already worth €500,000 more than I had paid for them.

Everybody was being advised to put their money into bricks and mortar and it made sense to me. Brian leaving had suddenly made Westlife seem precarious, and even now we were back on track, I knew we were only ever one bad album from being over. A safety net seemed a great idea.

Finbarr liked my idea and came onboard and we quickly took our plans a stage further. Instead of just buying houses, why not build a few to sell on? We started up a company and put our names together to name it: Shafin Developments.

Fired by enthusiasm, our first plan was to build four houses in a little village near Sligo, but that didn't work out. Then we spotted something that appeared to have a whole lot more potential.

There was a site up for auction in Dromahair, near to Sligo in County Leitrim, with planning permission to build forty-five houses. It was a five-acre site that would cost around €1m – a lot of money, but it looked like a fantastic investment.

My bank manager at Ulster Bank was very impressed with our plan and the fact that I had already made money on my property dealings, so we went for it. When the site next door also became available, for more than €1m, he was happy for Shafin to go for that too.

It was all pretty exciting but a lot of people were going mad for buying property in Ireland at the time – I was just lucky enough to be able to try to do it on a bigger scale.

Yet I also got some less welcome news on the property front that put a chill into my heart.

Sligo had always been a quiet, underdeveloped sort of place but suddenly, now the Celtic Tiger was rampant, everybody was looking to cash in on the property explosion – and a developer got permission to build a 15-storey hotel next to our bespoke house in Carraroe. This was despite 100 objections from locals.

Shit. I couldn't believe it. The hotel was to be built on a big traffic roundabout three fields from Castledale, the name we had decided to give our dream home. Because the hotel was so tall, anybody in it would not just be able to see our home – they would be able to see right into the windows.

Gillian and I were devastated. One reason we had chosen that site to build Castledale was that it was secluded, a lovely quiet location where we could relax away from the celebrity and the pressure of the goldfish bowl I lived in with Westlife. At a stroke, this was getting torn away.

I was outraged. We had spent four years and a fortune getting the Carraroe house built, and now we were about to lose our privacy even before we'd moved in! It felt wrong, just so unfair – and I was determined to fight it at any cost.

One of the two fields between us and the hotel site came up for sale. Jesus Christ! I feared the worst – if the council had already given permission for a 15-storey hotel, what was to stop them allowing the same, or worse, right by the house? I felt panicky, and powerless.

I made a decision. There was only one thing for it. We would have to buy the Carraroe site and develop it ourselves in order to protect my home, my family and our privacy.

Finbarr and I had not intended to expand Shafin so much or so quickly. The Dromahair site was quite enough for us to be getting on with. But suddenly buying this four-acre field in Carraroe became a priority.

I spoke to Ulster Bank again. Once more, they facilitated us in going for it and could not have fallen over themselves any more to help. They happily gave us another loan, and Finbarr and I started bidding on the site.

Our initial offer was €1m. Our final offer was €2.5m.

Even for a pop star, this was serious money, and for the first time I began to feel a bit of pressure from the property thing, rather than seeing it as a low-risk, enjoyable sideline. Even so, I knew that I had to buy that site. I couldn't have just stood back and seen our perfect home ruined before we had even moved into it.

The property dealings were interesting, but the band was still by far my main priority – and we were about to take a very interesting and unexpected left turn.

We had just finished the first, arena leg of the *Turnaround* tour and had a short break before playing outdoor shows later that summer. We knew now we were definitely going on without Brian, so Simon called us in for a meeting.

Westlife always released an album in November, so it was time for us to start planning the next one – and Mr Cowell had had one of his ideas.

Simon had been spending a lot of time in America of late, getting even more famous as *American Idol* went crazy over there, and maybe that had given him his latest brainwave.

'I know exactly what you're going to do next, kiddos,' he told us, dressed all in black, smoking a cigarette behind his desk, and looking more like James Bond (in his dreams) than ever.

'You've lost a member, lost a voice, so we need to change things around a bit. You need to do something big. You're going to be the Rat Pack.'

Wow. We certainly hadn't seen that one coming. As we all looked at each other, the general reaction was that it was a totally bonkers idea… so bonkers that it might just work.

Simon talked us through the idea. We would make a one-off album of covers of songs made famous by Rat Pack stars like

Frank Sinatra and Dean Martin; we would record them with orchestral backing; and we would make the videos in Las Vegas. The tour would be suitably lavish and spectacular.

We weren't totally opposed to any of this – I had grown up hearing and loving Frank Sinatra songs at home, and Nicky's dad was a showband singer who did all that stuff – but we were quite wary. It sounded a bit of a stretch, and would certainly take us out of our comfort zone. Was Simon quite sure about this?

'Trust me, kiddos! It will be magic.'

Louis was into the idea too, so the Rat Pack it was. Before we did the outdoor *Turnaround* dates, Nicky and I went on holiday that July to Miami, with Gillian and Georgina, and we had a good laugh sitting around the pool imagining how we were going to look in 1950s-style suits and slicked-back hair singing 'Fly Me to the Moon'.

While we were out in Miami, I got a phone call from Finbarr. Our bank had come through with the money, and we had got the €2.5m site at Carraroe next to my house. I got the news on my twenty-fifth birthday. It felt like a fantastic present.

Back home, Finbarr and I set to thinking about what we should do with the Carraroe site. We also hired an architect and drew up plans to build ninety-one houses and a crèche at Dromahair. We got in touch with McInerney's, one of Ireland's biggest builders, and they were keen to be involved. Everything was moving very fast. It was thrilling.

Meanwhile Westlife were set to make the entire Rat Pack album, which was to be called ... *Allow Us to Be Frank*, with Steve Mac, so we decamped to London for a few weeks. The vibe in the band was great. It was as if losing Brian had made us pull tighter and become more of a proper gang again.

Simon had already picked the songs for the album. He was a huge Sinatra buff, and I think to a degree he was living out a fantasy in getting his boys, his kiddos, to make his dream album for him.

The recording sessions were quite a weird experience. We started off unintentionally singing in American accents, although we weren't trying to impersonate the Rat Pack (even though Mark did look the absolute spit of Dean Martin, with his hair back and his tanned skin). We were just trying to pay homage to the spirit of the originals.

Mostly, it was a blast. We were playing a part, and in a funny way it reminded me of performing *Grease* at the Hawks Well – putting on the costumes and getting lost for a while in being somebody else. I loved crooning Ol' Blue Eyes classics like 'Fly Me to the Moon' and 'Let There Be Love'.

Yet we had some fallings-out during the recording of the album. The idea was that with Brian gone, Kian and Nicky would step up to the plate and take on more vocals, and some leads – but Nicky was very unhappy with how few parts Steve Mac was giving him.

There were two factors here. One is that Steve Mac is a perfectionist who is concerned only with getting the best results, even if it needs twenty takes, and is no respecter of egos. It can make recording sessions gruelling – 'C'mon, do it again with a bit of fairy dust!' he'll keep saying – but the results he gets make it all worthwhile.

The other element was that unlike Kian, Mark and me, with our experience of being Danny Zuko and Kenickie, Nicky had never done any acting or played a different character before, which to an extent was what we were doing now. It was all totally new to him, and maybe it showed.

Steve would try us all out on a song but then give hardly any parts to Nicky. Mark and I were expected to sing most of the leads, but Kian was doing way more than Nicky, which hurt him because they were supposed to be on the same level.

We were staying at a nearby hotel, and Nicky would give out to me every night: 'Why won't he give me a f\*\*king chance?' The next day at the studio I would take Steve to one side on Nicky's behalf, but he was adamant: 'He just doesn't suit the song!' Steve was very black and white like that.

It came to a head when Nicky flew into a rage at hardly being on the album and threatened to fly back to Dublin. He even talked of quitting the band. I don't think he would have – but after Brian, we were very vulnerable to that kind of talk.

I explained to Steve how serious things were getting. 'Look, Steve, Nicky is in the band and we've got to use him!'

Steve gave Nicky another chance on a few tracks, and he went in and absolutely nailed it. Ultimately, it was probably another example of Steve Mac's hardline methods getting results.

Simon was true to his word and flew us out to Las Vegas to make the videos. It was my first time in the city, and what a place! As soon as I set eyes on America's capital of tack, I could see why people called it Disneyland for adults.

Our first night in Vegas was mental. Record-label boss Clive Davis had invited us to a huge party he was throwing on the top floor of the Bellagio hotel. As we got out of the lift, with jet lag kicking in, Whitney Houston swept out of the party, nodding hello to us as she left.

The party was a super-glamorous affair, and Alicia Keys and Usher were there. We were all wearing our Rat Pack suits and we crowded around Usher for a photo. An Irish paper was to run the picture a day or two later, with the caption: 'US star Usher with his accountants.'

The jet lag ensured we got steaming drunk. We had a video shoot the next day, and our stylist had only let us wear our suits to the party on the condition that we left them outside her hotel room door when we got back.

Gillian reminded me as we got back to our hotel with Mark. At first I said I couldn't be bothered but Gillian insisted, so Mark and I stripped down to our boxer shorts in the lift on the way up to our floor. Half naked, I pulled my socks up to my knees and ran up and down the corridor singing Sinatra songs. The night ended with a giggling Mark and I wrestling on the carpet.

What happens in Vegas stays in Vegas, right? Well, until I told you about it, now…

We made three videos along the Strip and loved putting on our super-sophisticated Savile Row suits. Then we'd stay up in the casinos all night playing blackjack. I never strayed from the $20 table, although the staff ply you with drink all night to try to coax you onto the $100 big-boys table.

While we were in Vegas, we took the chance to go and see a Rat Pack stage show. It was cool to see such great renditions of Frankie and Dean, and it gave us a few ideas for when we came to tour the album.

... *Allow Us to Be Frank* had been mostly fun to make, but we were apprehensive when it came to putting it out. We just didn't know how people would react. We figured a lot of our older fans might like it, but we knew the Rat Pack wouldn't mean a thing to our teenage followers.

We also found we had an unexpected rival in the charts. Just six months after he had quit Westlife, Brian reappeared with a debut single, 'Real to Me', in September 2004, along with an album, *Irish Son*.

This surprised us because we thought Brian left because he wanted to spend more time with Kerry and his girls. Was he planning a solo career even then? Who knows? The truth is, I still don't know for sure even today.

His first single was good and for a short while we wondered if he would do a Robbie Williams. I never really thought he would, though – there is only one Robbie Williams. And then, of course, Brian and Kerry split up. I never saw that one coming, either.

As it turned out, Westlife had been right to be nervous about the Rat Pack. The album was no disaster sales-wise, but it only went into the chart at number three – our first album not to go straight to the top since our debut had been pipped by Steps five years earlier. It was a bad blow and we were disappointed.

Maybe it also had an adverse effect on how we viewed the record, because we had a bit of a downer on it when we came to get on the promotional treadmill. It had been good craic when we were making the album and the videos, but now that we were dressing up like Sammy Davis Jr to do TV shows, we began wondering if it was all a bit... silly.

Nicky and I weren't too hard on the whole thing but Mark and Kian were definitely starting to think it might have been a mistake. There were already enough people who thought Westlife made dreary music for older people – dressing up as forty-year-olds wasn't exactly helping!

Luckily, I had a very welcome distraction in my life, as on 17 November 2004, four years after we had started building it, Gillian and I finally moved into Castledale.

It was such a beautiful place. The architects and builders had done an extraordinary job, and as you pulled up the drive to the imposing façade, the subtle lighting made it look like a fairy-tale castle. It was truly magical.

We had seen it going up for years, but even so, when the key was finally in my hand, I did a double take. *Wow. Is this* really *where we live?* It felt like home from the second that Gillian and I walked through the door. The top floor, with its bar, cinema and pool table, immediately became my favourite place on Earth.

Castledale had been a long time in the building and a lot had changed. We had shifted from our original plan of moving in with our extended families and were now more inclined to make it our own family home.

There was one very good reason for that – because, before too long, Gillian was pregnant.

It was fantastic news. We had both been broody to start a family for a while, but Gillian had been keen to wait until we had finally moved into the house, so we didn't have to go through the whole moving process with a baby. Now we had our dream home – and a baby on the way to go with it.

When we moved into Castledale, my mum and dad finally quit the café and moved into our old house over the road, renaming it Carlton Lodge. It was the perfect place for them and they loved it – as they still do.

It was an exciting time all round, as just before Christmas 2004, Finbarr and I officially put in a planning-permission request for the housing estate at Dromahair. We had calculated that the development would cost in the order of €10m, and had gone back to Ulster Bank. They had indicated that that level of loan shouldn't be any problem.

Looking back now, ten years on, it's utterly bizarre that a bank was willing to lend so much money to a twenty-five-year-old pop star with virtually no knowledge of the property market. But at the time, booming Ireland was turning into the Wild West, and I certainly wasn't about to question it.

And I suppose, at that point, money really was no object for me. I was always flying back and forth between Sligo and Dublin and sick of the journey, so when a local guy asked me to go halves on buying a helicopter, I jumped at the chance. It was cool, it came with a pilot – and it halved my travelling time.

The papers made a bit of a big deal about Gillian and me moving in to Castledale, and Westlife fans began beating a path to our gate. The doorbell would ring two or three times a day, followed by a nervous voice on the intercom: 'Could Shane come down, please?'

They were never too intrusive and I didn't mind. The fans were always happy to wait for half an hour if I was busy, and they were so grateful and excited for an autograph or a photo that I never begrudged them a gawp at my house through the front gate.

I would never begin to compare myself with John Lennon, but I did like one thing he had said on a similar topic. I had read that fans scratched messages into the paint of his white Rolls-Royce. When he was asked if it bugged him, Lennon said, 'They paid for it – they're entitled to do it!' I was with him on that one.

In the early months of her pregnancy, Gillian got sick a lot. She lost weight even though she developed a chocolate craving. Those things aside, the pregnancy was largely trouble-free as we both eagerly awaited the life-changing arrival.

Before that, there was the little matter of a Westlife tour – and it was looking extremely ominous.

The next jaunt was to be called *The Red Carpet* tour and it was not selling as quickly as our previous ones. Sales weren't terrible, but they were sluggish. It seemed that a lot of our fans assumed that they would be sitting down all night listening to Rat Pack songs, and they didn't fancy it.

We were starting to think that the whole Rat Pack concept had been a blunder by Cowell, and were moaning that he was getting too distracted by being a superstar in the States – because you obviously always look for a scapegoat – when our live agent, John Giddings, saved the day.

John is a smart operator: he came down to a band meeting and simply said, 'Look, why don't we change the name to the *Number Ones* tour?'

We did exactly that, and sales started to pick up once fans realized it wasn't a Rat Pack-only show. It was our smallest-selling tour to date, though, and we were just doing two or three nights in arenas where we had usually done four or five. Nevertheless, the gigs still went down grand once we hit the road in spring 2005 – including the Rat Pack section.

Even so, it wasn't the most enjoyable tour we had been on. We knew that the album and ticket sales had been massive by most bands' standards, but we were Westlife and we were used to everything being off the scale. We had a huge reputation as the band that always got to number one and sold out every show and we didn't want to lose it.

Mark, in particular, liked Westlife most when we were doing fresh, original material, and recording an album of 1950s covers was never going to please him. It was clear on the *Number Ones* tour that he and Kian were pretty discontented with how things were going.

Nicky and I were the total opposite and desperate to keep things going – as ever, I was scared shitless at the thought of Westlife ending. Mark and Kian never said they wanted to quit, but on that tour a lot of our chats in dressing rooms and on tour buses found them declaring, 'I think things are going south,' or asking, rhetorically, 'Is it over, lads?'

The Rat Pack project had been fun at the start but it wasn't fun by the end. We had spent too long pretending to be middle-aged men and at least half of the band was sick of it. We had a meeting with Louis and Mark spilled out what was on his mind.

'Louis, we're going down a slippery slope here,' he said frankly to our manager. 'We're going downhill, and if we go any further we are going to be f**ked. We need a miracle.'

Louis, of course, was ever the man with the optimism and the wisecracks. 'We'll find a miracle!' he told him.

Mark wasn't convinced and kept trying to tell Louis how bad he felt things were. 'We're sick,' he said. 'As a band, we're sick. It's like we have cancer.'

'Ah!' said Louis. 'I know a doctor!'

'There is no cure for cancer,' said Mark.

'We don't have cancer, we're just a little bit sick!' chirped Louis. 'We'll get better because I'm going to find a cure!'

Eventually, even Mark had to laugh at Louis's relentless, limitless positivity – but I think we all knew that our next move, and what Mr Cowell decided to do for our next trick, would be crucial.

Simon had toyed with the idea of a second Rat Pack album, but abandoned it pretty quickly when Louis told him about the mood in the band. When we all trooped in to see him a few days later, he had a better idea: 'Let's go back to what we do best. Let's go back to being Westlife.'

It's important to say that at this stage, Simon Cowell did not need Westlife. His astronomical fame and success in the US and around the globe was ludicrous. He was still the love-to-hate figure of *American Idol*, he had just launched *The X Factor* at home, and he was earning at least £20m per year.

Simon could have decided we were old hat and left us in his dust – but he didn't, because he still cared for us. He had helped to shape us from the start, and he definitely didn't want us just to fall apart.

So he agreed that the next album – which would be called *Face to Face* – would comprise textbook Westlife original ballads and pop songs, and he sent us off to our usual studio haunts in London and Stockholm to make it. For me, though, it was to prove anything but the usual recording process.

Gillian was due to give birth in August and there was no way I was not going to be there. There was a good chance that we would still be working on the album then, so I went into the studios early to record all of my vocals on my own.

It was like making a solo record. I would turn up, be given the songs by the producers and sing all of the vocal parts so that they could choose what to use later when the other lads had done their bits.

I found it a weird way to work, but the album was coming together nicely – the Swedes wrote us a great song called 'Amazing' and we were excited to learn that we were going to do a collaboration with Diana Ross, 'When You Tell Me That You Love Me'. But as the weeks went by, Simon was telling us that we still didn't have the big single – and he was right.

That was until Louis came to the rescue. Our manager had said that he would find the miracle to save the band, and he did it. He cured our sickness.

At first, it seemed unlikely medicine. For a couple of years, Louis had been banging on about a song called 'You Raise Me Up', which had been a minor hit for its authors, Secret Garden. Brian Kennedy had sung it with them in Ireland and Josh Groban had recorded the track in America, but even so it was still very obscure in the UK and not many people had heard of it.

Louis was always giving out that Westlife should do a cover of it, but we were never convinced. We thought it was a beautiful song, but it sounded kind of churchy, like it could be a hymn. We had never thought it was right for us.

Louis started on about the song again and at first I was like, 'Ah, not this again!' But this time, he was really persistent. He kept phoning, asking me to give it a go, and eventually I said, 'Oh, f**k it! What have we got to lose?'

There was certainly a feeling at that point that *Face to Face* could be our last album. The Rat Pack experiment had not been a total success, and if we had followed it up with an OK, middling album with no big song in it, we might very well have called it a day. The cancer might have won.

I went into the studio with Steve Mac to put down a guide vocal on 'You Raise Me Up'. As I sang it, I realized for the first time just what a beautiful song it was – a f**king serious tune. The words of the chorus really hit home to me:

You raise me up, so I can stand on mountains
You raise me up to walk on stormy seas
I am strong when I am on your shoulders
You raise me up to more than I can be.

The lyrics made me think of my parents, of how they had always supported me and been there for me, and as I sang I felt I was saluting them. It made me feel quite emotional; it was a way more powerful song than I had first thought.

I was converted to Louis's brainwave but I wasn't sure how Mark would feel about doing another cover, so I phoned him. He wasn't jumping up and down for joy but he agreed to give it a go.

I think, like me, he knew that Westlife were nearing the last chance saloon.

Simon and Louis both loved Mark and my vocals on the song, and they sent the whole band back into the studio to do it properly. With Steve Mac we really threw the kitchen sink at it, with strings, pipes, gospel choirs, the whole shebang.

When Steve played it back for us at the end of the session, we all had tingles going down our spines. Hey, this one was special! The last time we had reacted this strongly to a song was for 'Flying Without Wings'. But lightning couldn't strike twice... could it?

Simon had no doubts and immediately proclaimed that it would be the first single from the album. We didn't know if he was right or not – we were just glad it wasn't us making the decision. And, Rat Pack aside, he normally got these things right.

We were still nervous about what people might make of 'You Raise Me Up', but it was nice to feel that we had the big single in the bag at last. For me, I just wanted to get it sorted so that Gillian and I could focus on the main event: the baby.

The two of us had been trotting off dutifully to all of the tests and scans but had asked not to be told what the sex was. I thought it would be a boy; Gillian was sure it was a girl. We were at a scan at Sligo Hospital more than three weeks before the due date when the doctor dropped a bombshell.

'There is no amniotic fluid around the baby,' he said, peering at the fuzzy shape on the screen.

My heart missed a beat. *What?*

'What does that mean?' we asked him, worried.

'It means you're going to have a baby tomorrow,' he said. 'I strongly recommend a planned Caesarean in the morning.'

Over the next couple of hours we had a few more detailed scans that confirmed the original diagnosis. There was no real decision to make. Gillian was tearful because she had wanted to give birth naturally, but obviously we were going to do what was best for the baby.

The doc booked us in for eight the next morning, and then we headed off in a daze. We stopped off for a pub meal at a local pub we liked, the Fiddler's Creek, then told our parents the news that had still not sunk in for us.

When we got back to Castledale, Gillian went to bed early for the dawn start the next morning, but I knew I wouldn't be able to sleep for a while. I went outside and walked around the drive and garden, trying to grasp it. *My life is going to change tomorrow. I'm going to be a dad!* The alarm went off at 6 a.m. and I leapt out of bed like the Duracell bunny, feeling like a kid at Christmas. I think that I might even have said, 'Woo hoo! Today's the day!' Gillian was more level-headed and apprehensive – understandably, as she was the one being cut open.

The medics and midwives wouldn't let me into the theatre while they made the cut – husbands can find it upsetting, and I'm sure I would have. When I went in, looking an eejit in a surgical gown, all that I could do was stare at Gillian. She didn't seem in pain at all; she couldn't feel a thing.

Inside ten minutes, the doctor said, 'I can see the head,' and then as I heard the baby cry and the doc pronounce 'It's a beautiful girl!' my legs went to jelly. It was a wonder that I didn't pass out.

The midwife wrapped her in a blanket and handed her to me. I looked into her big blue eyes and gave her a kiss before holding her by Gillian so she could kiss her. I had never known that life could be so magical.

*Here was our child. Our daughter.*

We had chosen the name Nicole Rose the night before. We loved Nicole Kidman's name and thought Nicole sounded cool and had a lovely ring to it, and Rose was a big name in Gillian's family, including her mum and grandmother.

Nicole was a little jaundiced and needed to recuperate, and as I wheeled our new little girl down a corridor in an incubator, I was bawling my head off with happiness. *What a wonderful, amazing moment.*

Becoming a dad was such an adventure. Like every new, young father, I was full of joy and terror. Nicole would sleep in a Moses basket on Gillian's side of the bed and I used to wake up in the night, go around and put my finger by her mouth, to check she was breathing.

Nobody can know what the sleep deprivation bit of having a baby is like until you go through it. Nicole would wake up at 3 a.m. most nights and I'd be changing her nappy or feeding her like a zombie.

You worry more about kids than about anything else in your life, but you also love them more, with a deep, profound love. Nothing compares to parenthood – and Gillian was a natural, just a brilliant mother from the start.

Interestingly, just after Nicole was born, I sold my share in the helicopter. I had been fine choppering back and forth, but I didn't like the idea of my little baby going in such a precarious form of transport.

We spent all the family time we could in Castledale, but Gillian and I had also bought an apartment on the Fulham Road in London for when I had to be in the capital for any length of time.

Nicky and I were staying there the night that Mark told us he was gay.

It wasn't a huge surprise, to be honest. Kian, Nicky and I had speculated about it, simply because Mark was hardly ever with girls and never had serious relationships. We knew he was a shy person, but we were 90 per cent sure he was gay.

We were in London for a photo shoot, and at the end of it Mark asked, 'Lads, do you want to go for a drink tonight?' Kian was busy (plus Mark had told him already) but Nicky, Mark and I headed off to a bar.

We chatted away and Nicky and I sank a few beers, but Mark was throwing down vodka and Cokes; looking back, I guess he was probably nervous. After a couple of hours, we decided to go back to my flat and watch some TV or a DVD.

We got in, sat down, and Mark told us, 'I've got something to tell you – although you probably know already.'

'What?' we asked him.

'I'm gay.'

We jumped on Mark and hugged him. We could see the relief in his face from finally unburdening his secret. 'Yes!' we laughed. 'That's amazing – we're so f\*\*king happy for you!'

'Did you know already?' he asked us.

'Of course we knew – but we didn't *know* until you told us,' I said. It was a strange statement that made absolute sense.

It was a lovely moment. I had always been close to Mark, but I guess there was always a sense that there was something he just wouldn't talk about. Now he was out, and I was a dad, it felt like we were growing more mature – and it helped our friendship become even closer.

In that autumn of 2005, Finbarr and I got more heavily into Shafin Developments. We received the planning permission on the expanded plan for the estate at Dromahair and spent time with the architect and McInerney's to ensure that the building could start early the next year.

Things were also looking up for Westlife – because it was rapidly becoming clear that 'You Raise Me Up' was going to be a phenomenally huge song.

It was a dream to sing. I sang the first verse and chorus on my own, and I loved how the song started so low and built up through my part and an instrumental section to where Mark came bursting in with his amazing, enormous voice.

It was just so powerful – it affected us every time, never mind the listeners.

Simon had had the idea that we should all sit on our stools to sing the start of the tune and then stand up when we came to that huge, swelling chorus. It could easily have looked corny as hell, but somehow when we rehearsed it with Priscilla, it didn't seem that way. It seemed rich with emotion.

We first realized how big 'You Raise Me Up' could be when we previewed it at the Tickled Pink gala at the Royal Albert Hall. It was a big charity show to raise money to fight breast cancer, and we were headlining it over Mariah Carey, Sheryl Crow, Sugababes and Simon's latest project, Il Divo.

We totally nailed the song from the first note that night. You could have heard a pin drop during the quiet, poetic opening verses. We had a full gospel choir with us, and as they came in for the dramatic, towering chorus, and we got up off our stools as one on the big key change, the Albert Hall erupted. Jesus. We had goose bumps on goose bumps!

We hadn't felt as charged and powerful as a band for a long time. We knew we had the crowd in the palms of our hands, and the applause as they gave us a standing ovation at the end was deafening.

Backstage after the show, we all knew that something spectacular had just happened. Sonny from Simon's office came running in. His eyes were wide. 'Wow, what was that? It was like the crowd was under a spell!' He was right.

'You Raise Me Up' was such a powerhouse and it was about to give Westlife the new lease of life that we so desperately needed. It was like 'Flying Without Wings' all over again. It was such a massive song – when it was released as a single a few weeks later, it simply obliterated the opposition.

It was the best cover version we ever did, and to this day 'You Raise Me Up' is my favourite Westlife song, even over 'Flying Without Wings'. The day Louis persuaded us to sing it was the day he saved the band.

Our manager had done what he'd promised. He had found our miracle cure.

We even broke Australia purely off the back of that song. It totally rebooted the band. Occasionally Simon will claim it was his idea to cover it. It's typical Simon, and Louis and the lads just laugh because we know *exactly* where the credit lies.

One great thing about the success of 'You Raise Me Up' was that it pulled the *Face to Face* album along in its wake. Our LP leapt into the chart at number one on its release in October 2005, selling more than twice what the Rat Pack album had in the process, and quickly became our biggest record since *Coast to Coast*.

It was an amazing turnaround. Suddenly we were as big as we had been five years ago and Sony BMG wanted to hang on to us and keep us happy. They extended our contract by two years, on improved terms. Everything in the garden was rosy.

We hadn't met Diana Ross when we did 'When You Tell Me That You Love Me' with her for the album. We had recorded our vocals separately. But we did meet up when the label decided to shoot a video and put the song out as a Christmas single.

Before the shoot, one of her many people came in and told us we had to address her as Miss Ross. I thought it was daft. I mean, f\*\*k that shite! When she appeared, though, she was pleasant, professional and not at all diva-like, which was a good thing as the video shoot took fourteen hours. She didn't even seem to mind at all when I called her Diana.

The single did great and even seemed to have a chance of being the Christmas 2005 number one – but we lost out to our boss. Simon had turned *The X Factor* into a monster by then and we finished up being number two, behind that series' winner, Shayne Ward.

Frankly, who cared? Maybe it would have bugged us once, but now we were just delighted that Westlife were back, reborn and on form again – because we knew it could so easily have gone the other way.

The end of that year brought another major change for Gillian and me. Now Westlife were back on the rise we knew I would have to be spending a lot more time in London, and I didn't want to miss out on seeing Nicole grow up. We decided to buy a place in the UK so she and Gillian could always be near me.

Steve Mac recommended looking around Surrey, where he lived, and Gillian and I saw a lovely Georgian-style house in Cobham, near the Chelsea FC training ground. It was on the market for a bit more than we ideally wanted to spend but we loved it, so we took the plunge and bought it.

In the meantime, Finbarr and I were pressing on with Shafin business back at home. We were ready to begin construction on the Dormahair site, and it was brilliant to see McInerney's diggers and builders go in as our architect's plans for the estate leapt off the drawing board and began to become a reality.

More pressingly, now that we had bought the site next to my house in Carraroe, we had to work out what to do with it. We were quite keen to keep the development low-rise – after all, the reason I had bought it in the first place was to try to stop some monstrosity towering over my home like a spaceship!

Carraroe only had one shop, one church and one school, so we got together with our architect and worked out plans for a development to benefit the village. It would have a few houses but also a supermarket, crèche, gym, doctors' and dentists' surgeries, restaurant, takeaway, laundry and coffee shop – all things the village currently lacked.

The town planner we were initially working with wanted a higher-rise development and asked us to feature a tower near the entrance to the site. He seemed to have some sort of bizarre vision that this structure and the 15-storey hotel could become Sligo's own Twin Towers.

This was the last thing that Finbarr and I had envisaged, but we took the planner's comments on board and started sending plans back and forth to his office.

I had only bought the land to protect my family's privacy and this was all starting to get a bit complex and wearisome, but I felt confident. Developments were shooting up everywhere and an estate down the road had sold forty houses in a single day.

We knew that we had a great site. What was there to worry about?

We also got approached about another site at Orchard Lane off the Strandhill Road, one of the main streets that ran through Sligo. We kind of felt we had enough on our plate but when Finbarr and I mentioned it to Ulster Bank, they again advised us it was potentially a lucrative project and introduced us to a developer from Galway.

Finbarr and I liked this guy straight away, we went to see a few of his developments and they looked fantastic, and it was clear he knew exactly what he was doing. OK, we were in: we took out another Ulster Bank loan and bought the site.

These loans were all to Shafin Developments, but I stood as the personal guarantor to all of them. Why would I not? I was the millionaire pop star, not Finbarr – and in any case, we would make our money back on these investments, and more. Wouldn't we?

Had I sought out advice from Louis or the band's financial advisers when I got into Shafin, they would probably have told me not to guarantee the loans personally. But I never asked them. I just went ahead and did it. With hindsight, this was not my wisest move.

I did mention what I was doing to the other lads in the band and they just went, 'Oh yeah, cool.' No one questioned it. At the time, it seemed like everybody in Ireland was doing it.

In my downtime from the band and the property developments, I was just loving being a dad. Gillian did the lion's share of looking after Nicole, as many mums do, but some days I would get up at the crack of dawn to watch TV with her: *The Wiggles*, *Noddy* and *Balamory*.

I was the textbook doting dad who thought everything that Nicole did was adorable. When I was rooting in the fridge one day and she said her first word, 'ham', it seemed the most amazing thing ever. Oh, and she said 'Dadda' before she said 'Momma'! Gillian doesn't agree, but she is wrong...

We were having such a perfect family time together that when it came time for the band to head off on the *Face to Face* tour in spring 2006, I couldn't bear to leave Gillian and Nicole behind. Instead, we hired two buses instead of the usual one and they came with me.

The *Face to Face* tour was a big success. We were confident enough to open our set with 'Flying Without Wings', happy in the knowledge that we had another killer track to finish off with in 'You Raise Me Up'. It was also just a really settled, happy time for the whole band.

Nicky brought Georgina, whom he'd married in 2003, on the road with him a lot and Kian was with Jodi Albert; they'd been dating for a couple of years. Mark had a lovely boyfriend, Kevin McDaid, who was a photographer and also came along and took lots of great shots of Nicole.

If we were travelling overnight, Nicole would sleep in a bunk bed on the bus, but mostly we would be in hotels and Gillian would put Nicole to bed while I was onstage. It was such a buzz to do a gig knowing my wife and daughter were waiting for me, and then heading back to them afterwards.

Westlife rarely felt like a treadmill but I suppose it was true that each year followed the same routine. Every autumn without fail we would release a new album, then start promoting it non-stop: Britain and Ireland, Europe, Asia. November would bring the first single, then the album.

After a break for Christmas, we would start rehearsing for the tour, which would take us through from early spring into high summer. In June or July, we would go in to see Simon to talk about the next album, and the cycle would begin again.

That year, we had a month off from the *Face to Face* tour before going back on the road to play a load of huge outdoor British dates and then Asia. It was a gorgeous sunny day in Sligo in summer 2006 and I was in the garden with Nicole when Louis called me.

'Simon's back from America and he knows what he wants to do,' he told me. 'It's a covers album of love songs.'

Oh, really? I must admit, my first reaction to this news was extremely lukewarm. I felt as if Westlife had just fought our way out of a slump with a strong album of mostly original songs – it felt like taking a step back to be doing covers again.

Could we not keep looking for great new material? After all, Take That had just reformed – without Robbie – after ten years, and we knew that they were recording an album of all-new original material. Why couldn't we do the same thing?

We argued our corner and didn't agree to Simon's plan straight away. Over the next few days, there were a lot of serious conversations within the band, and with Louis. As usual, Mark was the most opposed to doing covers and the keenest to do our own thing.

Kian, Nicky and I were a bit more into the idea. It wouldn't have been our first choice, any of us. On the other hand, we wanted to keep our new success going, and Simon did have a fantastic track record of getting things like this right (well, apart from the Rat Pack album).

Really, it was just Simon taking a cold, hard look at what had worked and wanting more of the same. We had just had an enormous hit with 'You Raise Me Up' so now he was looking for an album of the same sort of thing.

By now, as well as attracting screaming girls, Westlife had a lot of fans in their thirties, forties and even fifties, and this album was to be aimed fairly and squarely at these women. Simon knew they would go for covers of big romantic hits they had loved when they were younger.

It was very Cowell and typically clever. He even asked us for a list of our favourite love songs for possible inclusion on the record, to make us feel involved rather than as if we had had the idea foisted upon us (which we had). I don't think too many of our choices made it on the final album.

We wavered back and forth but Simon still had this gift of making his ideas always seem like the right ones and in the end he got his way. When the *Face to Face* tour finally finished with the usual scenes of hysteria in Taiwan and Indonesia, we went into Steve Mac's studio to record *The Love Album*.

Steve gave the album his best efforts, as always, but I think he was secretly disappointed that we were plodding down the covers route again. It was a quick-fix album and it was done and dusted in three weeks, with songs by artists as mixed as the Righteous Brothers, The Judds and Leo Sayer.

The lead-off single was 'The Rose' by Bette Midler, which was probably my least favourite Westlife single of them all – in fact, I don't think any of us really liked it. It was a blatant, cynical attempt to come up with 'You Raise Me Up II' – and it worked, in that it leapt straight to number one.

It was the credibility versus commercialism battle again: and once again commercialism had won. *The Love Album* was a great idea in terms of selling records, but it did nothing for our image, once more playing into the hands of the many critics who saw Westlife as purveyors of lame, dreary karaoke.

We were used to being slagged off by now, of course, and normally we didn't give a shit about it. There are always people who love to criticize. We knew we would never be a cool critics' band, but we did have fourteen number-one singles, multi-platinum albums and sell-out arena tours. F**k the haters – they could write what they liked!

*The Love Album* was up against some serious competition when it was released in November 2006. It wasn't just out in the same week as an Oasis Greatest Hits record called *Stop the Clocks*, but also a Beatles compilation, *Love*, and a U2 'best of' record named *U218*. No pressure, then!

Oasis were a proper rock 'n' roll band that journalists loved, of course, and in the week leading up to the release, the *Sun* newspaper in Britain had a campaign to get Oasis to number one ahead of us. They told their readers to buy multiple copies of the Oasis album to keep Westlife off the top.

Noel Gallagher was giving out absolute stink about us in the *Sun*, saying that our album was a load of shite and caning us day after day. The *Sun* didn't just run the front-page headline 'STOP THE COCKS' (the 'cocks' being us, Westlife): they even printed and sold T-shirts with the slogan.

It was nasty stuff but Simon and Louis loved it and just told us it was the kind of advertising that money couldn't buy. By now the two of them were judges on *The X Factor*, of course – bona fide high-profile stars – so they both put their two penn'orth in as well and kept the publicity fires burning.

The *Sun*'s campaign was in vain. When the eagerly awaited album chart appeared, Westlife were number one, ahead of Oasis. The Beatles were at number three and U2 were fourth. I loved the top of that chart so much that I cut it out of the paper and carried it around in my wallet for ages.

*The Love Album* was a massive record for us. It ended up selling well over a million copies and even outsold *Face to Face*, establishing beyond doubt that we were one of the biggest bands in pop.

The downside was that it once again had people thinking of Westlife as a band that did covers.

We had some fun promoting it. Singing a cover of 'Easy' live on TV with Lionel Richie a couple of times was a real blast. Yet at other times our dissatisfaction and uneasiness with the project showed through.

The second single from the album was supposed to be Bonnie Tyler's 'Total Eclipse of the Heart'. It was a song that none of us really liked. It was just too naff, a step too far, beyond even Barry Manilow. It wasn't cool in any way and we didn't know why we were doing it.

We launched it live on TV on the National Lottery show and it would be an understatement to say that our hearts were not in it. We were promoting our new single on one of the biggest shows going and we just did not want to be there. The Saturday night TV audience certainly got cheated if they were hoping for a rip-roaring version of 'Total Eclipse of the Heart'. We all felt depressed and we looked it, and in truth we were barely going through the motions. How the hell had we come to this?

The day after the programme, Louis phoned us to say that Simon had seen it, had thought we looked bored off our tits and was pulling the single release because he thought there was no point. We didn't object to this. In fact, if I am honest, we felt relieved.

Westlife were back on top of the pop world – but we had paid a heavy price to get up there, and maybe that price had been our artistic integrity. Enough was enough.

Next time around, we swore, we would not be doing covers.

# 10

# WE'RE GOING OUT AND WE MAY BE SOME TIME

Shafin Developments and my property dealings had always effectively been a sideline to my main love and career of being in Westlife; a nice little extracurricular activity to try to build up a nest egg for when the band was finally over.

To my concern, this appeared to be changing as it became notably more time-consuming. As winter fell and we headed towards Christmas 2006, Shafin was getting dangerously close to feeling like a full-time job.

It seemed to be taking over my life. Every day off from the band seemed to be filled with Shafin meetings and I was not getting enough time to spend with Gillian and Nicole. It was all too much. I had never wanted to be a full-time property developer.

Finbarr and I were certainly trying to juggle plenty of balls. Having finalized our plans for the Carraroe site near my house, which as requested included a tower and more medium-rise buildings, we lodged our planning proposals with the council. By now we had been working on them for nearly a year.

We were pleased with the plans, which we really believed we had sensitively thought through to provide plenty of local amenities that that part of Sligo was currently lacking. But when the council published the plans, they received eight formal objections from people living nearby.

Five of the objections came from one guy who lived right next to the site. They were to do with how tall the buildings were, how close together, what colour they were, the effect on locals – everything, really. They ran to pages and pages.

The council asked us to go away, supply them with further information and recalibrate our plans in the light of these objections. This was a major setback for us, especially as the hefty mortgage on the site was costing me well over €100,000 per year.

I was also surprised at the nature of the objections. There had been around 100 objections to the proposed 15-storey monstrosity of a hotel down the road, which had been granted permission – surely our plans made more sense than that? I was baffled, and slightly angry at the whole thing.

Around the same time we applied for planning permission to build sixty-three apartments on the Orchard Lane site we had bought at the start of the year. This also hit objections, with the main one being from the residents' committee of a nearby estate. So now Finbarr and I had two projects going, quite literally, back to the drawing board.

The good news was that building was well underway on our first, the Dromahair site. We had already sold twenty-five houses there, and the first tenant had just moved in. Fired by this success, we had been looking at another project in the area.

We had noticed that Dromahair was very poorly served by shops, especially as there were four new estates being built around the town, including ours. Staking out the centre of the town for prospective retail sites, we discovered an old ballroom that was now closed up and disused.

Another bank, Anglo-Irish, had approached us wanting to work with us and we looked at the ballroom site together. They agreed it had huge potential, and agreed to give us a loan to convert it into a convenience store, crèche, small gym and community room. We bought the site.

Were Finbarr and I getting carried away? It may seem that way now, but at the time banks were beating a path to our door and falling over themselves to give us money, and the upsides to all of these projects seemed limitless. We could just see potential everywhere we looked.

I also had another, major motivation. I had always loved Sligo and had stayed there and made my home there even after Westlife became so big. Shafin was a business venture, sure, but I thought I was really giving something back to the place that had raised me.

That was why I was putting my money into Sligo rather than into Dublin or Dubai. It may sound simplistic, and maybe it is, but I thought I was making things better.

It was a relief to get back to Westlife business in the New Year. On the back of the enormous success of *The Love Album*, the *Love* tour had sold out very quickly and things were looking extremely good for our latest mega-jaunt around the globe.

Westlife had never done especially well in Australia, but that had all changed with the arrival of the all-conquering 'You Raise Me Up' and we kicked off the tour with a week down under in spring 2007, playing arenas in Perth, Adelaide, Melbourne, Sydney and Brisbane.

It was a fantastic start. My mum and dad flew out with us for their first-ever trip to Australia. My brother Peter was by now living in Melbourne with his family, working as a doctor, so it was great for us all to catch up.

After a week in South Africa, we came back to hit the British and Irish arenas. We were all getting on grand and having good craic but at the same time we all still had this bubbling undercurrent of resentment that had been simmering ever since Simon had blindsided us into doing *The Love Album*.

It was very simple. We were just tired of being regarded as a covers band. Some of our best, most powerful and most successful songs had been original material, but even so we were finding it hard to shake off this perception of Westlife merely being slick karaoke. It was misleading, and wrong. We were a lot more than that.

Mark still felt the strongest about this, but really we were all on the same page this time around. We admired the amazing way Take That had come back after ten years with a brilliant album of original material. Well, if they could do it, so could we. There was no way that Simon was going to shoehorn us into a covers project this time.

We rounded off the *Love* tour with ten days at the Point in Dublin and headed home to await developments and contact from Mr Cowell. It came via a message from his right-hand man, Sonny.

Simon had decided on our next project, Sonny told us. It was to be an album of cover songs from the movies.

Sonny may not have been entirely expecting the strength of the reaction that he got back from us.

'What?'

'Is he joking?'

'No way!'

'No f\*\*king way!'

We gave it to Sonny straight. We had had it up to here with covers. We were a band, a proper pop band, not a bunch of *X Factor* contestants. In our career, we had sold millions of copies of great, original songs. It was what we did best and it was what we wanted to do again.

We had done *The Love Album* that Simon had wanted from us, and fair play to him it had been a massive success, but no more. We were drawing a line in the sand. We wanted to go back to being Westlife, and to doing what Westlife did. It was a new album of original material, or it was nothing.

To summarize, then: we would not be singing an album of songs from the movies.

Sonny went away with a flea in his ear, knowing exactly how we felt. There were conversations between him and Simon, and between Simon and Louis. Louis called us to tell us that he could see our point, and he sympathized, but we should be careful not to piss off the record label too much. If they lost interest in us, it could be curtains.

We stood firm. We had gone along with what Simon wanted so many times, right from the start of our career, but this time it was non-negotiable.

A couple of days later, we got a message from Simon, via Louis: 'Why don't you come in, and we'll have a chat?'

Uh-oh, we told each other. Here we go. Time for yet another session with the Great Persuader. We had lost count of how many times we had gone to meetings with Simon, ready to tell him that black was black, only to come out with him having somehow convinced us that it was actually white.

Well, not this time. This time would be different. As we all waited outside his office with Louis, we were still geeing each other up: 'OK, no giving way! No agreeing to any more covers albums!' We waited.

'Come in, kiddos!'

Simon greeted us at the door as usual with his perfect white-toothed smile, all in black, perma-tanned, every hair in place. We all got the welcoming hug with a little intimate double pat on the back. The confidence that everything was going to be OK simply oozed from him.

That's what Simon Cowell does. He gets you from the start.

We all took a seat as Simon went and sat back behind his desk, his usual little arsenal of cigarettes, tea and custard creams in front of him. We looked at him and all our anger and tension just dissipated. We couldn't help but laugh.

If a picture dictionary wanted an image to epitomize success, it would choose a photo of Simon Cowell that day. As he sat grinning at his desk, his face also beamed from the framed front covers on the wall behind him: *GQ*, *Esquire*, *Forbes* magazine. Man, he looked more of a superstar than we did!

We had all our arguments readied – and then Simon disarmed us from the start.

'Well, I get that you don't want to do a covers album,' he began. 'I see your frustration and it's no problem.'

Huh? Was it going to be this easy?

'So we will make a classic Westlife album,' he went on. 'We will use the best songwriters for fantastic original songs, and we will have maybe just a couple of covers. And this will be our first single.'

Simon leaned back in his chair towards the sound system. It was 'Mandy' all over again. He pressed a button.

Soft guitar chords swelled around the meeting room, then a lovelorn vocal: 'Another summer day has come and gone away, in Paris and Rome / But I want to come home...'

'Home' by Michael Bublé. Shit, I loved that song – but hadn't it been out recently? And hadn't Simon just said, 'No covers'? Ah, but it is a great song, mind...

Those two ideas were fighting in my head. I looked up and Simon caught my eye and smiled. His look seemed to be saying, 'Wouldn't you just *love* to sing this song?' I may even have nodded. He winked.

When it ended, we raised the objections: hadn't it just been out? Simon had his answers all prepared: 'It wasn't a hit. It got a few plays on Magic FM and that's all. Nobody will know it. It's a great first single. We'll take you to LA to do a video – and then you get your album of original songs.'

I could see from Mark's face that he wasn't keen on this but I could also see that Simon's plan made a lot of sense. It was textbook Cowell. We talked it over a little more, had a couple of custard creams and said we'd get back to him.

'I got a wink from Simon,' said Nicky in the taxi afterwards.

'I got two,' said Mark, glumly.

The thing was that Westlife were always on a deadline. Our crazy schedule meant we always had just a month, or six weeks at most, to make an album. It would be lovely to spend the next few weeks searching for the perfect, original song for a first single – but, as ever, the clock was ticking. *Tick tock. Album time.*

In the end, it was Kian who talked Mark round. 'Look, we're getting to do the album of new songs we wanted,' he said. 'It's not *The Love Album* part II. It's not *Songs From the Movies*. Let's just do it.'

We just did it. The Michael Bublé version of 'Home' was quite jazzy, but in the studio Steve Mac added big piano chords to the song and made it into a proper tear-jerking Westlife ballad. And Simon was right. I did love singing it.

We ricocheted between London, LA and Sweden during the summer of 2007, making the album which became *Back Home*; spending longer than usual in Stockholm. Nicky was eager for us to cover a song by Lonestar, 'I'm Already There', and the Swedish producers asked me to try out for the lead vocal.

At that time, for one reason or another, I had been away from Nicole for about three weeks, which was our longest separation since she had been born. I went into the vocal booth, the producers cued up the track, and the lyrics just hit me:

He called her on the road, from a lonely cold hotel room
Just to say I love you one more time...

It was just how I felt right then. I was away, staying in hotel rooms, missing my family, missing my baby. The emotion welled up in me. It was the end of the first verse that got me:

A little voice came on the phone, said, 'Daddy, when are you coming home?'

Suddenly, I was sobbing in the studio, really bawling. One of the producers flicked a switch on his console, concerned: 'Hey, man, are you OK in there?' I wasn't, really, but I stayed in there doing that one song for an hour or more, getting into the heft and weave of the words, opening up my heart, trying to get it just perfect. I'm so proud of my vocal on that song.

I have been lucky enough never to have any major health issues – but I have always been prone to hay fever. While we were making the *Back Home* album, I came down with a particularly bad case of the sniffles.

My tablets weren't doing the job but a doctor gave me an injection of a steroid that targets hay fever. It seemed to work and over the next few months I saw a few different doctors who gave me the same treatment.

While we were making the album, Finbarr and I were hitting more problems with Shafin Developments. The Dromahair estate was going great and we'd sold another ten homes in the first half of the year, but suddenly local rumours began to circulate that the houses were poorly designed and built – and even in danger of falling down.

To this day, I have no idea where these stories came from. We had spared no expense on the budgets and deliberately worked with top architects to ensure the homes were high quality, and McInerneys were one of the biggest builders in Ireland.

It made no sense, but it brought sales to a standstill. Finbarr and I were concerned, but it was no crisis. The sales on the estate were still ahead of our original projections, and so we decided to hold fire, let the nonsense rumours pass, and relaunch the next year.

We were far more anxious about events surrounding the site by my home at Carraroe. We had adapted our plans for the development to include a tower at the express request of the town planner we were working with, even though it was our instinct to stay low-rise.

Now, suddenly, there was a change of personnel in the town council's planning department, and the new guy in charge was totally opposed to our tower. We withdrew our plans to rethink them, as they were clearly not going to get approval as they stood. It was back to square one.

This wasn't just an inconvenience in terms of delaying work starting on the site, on which I was still paying a prodigious mortgage and interest. It also hit me hard in the pocket in other ways. For a site that big, every time we commissioned fresh plans to be drawn up, it cost big money.

Everybody we hired wanted part of the fee upfront and the rest when the job was done – it was just normal business practice. That was fine, but it meant that Shafin was shelling out non-stop and getting nothing back.

More than half of the objections to our previous plans had come from one house right next to the Carraroe site. As our architect went back to the drawing board again, Finbarr and I figured it might make sense to buy the house to take the objector out of the picture.

We got in touch and began to negotiate. We made what we thought was a great offer – we'd buy the house. It was on no more than a third of an acre, but after months of negotiation, we offered more than €1m for it.

We were desperate to break the deadlock because the upside for the estate was looking so exciting. We had got in touch with

LEFT: With Gillian: My birthday in Benihana's restaurant, London.

BELOW: 'Queen of my Heart': Just married, Ashford Castle, 28 December 2003.

LEFT AND BELOW: Singing for Obama at the Nobel Prize ceremony, 2009 and meeting him backstage. What a guy! *Sandy Young/ Getty Images for Nobel Peace Prize*

LEFT: On stage as part of the *Where We Are* tour, O2 London, 2010. *Rune Hellestad/ Corbis*

BELOW: Performing at Lissadell meant an awful lot to us. *Framelight.ie*

LEFT: I had the pleasure of playing with the legend that is Zinedine Zidane at Soccer Aid 2010. This is one for the mantelpiece!

BELOW: Me and the boys surrounded by our success. *Ben Riggott/Corbis Outline*

China and Southeast Asia were some of the most enjoyable dates we had played in a few years. Here I am with the boys on stage in Beijing and messing about on a night out in Hong Kong. Getting to meet a panda cub in China was also a very special experience.

Patrick and Shane playing on the bumper cars that were part of our set for the *Greatest Hits* tour.

In the empty stadium before the final Croke Park gigs.

ABOVE: 'The city of twinkling lights': Croke Park, 23 June 2012.

BELOW: Saying goodbye – what an emotional night.
*Colin Bell*

'Going for a Song': The local media reaction to my bankruptcy.

My manager, my mentor, my friend: Back stage at *The X Factor* with Louis.

Performing with Nicholas on *The X Factor* final.

ABOVE: Singing on stage to Nicole.

BELOW: Performing at the Olympia, Dublin. What a great crowd!

ABOVE: Celebrating a sold out UK Tour with my amazing tour promoters. *Left to right*, Louis Walsh, Sarah Sherlock, Maria Barry and Barry Clayman from Live Nation, John Giddings.

TOP LEFT: I travel the world with my tour manager Liam. He's amazing! But who's copying whose style here?

TOP RIGHT: This is what happens when my bass player, Jimmy, misses a note on tour …

LEFT ABOVE: At my EP launch in Asia. I love going there so much.

LEFT: Irish flags in Hong Kong, September 2014. What a great concert!

LEFT: My amazing family and crew on the road!

BELOW: 'Ah, Shane Filan from Sligo – look at him now!' My name above the Hammersmith Apollo.

ABOVE: Me and my band having a laugh on stage. Such a great bunch of lads. *Left to right*: Jimmy, Henry, Ben, Isaac, Matt. Belfast, December 2014.

ABOVE: A Christmas pint with my mates from Sligo, *Left to right:* Philip, Cathal, Keith, Brian (Brig) and Paul.

LEFT AND BELOW: As Gillian said, 'You have me, Nicole, Patrick and Shane – what more do you need?'

one of Ireland's biggest supermarket chains, SuperValu, who came to look at the Carraroe site. They agreed to open a 10,000ft superstore on the estate.

It was perfect for us and would have been great for that part of Sligo, because there was nothing of the sort around there. But first we had to build it.

Buying out the chief objector, even over the odds at more than €1m, seemed like sound business – but after a few weeks, they came back to us and said they would not accept the offer. They didn't want to move at all. Square one, here we come again.

The ballroom development in Dromahair centre was also running into difficulties. Our meeting with the town planner for Leitrim had been our shortest ever. He loved our plans to convert it into a convenience store, crèche and gym and said he couldn't foresee any objections from the locals.

But there *were* a few objections: sixty-three of them!

The opposition came from some existing local retailers. They began campaigning against us and issued people with a template for their objections. One confused soul merely signed the template and submitted it.

Finbarr and I found it bizarre that these traders objected so virulently to our plans. When Tesco had applied to build a store in the next town down the road, Manorhamilton, they had received only three objections.

What was so different about our proposals? We were also trying to address local needs. Dromahair badly lacked crèche facilities, with only ten or so childcare places available in a village about to have three estates built on its outskirts. We felt like we were being thwarted at every turn.

The planner told us to sit tight – he would be in touch. Of course, every time we sat tight on a site where nothing was happening, we were still paying out mortgages, interest on loans, architects' and lawyers' fees and countless other costs. We badly needed something to start happening.

As the autumn of 2007 turned into winter, Sony BMG put out 'Home' as Westlife's lead single from the *Back Home* album. It went into the chart at number three, behind another of Simon's *X Factor* winners, Leona Lewis, with 'Bleeding Love', and Take That with one of their original songs, 'Rule the World'.

We were disappointed 'Home' wasn't number one, because we thought our version of it was pretty good, but we also attracted some critical flak for putting it out as a single so soon after Michael Bublé's version. Maybe it was another of those rare Simon Cowell missteps.

In any case, the important thing was the album, and *Back Home* went straight in at number one. We should have been used to this by now, but it was still a big deal for us – and this time around it was also a relief. We felt vindicated for having stood firm and refused to make another covers album.

Who knows? Maybe *Westlife Sing Classic Movie Songs* would have done even better. But we wouldn't have felt as proud of it – and at least this way we were getting a break from being accused of being karaoke artistes.

The band pushed Sony BMG to release 'I'm Already There' as a single, the song that I had recorded in tears in Sweden, but they didn't want to do it. Even so, we sang it on *The X Factor* at Christmas and fans loved it. A lot of people still assume it was a single.

It was mixed feelings in the house in Sligo that Christmastime. On the one hand, Gillian, Nicole and I were blissfully happy, and Westlife were coming off the back of yet another number-one album. On the other hand, I was worried that so many Shafin projects were bogged down in objections and delays.

These problems worsened at the start of 2008 when the Leitrim town planner came back to us with a request for twenty-five more points of information on the Dromahair ballroom site. This was the guy who had absolutely loved our plans when we first lodged them. There was a certain irony there.

Shafin thought we had better news when the council granted planning permission for our 63-apartment development at Orchard Lane, but inevitably there was an objection and we had to go to yet another An Bord Pleanála – the board that hears appeals against council planning decisions. We were getting very used to those things.

As Finbarr and I struggled to get our Shafin projects moving, and Westlife went into rehearsals for the *Back Home* tour, I had a rare but very welcome shaft of good news: Gillian was pregnant again.

Gillian and I both came from big families and we wanted lots of children ourselves, so we were delighted that Nicole was going to get a little brother or sister – as was she. Even so, I couldn't help worrying that the property side of things was starting to look troublesome.

Thank God I still had Westlife.

Or did I? The *Back Home* tour was a massive jaunt, starting off with more than twenty sold-out British and Irish arena dates. After a month off, we were heading to New Zealand for the first time, before a second wave of gigs at home through the spring and early summer of 2008.

It was another four months on the road – and as the tour got underway, it became clear a few of us were flagging.

Westlife on the road had changed so much. Where our first-ever tour had been non-stop hedonism, alcohol, puking and deely-boppers, now we were far more mature, measured and professional. Put simply, we weren't kids any more.

We might have been on the verge of releasing a single from *Back Home* called 'Us Against the World' but we were no longer a gang of teenage tearaways. Two of us were family men – Nicky and Georgina had their twins, Rocco and Jay, by now – and we took our families with us. We travelled on two tour buses and we all had separate dressing rooms.

Plus, of course, we could not keep up this crazy pace forever. Westlife had released eight albums – eight! – in nine years, toured every summer and never had a break. We had spent close on a decade riding this pop rollercoaster... and we were exhausted.

As the *Back Home* tour rolled through all our familiar old haunts, from Belfast Odyssey Arena to the SECC in Glasgow, we began having a conversation about an idea that had never even occurred to us previously.

Maybe we needed a year off.

Mark was the most vociferous on this theme. He had still not totally got over how much Westlife had become perceived as a covers band, and increasingly felt we had become stale and would benefit from a year away from the treadmill.

'Lads, we need to take a break here,' he would tell us as we talked in backstage dressing rooms or hotel suites. 'We can come back a lot fresher. If we don't do it, it will kill the band.'

Mark might have been the first member actually to come out and say it, but he certainly wasn't alone in his wish. Kian and Nicky had their moments of being sick of it all, and had it not been for my unravelling financial state, I might have jumped at the idea. However, the very thing that we felt we needed also scared us.

I guess the danger for any pop band, particularly a boy band like us who had been going for nearly ten years, was this: if we go away, will anyone care when we come back? Pop is a young person's game. We might think that we were saying '*Au revoir…*' but would we really be saying goodbye for good?

We talked it over and went back and forth as the *Back Home* tour wended its way up and down Britain – but we kept on coming back to the same conclusion. We were grateful for all we had, and all we had done, but we were knackered and we needed a break. We decided to talk to Louis and Simon.

They obviously wanted to keep things rolling along. Westlife had been a phenomenon and a cash cow for a very long time: why on earth would they want it to come to a halt? But they also understood our point of view, and didn't try to persuade us out of it.

I suppose the band's thinking was partly that by now we were all wealthy, we were all millionaires, and it was an opportunity to take some time off and enjoy what we had earned.

I had not given Mark, Kian or Nicky the slightest clue that, for me, this was now very much not the case.

All the time we were talking about taking a year off, a voice in my head was screaming, 'F**k, no!' Over the last two or three years, I had shovelled most of my Westlife income into Shafin Developments.

What the f**k would I do if that income was no longer there?

I was the personal guarantor to all of Shafin's commitments, which covered millions of euros worth of bank loans, huge mortgages on four different property developments and vast fees to architects, builders and lawyers. The idea of keeping this afloat during a year off was terrifying.

So why didn't I say a word about it to anybody in Westlife?

I guess one reason was stupid male pride. I had gone into the property business looking to create a nice nest egg to look after my family after the band had finished. I just didn't want to admit that I might have bitten off more than I could chew.

Also, I didn't want my plight to impinge on the band. Mark was right – we *did* need a break and a year off, and I wasn't about to ask Mark, Kian and Nicky to postpone it because I had a few financial worries.

I would feel humiliated and awful asking them, and I also felt it would not be fair to put them in that position. I had got myself into this situation. It was down to me to get out of it.

In any case, a year off would give Finbarr and me ample chance to focus fully on Shafin and get everything moving back in a positive direction. I have always been one of life's optimists, and I strained hard to see this particular bottle as half-full.

The first leg of the *Back Home* tour ended at Wembley and I got a severe dose of my hay fever. This was the last thing I wanted, as I was about to head off to Spain on a short golfing holiday with my brother-in-law, Cathal.

I called in an on-call doctor and he gave me a double dose of the injection that had worked so well before. It was just as effective again, and by the time I got on the plane to Spain, my sniffles had totally cleared up.

However, I didn't stay well in Spain. Once I got there, I felt restless, itchy and anxious. I had the weird sensation that the tips of my fingers were buzzing. I figured that it was all of the stress of Shafin finally catching up with me.

I have always slept like a log but one night I didn't get a single wink and was in and out of the toilet all night. I was so bad that Cathal stayed up all night with me. This was not the relaxing golfing break I had hoped for.

Back home, as the second British and Irish leg of the *Back Home* tour got underway, one date leapt out of the itinerary: headlining Croke Park in Dublin on 1 June.

It was Louis's idea and we were all pretty wary about it. OK, we had done thirteen nights in a row at the Point before, or ten at Wembley Arena, but this was a full-on, 85,000-capacity national sports stadium.

Croke Park was a special place for me, as it is for most Irish people. As a tiny kid, I had been a mascot there when my three brothers played in a hurling final. After they had won, I had been photographed with the cup on my head.

I had been to Croke Park with my dad to see Gaelic football matches. I had seen U2 there on their *Vertigo* tour three years earlier. But to play there myself, to try to sell the place out… I didn't know.

If I am honest, the idea both exhilarated and terrified me. Was Louis overreaching himself? Was this finally going to be the point we embarrassingly fell flat on our arse?

We soon got the answer. The initial 56,000 tickets to go on

sale all went on the first day. Within ten days, the gig was sold out. Wow. This was going to be quite something… We were playing arena dates throughout May 2008 but all of our thoughts were on the big one coming up. We wanted it to be truly spectacular, and at a series of planning meetings, we kept adding stuff to it. We would start with female dancers; we would add additional pyrotechnics; we would have an extra stage in the middle of the stadium and a walkway leading to it…

On the day before the gig I felt like I was coming down with hay fever again. No! I couldn't sing to 85,000 people in Croke Park with a blocked nose! I managed to see an on-call doctor in Dublin who gave me a double-dose injection of the magic treatment.

That night, I checked into the Four Seasons hotel in Dublin with Gillian and Nicole. It was where Westlife had staged our awful press conference when Brian had quit the band, and I had a fleeting thought of how much he would have loved to play Croke Park with us.

Ah, well. He had made his decision…

In the days leading up to the gig, I had tried to play it down in my mind, figuring there was no way that it would be able to meet my fevered expectations.

It didn't. It surpassed them.

From the moment that Mark, Kian, Nicky and I rose up on a platform in the stage floor, the show was a mad, intoxicating dream. The fans seemed to stretch to the horizon; I couldn't even see where the crowd ended. The screams went beyond deafening. It was just white noise.

We did the first two songs – 'Hit You with the Real Thing', from *Face to Face*, and 'World of Our Own' – from memory at the heart of the madness, then managed to regain control and enjoy the show. Now and then we'd shoot each other boggling glances: *can you believe this*? We had had some amazing shows, but this was the best night of our career.

Just when we thought the screams could get no louder, we'd unveil a crowd favourite and the noise would go up another notch: 'What Makes a Man', 'Uptown Girl', 'If I Let You Go', 'Mandy'. Our medley section included Robbie Williams's 'Let Me Entertain You' and 85,000 people freaked out like they were at a full-on rock show.

How had this happened? How did we sell all these tickets? How the f**k did we ever get this big?

If only these people knew it was all about to come to an end – for a year, at least.

They say always leave them wanting more, and we closed the main set with 'Flying Without Wings' and the encore with 'You Raise Me Up'. As the last strains fell away and the platform sank bank into the stage, I stood on my tiptoes to drink in the crowd and their reaction to the very last second.

It had been unbelievable. Would we ever do it again?

It was such an adrenaline rush and after it was over I felt totally drained. I went to the aftershow party, but was too tired and emotionally wrecked to drink and talk. I think I was in bed by midnight.

After a couple more arena dates, Westlife had an enjoyable extracurricular jaunt – we played at Wayne Rooney's wedding.

Our agent had told us that we had been offered a huge celebrity wedding in Tuscany in mid-June. We figured that it might be a footballer, and looking at the papers, you didn't have to be Magnum PI to work out that it might be Wayne Rooney and Coleen McLoughlin.

We knew Wayne was a Westlife fan because he had come to one of our Manchester gigs a few years earlier, when he was still at Everton, and had a brief chat with us after the show. For our part, Nicky and I were big Manchester United fans, and could not believe our luck.

It was a classy affair from the start. They sent a private jet to fly us out to Italy, and no matter how many times you travel that way it is always cool. We were booked to play their wedding party in a gorgeous castle in Portofino.

Coleen had booked us as a surprise for Wayne but the press got hold of the story and, as usual, spoiled it. Wayne, Coleen and their families were welcoming and down-to-earth and had only one request for our set list – that we start with 'I Do' from the latest album.

It was their first dance, and it was the first, and only, time we ever sang that song live.

We did a 45-minute set and it was great craic. Wayne got up to sing with us on 'Swear It Again' – well, I say sing: he was kind of half-rapping it, like an Eminem vibe. Lovely guy, but as a singer, he makes a great footballer.

When we finished, Wayne and Coleen were chuffed, and invited us to stick around, have a drink and enjoy the rest of the party. After the stresses and euphoria of Croke Park, it was a brilliant, relaxing, chilled-out break.

The *Back Home* tour still had another week of dates to go, including stadium shows in Galway and Killarney, before it finished up in Liverpool. Yet as soon as we came back from

Italy, I was consumed with thoughts of our year off. The morning after the Liverpool gig, Louis announced on Irish TV that Westlife were taking a break for exactly a year, until 1 July 2009.

So, this was it. I knew that I had things to look forward to – becoming a dad again in September, playing a lot of golf, chilling out – but a huge part of me was just deeply anxious.

What if Mark, Nicky and Kian enjoyed their time off so much that Westlife never came back? And what were Finbarr and I going to do about the almighty mess Shafin Developments was getting into… how were we going to sort that out?

I was about to get some very worrying answers.

# 11

# I DON'T LIKE THIS HOLIDAY

The first morning of our year off from Westlife, I woke up absolutely petrified.

I guess this was partly down to the fact I was taking a leap into the unknown. Since my teens, I had lived in the Westlife bubble, loving my charmed life of being in a gang with my best mates, enjoying phenomenal success, and happy to be in the cosy, familiar cycles of making albums and touring. Suddenly this had all been snatched away.

Yet my biggest anxiety by far was Shafin. When Finbarr and I had launched the company it had seemed rich with potential to safeguard our families' financial futures and help the northwest of Ireland to realize its potential. Now it had become a source of stress, hassle and negativity.

Shafin had promising projects waiting to roll, but nothing was happening. We had done the hard part in finding and buying the sites for development and lining up clients – supermarkets, pharmacies, agencies – who wanted to move in. In theory, our property venture should be booming.

Instead, the Dromahair retail project, Orchard Lane and the

big, all-important development next to my home in Carraroe were all bogged down in objections, planning delays and red tape. We had never for one second imagined that everything would take so long and prove so difficult.

While these interminable delays were dragging on, I was still shelling out vast monthly sums in mortgages and interest on loans as well as architects', solicitors' and builders' fees – not that we were building anything yet. Even the sales on the residential estate at Dromahair had ground to a halt as Ireland began to feel the effects of the global financial crash.

The banks had been falling over themselves to give Shafin Developments money back in the day and we had raced ahead, fuelled by the optimism of the boom years. By now our loans ran to well over €10m and these same banks were starting to worry that all of our projects appeared to have stalled.

Something needed to happen – and fast.

A few days after Westlife went on hiatus, An Bord Pleanála, who had been considering our plans for Orchard Lane, withdrew permission for the 63-apartment development. They asked us to redesign the project and resubmit our new plans.

As we were seeing to our horror in Dromahair, the bottom was falling out of the Irish housing market. Casting around for alternatives, Finbarr and I decided to try a different tack entirely and apply for permission to build a nursing home at Orchard Lane.

This made a lot of sense. The estate next door's residents' committee, who had blocked our housing proposal, would be far less likely to object to a care home. More importantly, it would meet a major need in Sligo, which suffered from a chronic shortage of nursing-home beds.

The planners were very keen on this so we commissioned another expensive redesign and contacted the Alzheimer's Ireland charity for advice. Our new idea was to build a state-of-the-art nursing-home/respite-care centre and a retirement village. These plans would be a year in the making.

In truth, if Finbarr and I could have got out of property now, we would have done it in a flash. Shafin was fast becoming a living nightmare and I would have even taken a hefty loss to be able to wash my hands of the whole thing and go back to my easygoing, trouble-free life.

Yet we knew we couldn't do that. We were in too deep. We needed to get at least one of the projects moving and generate some sales to give some money back to the banks and reduce the crippling mortgage on the Carraroe land. In any case, the banks were still supportive and we believed they were all good, strong projects.

We just needed to catch a break.

In the midst of this barrage of bad news, it was good to have something to celebrate. On 15 September 2008, Gillian gave birth to our second baby, Patrick Michael.

After the drama of Nicole's birth and the Caesarean section, Patrick's was a far more straightforward arrival. He came two weeks early, and while we hadn't known the sex in advance, I guess we had both been secretly hoping for a boy.

Nicole, who was three by now, was delighted to have a little brother, and Gillian and I were far more used to the sleep deprivation that had killed us first time around. In terms of me being at home for a year, the timing was perfect and I got some quality time to bond with Patrick.

My son arrived into a loving home, but also a very stressed one. Kian, Mark and Nicky might have been chilling but my year off was proving to be anything but relaxing as Finbarr and I cast around for ideas to try to release the pressure on Shafin.

Our biggest albatross was the enormous mortgage on the site at Carraroe, and we were desperate to build something that we could sell, so we could give the money back to the bank to reduce that burden. Another supermarket chain, Centra, was keen on moving into that part of Sligo, and told us they would be interested in buying a site from us if we had sorted the planning permission.

Finbarr and I talked over our plight every day, and we told our parents we were having difficulties, but my sole other confidante at this troubled time was Gillian. She could not have been more understanding as I spilled my heart out in frustration and despair night after night.

In October 2008 we put in a revamped planning application for the site at Carraroe. The tower had gone and the stylish, tasteful design for the supermarket and businesses, plus forty apartments, was all low-rise. We had to wait four months for a decision, but people seemed to like it and it appeared less likely to be objected to.

Just in case we thought things were going our way, we had another setback. The council in Leitrim refused us planning permission for the former ballroom site, even though we had reduced the floor area of the shop and taken out the gym completely.

It seemed to us that the weight of the orchestrated local protests had shaped the council's decision. For now, though, there was little we could do except give a deep sigh and appeal to yet another An Bord Pleanála.

By now my panic at our failing business was beginning to mix with paranoia. Why, exactly, were Shafin's proposals – which were all carefully thought out to try to benefit local communities – meeting so many objections, where other firms' proposals seemed to sail through?

It was hard not to think that some of the obstructions and protests were happening purely because of who I was. I might have been a local boy made good, but not everybody appreciates success, and perhaps a lot of people thought I was a cocky pop star getting above myself and thinking I could do whatever I wanted.

If they just knew the reality, and could see how frightened and in over my head I was, they would see nothing could be further from the truth. I was going mad with worry – but nevertheless Sligo and Leitrim suddenly appeared to me to be full of people queuing up to bring Shane from Westlife down a peg or two.

That November of 2008 was really weird for me. It was the first time in eight years that Westlife had not got a November album out and this gave me a spooked, empty feeling. Tellingly, after spending the last decade in each other's pockets, Mark, Kian, Nicky and I had not spoken once since the last tour. Maybe we had needed a break after all.

I did see the lads just before Christmas when we interrupted our year off to appear on *The X Factor* final show, singing 'Flying Without Wings' with the latest hot new boy band, JLS. I guess it was Simon's clever way of reminding the world that we still existed.

That Christmas, in the middle of a year's holiday and with two kids to pamper rather than one, should have been a joy for Gillian and me, but it was just incredibly tense. I found it impossible to relax. My last thought before I went to sleep every night, and my first when I woke up each morning, was: *What the f\*\*k am I going to do about Shafin?* In the New Year, I had yet another anti-hay fever injection. It had been coming back at regular intervals and I had been caning this super-cure. You were only supposed to have one or two injections per year but I had had five or six, some of them double doses. The doctor swore by them.

Would my luck change in 2009? It looked like it in February when Finbarr and I finally got planning permission on our biggest and most important project – the €10m development by my house at Carraroe. At last! Our new subtle, carefully recalibrated low-rise plans had paid off!

No such luck. The same neighbour who had refused our €1m offer to buy his house objected again a couple of weeks later. It was back to An Bord Pleanála for us. We wouldn't have a decision until the end of the summer.

There was one massive irony towering – or, rather, not towering – over all of this. I had only bought the Carraroe site to protect my family's privacy and our quality of life after the council had given permission for the 15-storey hotel a few hundred yards away. The idea of buying the land would never even have occurred to me otherwise.

Well, three years on, building work had not started on the hotel, and there were no signs of it starting. The developers had faced more than 100 protests, and were even more mired in objections and An Bord Pleanálas (rightly so, in their case) than we were.

The hotel would probably never happen and the site would remain what it had always been – a peaceful country field with cows grazing on it. There had been no need for me to get into this f\*\*king mess in the first place. The whole thing was a joke, but Finbarr and I certainly weren't laughing.

The banks were becoming more and more concerned and kept calling, sending emails and wanting meetings to talk about why nothing was getting built. They started making noises about needing to have loans repaid. As the weeks ground by with no breakthroughs and no let-up in the pressure, I started to get seriously ill.

I have always been a fairly happy-go-lucky character but now I was becoming horribly stressed. I could hardly sleep for worry, and even when I did drop off, I would wake up to pee five or six times in the night.

I had the thing I'd had on my golfing trip to Spain again, where my fingertips were buzzing all the time and I couldn't think straight. Then things got worse. I was getting really bloated, and huge boils were breaking out all over my face. When I went out, I tried to cover them up with make-up.

What the f\*\*k was wrong with me? I didn't know what to think. Of course, you fear the worst. Was I cracking up?

Normally, Gillian could talk me down from my worst panics. She would tell me: 'Look, of course you're stressed. You've a lot on your plate with the band and being up to your neck in property debt and all the negativity. But it will pass. You, me, Nicole and Patrick will be fine. We'll be OK.'

Yet even she was horrified at the bad way I was in now. She had never seen me this way before – shit, I had never *been* this way before.

I still have a great (well, actually, f**king awful) photo from that time that shows how terrible I got. I was out with my mum and dad at a function in Sligo when my phone rang. It was Ken Doherty, the snooker player, with whom I had become friendly. He was at an exhibition match in Sligo.

'Shane, it's Ken!' he said. 'I hear you've got a snooker table in your house – can I come out now and have a look at it? Oh, and I've got Steve Davis with me – can he come as well?'

*What?*

'Wow, yes, of course,' I told him, and quickly headed back to the house, rounding up a few mates by phone on the way. I knew they wouldn't want to miss the chance to play snooker with Steve Davis and Ken Doherty!

Ken and Steve arrived. I had never met Steve before but he was a real gentleman. We all hung out until four in the morning, drinking pints and playing snooker and pool. It was a fantastic evening, one of the rare chances I got in that year off to forget the fear and anxiety of Shafin and just relax and enjoy myself.

Even so, in the photos of that night, you can see just how ill I was. I was bloated, my face looked like a moon and there were smudges of make-up on my face where I was trying to cover up the boils. It is hard to imagine anybody who looked less like a pop star. I'm not sure Westlife fans would even have recognized me.

Gillian was crazy worried about me. She said I should see a doctor and, out of desperation, she bought me a book about how to cope with stress called *Anxiety for Dummies*.

I was at my wits' end and willing to try anything and I started reading the book as soon as she gave it to me. I skimmed over the opening blurb and read a bit to Gillian: 'The main causes of anxiety include stress and steroid use...'

'Well, at least I don't have to worry about one of them,' I told her.

'Yes, you do,' she said. 'Your anti-hay fever injection is a steroid.'

Eh? Could it be that simple? I went to the doctor for a test and got the results straight away: allergic to the steroid.

F**k! That explained the lack of sleep, the being bloated, the buzzing fingertips, the boils... everything! It wouldn't take away my problems and my stress, but at least I now knew I wasn't going mad.

We needed a break away from the angst and the negativity of Sligo and we got one. Kian married Jodi in Barbados in May 2009 and Gillian, Nicole, Patrick and I flew out for the wedding.

It was an amazing trip. Kian and Jodi got married in a truly stunning tropical garden and had the reception in a huge mansion on the edge of a cliff. The Caribbean sun was blazing down and the day was picture perfect.

It was great to see the other lads again and there was no awkwardness about it – we just picked up where we left off. Mark was looking fantastic: he had been training hard and also travelling a lot, and he had lost a lot of weight.

Nicky looked in grand shape, too. The rest of the band had clearly been having a far more relaxing year off than me. Kian had hired out the big house for the whole of the wedding week and invited us to stay over after the reception for a holiday.

Nicky had to head back but Mark and Kevin, Gillian, me and the kids all stayed on for a week's sun, sea and sand holiday. It was just what the doctor ordered (certainly more so than steroid injections!) and for a week at least I could forget about construction sites and An Bord Pleanálas.

It became clear on the Barbados trip that while the other lads had all loved their year off, they were also raring to get together again and start work on a new Westlife album in a few weeks' time. That was a massive relief – because I had missed singing, and I needed money more than ever before in my life.

One reason for this, amongst the many others, was that Gillian was pregnant again. We were delighted by this news and had always wanted to have more than two kids – but it also increased my worries about having enough money to care for my family.

Back in Sligo, Finbarr and I were still trying to find a project we could develop and sell to give some money back to the banks to lessen our crippling debts. Tesco had applied to build a superstore by our Carroroe site, but had been turned down by the council, who felt it would suck the life out of the town centre.

Finbarr and I saw an opportunity for Shafin. We approached Tesco, proposing that we look for an alternative site for them around northwest Ireland and get the planning permission sorted for them. This played well with Ulster Bank, who figured any project with Tesco involved was a sure-fire winner.

Finbarr and I found a site that Tesco liked but we knew it would be too big a job for us to undertake on our own. Ulster

Bank agreed and said they would try to get one of their major Dublin developer clients to work with us.

This character arrived in a helicopter that was so big that it could hardly land in my garden. He was a pretty flash fella but he liked the site and agreed to partner up with us if we could get the site subject to planning permission.

Finbarr and I agreed a price with the guy selling the site on a Thursday afternoon. It's a sign of how mad the banks were to work with us and how they were still throwing money at us, even this late on, that the following Monday, Finbarr had a seven-figure cheque from Ulster Bank. In the end, there was a problem with the site and the deal didn't go through.

Our bad luck seemed to have turned when An Bord Pleanála, deciding on our application to turn the ballroom in Dromahair centre into a convenience store and crèche, found in our favour. It was such a relief... until we had a call from the Bord a few days later. They had messed up, failed to take into consideration one of the objections, and would have to appoint another inspector to hear the case again.

Logically, I could see this was fair if they had not heard all of the evidence they should have. Even so, it made Finbarr and I feel even more that the world was against us. Just how many black cats had we killed in a previous life?

By now the property crash had kicked in in a big way and sales on our housing estate at Dromahair, which had been our one success story to date, had ground to a halt. With no signs of them picking up again, Finbarr and I knew that we needed a plan B.

We decided to take a lead from our Orchard Lane project. Instead of more homes that nobody would buy, we would change the Dromahair planning application, and look to build a nursing home and sheltered-accommodation units. We set one of our architects to work yet again.

We worked closely with Alzheimer's Ireland to try to ensure that the residents in these nursing homes would have the best quality of life possible. We left no stone unturned. An experienced care-home manager was reviewing every detail of our plans; we even built a full-size bedroom in a warehouse to see how a wheelchair would function around a bed.

In the midst of all of the chaos and confusion of Shafin, I could not have been more relieved when the time came to hook up with Mark, Kian and Nicky to get Westlife moving again.

First of all, we met up with Louis at a hotel in London for a chat about how we all felt after our time off and if we were ready for a comeback. It was a really positive meeting. The other three were all looking relaxed, trim and in good shape. It was clear that the year off had done them a world of good.

We were all very bullish in the meeting. We wanted to keep Westlife going and we felt that we had to up our game and explode back with a really brilliant album. There was no point in going through the motions. We had to show that we were still a force to be reckoned with.

If we were secretly worrying that we were getting too old to be a boy band, Take That's return had settled those fears. If we were a dad-band by now, they were a granddad-band – yet while we had been away, they had got bigger than ever, and now they were on a stadium tour.

We didn't see Take That as competition, exactly; it wasn't as simple as that. But their triumphant return inspired us to think that if we had the right songs, we could do something similar. If they could do it, why shouldn't we?

One or two of the other lads were saying that Westlife could last another ten years, just like Take That, but that we wouldn't be able to keep up our usual insane pace of putting out an album and touring every year. We would have to space the albums out more and maybe do one every other year.

I saw what they were saying, but at the same time I thought, *F\*\*k! Let's carry on doing an album a year!* Because I knew that I was financially screwed, and chances were that things might get a lot worse before they got better.

Even so, I didn't say a word. Partly it was still my stupid pride, but mainly I still knew that Westlife's future had to be decided by what everybody naturally wanted to do, not by my financial woes. I wasn't going to beg the band to go into a studio to pay my bills.

The new album would show people where we were at after our time away, so we decided to call it that – *Where We Are*. It was the first album where we didn't work with Steve Mac and Wayne Hector. They had always been great, but we felt we needed a change. We did a couple of tracks with the Swedes in Stockholm, but mostly we were to record it in Los Angeles.

We decamped to LA at the height of the summer in 2009 to work with a load of new producers, including Ryan Tedder from OneRepublic and Sam Watters who used to be in Color Me Badd. It was fantastic to be back in the studio and I could feel the relief flooding out of me.

In the depths of my despair over Shafin in our year off, I had forgotten how much I loved singing and being in Westlife. It was brilliant to put on headphones again and lose myself in a song. At least here, I knew exactly what I was doing.

It is a blessing to find your vocation in life and I should never have lost sight of mine. Singing was my thing. *This was me*. I felt like I had been in hell for the last twelve months but here was my escape – back into the world that I knew, and loved.

Simon Cowell had relocated to America for a lot of the year while he continued his rise to effortless world domination on *American Idol*. He had a place in Beverly Hills – well, of course he did – and Louis was taking him our recordings as we finished them in the studio.

We liked the way the album was going, and so did Simon, but he felt that we were still missing the big single we needed to relaunch Westlife and kick-start *Where We Are*. Early in August 2009, he invited us over to his house to discuss progress.

Louis had hired a convertible, and as we cruised through the palm-tree-lined Beverly Hills streets in the bright California sunshine, we boggled at the opulent wealth on show. Well, that was before we saw Simon's house.

We knew that Simon was a superstar on both sides of the Atlantic now, and as we pulled into the drive of his lavish white mansion it was clear that he was living like one. He had bought Jennifer Lopez's house, knocked it down and built something even more impressive on the site.

Simon clearly fitted into Beverly Hills like a hand in a glove. When he opened the door to us, wreathed in smiles, he looked like Mr Hollywood incarnate. We couldn't help but laugh in admiration.

'Jeez, Simon, you're doing OK for yourself!' I told him.

'I'm just telling the truth, same as always, kiddos,' he grinned from behind his shades. 'And America seems to like it.'

He gave us a quick tour of his house, which was totally white with all black furniture. Staircases swept up to the heavens and art photographs of Sinatra dotted the walls. We all went out to sit around his pool for a chat.

Simon was up to speed with what we had done on the album so far, which was all original songs. He knew we wouldn't be up for coming back with a cover, so he delivered his latest proposal even more shrewdly than usual.

'The album is strong,' he said, 'but I still think that you are missing something. You're missing a song that is something like this.'

He had a laptop on his little table by the pool and clicked on a button. An unmistakably American soft-rock anthem wafted out: 'Shadows fill an empty heart / As love is fading…'

It was a power ballad called 'What About Now?' by a US rock band called Daughtry, who had got huge in the States after their singer, Chris Daughtry, reached the final of *American Idol*. Nicky knew it because he and Georgina had been on holiday in LA when it hit big. I had never heard it, but as I listened I could tell it was a fantastic tune.

'Jeez, yeah, it would be great to have a song like that!' we all agreed.

'I'm going to tell a few of the writers to write something like that for you,' promised Simon. 'We'll make it happen.'

We were all more than happy with that. Before we left, Simon took us to his home cinema, which was kitted out entirely in black leather, and showed us – what else? – some episodes of the next series of *The X Factor* that he had just finished recording in London.

The boy had done good, all right! Simon hugged us and bade us farewell next to his three immaculate black cars – a Rolls-Royce, a Bugatti and a Bentley. The next day we flew home to continue recording the album in London.

I was on a high from being back with Westlife and the trip to California – and suddenly it looked as if things were going to start going Shafin's way, too. Just after I got back, I woke up to a text from Finbarr: 'We got the planning on Carraroe.'

Thank f**k! After four years, many hundreds of thousands of pounds in fees and numerous objections, the final An Bord Pleanála on our main project at Carraroe had given us the green light. There could be no more appeals.

At last we could start building and the supermarket chain, pharmacists, coffee-shop owners and hairdressers that we had lined up could start buying from us, moving in and doing business. Thank you, Jesus! Finally I could pay the bank back most of what we owed them and get my peace of mind – no, get my *life* back.

I eagerly flew back to Sligo and we gave Ulster Bank the great news and met up to move things forward. Now we had planning permission, we had to arrange the next tranche of loans from them to give our builders their down payments so they could start building.

It was a meeting I will never forget – and one that was to haunt me for many years to come.

'Congratulations!' said the guy from Ulster Bank. 'But I am afraid that in the light of the downturn in the market at the moment, we are withdrawing from development business in Ireland. We can no longer finance this project.'

I looked at the fella. Time seemed to stand still. I could see his lips moving but I couldn't make sense of what he was saying to me. Or, I didn't want to.

'Wait, wait a minute,' I said to him. 'You loaned us the money to buy this site, you gave us money to pay the architects' fees and the solicitors' fees, you promised us the money to build the development – and now you're saying that you don't have it?'

'I'm afraid so,' the manager said, apologetically.

'So where the f**k does that leave me? How am I going to pay it all back?'

He grinned at me, awkwardly.

'I'm afraid that is really a matter for you.'

It was terrifying. It felt like Armageddon. That night, Finbarr and I were sharing out my spare Euros, panic-striken and raging with anger, on my snooker table.

*What would we do now?*

# 12

# THINGS FALL APART

Finbarr and I had been through some serious grief and pain with Shafin Developments – but nothing like this. In that one conversation, our problems worsened a hundredfold.

To say that Ulster Bank withdrawing all of our funding felt like a deathblow would be an understatement. The bank had been our support from the start, encouraging us to take on more investments and extend ourselves, assuring us that they had our backs – and now, suddenly, they weren't there.

Our problem was very straightforward. By now Shafin owed banks millions of euros in loans. The only way for us to repay those loans was to develop the sites we had bought with them. If we had no funding, we couldn't develop a thing.

We were trapped in a classic Catch-22 that could lead only to disaster. As Finbarr and I left that fateful meeting, we knew that we were in deep, deep shit.

It was truly desperate – but one possible solution presented itself. When I was first starting out in Westlife, I had initially been with the Bank of Ireland before moving to Ulster Bank for some reason or other.

Bank of Ireland had taken this desertion hard, and over the following years, as Westlife soared through the stratosphere, they had frequently written to me to try to tempt me back into the fold. They had continued to do so when we formed Shafin.

They seemed like an option, so I contacted them and Finbarr and I went into the local branch to see them. They could not have been more welcoming and seemed to think that all of our sites were fantastic. Their enthusiasm reminded me of what Ulster Bank had been like when we first started out.

We knew we were far from out of the woods, but at least Finbarr and I could see a glimmer of light and Bank of Ireland weren't just offering us a lifeline – they were all over us like a rash. Finbarr set about opening up Shafin accounts with them; I had Westlife business to deal with.

*Where We Are* was almost finished but despite Simon's fine words in Hollywood, we didn't yet have the big single in the mould of 'What About Now?' Simon had phoned us a couple of times, basically saying, 'No, we don't have the hit yet.'

The clock was ticking and Sonny from Simon's office called me for a big heart-to-heart. He seemed to be subtly dropping hints that without a single, the label might not even release the album.

*What? I can't bear the thought of another year off!*

'What if we were to cover "What About Now?"' I asked him. 'Would that be our first single?'

'Wow, that's a great idea!' said Sonny, as if the very idea had never occurred to him or Simon. I couldn't help feeling that I had just fallen into a clever trap.

And, in actual fact, I didn't f\*\*king care. I thought we had made a great, really strong comeback album and there was no way I wanted it to be in jeopardy because we were being precious about doing a cover. I told Sonny I would talk to the lads.

When I rang Nicky and Kian, they were pretty open to the idea. I called Mark last, because I knew he could be relied upon to feel the strongest on these questions, but to my relief, he was not actually too opposed to it.

'Look, it's a great song, there's a time and a place for a cover, and it's not well known at all,' he said. 'The rest of the album is great. Let's do it.'

So Simon got his way. Who would have thought it? It was the last track we recorded for the album and it was such a cool song that we didn't change too much about it. Simon was delighted and loved our vocals on the song.

Mark's boyfriend Kevin was a photographer who had done a few Westlife shoots and he and Mark had an idea for the video. The label agreed to fly us to Iceland. We were out in the glaciers and the icebergs, miming and posing away as usual, and man, it was absolutely Baltic.

It was something crazy like minus 30 degrees and we all wore these huge coats, took them off for a few minutes as the cameras rolled, and then ran to put them on again. We filmed the end of the video at night, under the Northern Lights, and they were simply breathtaking.

Simon got us in to premiere 'What About Now?' on *The X Factor*, so we were all confident when the week of release came – and gutted when it only went in at number two.

Cheryl Cole's 'Fight for This Love' kept it off the top and went on to become the biggest-selling single of the year. By then, Cheryl was also an *X Factor* judge and a national treasure. We felt disappointed to miss out on number one, but it was still a pretty successful comeback.

Cheryl also kept us off the top a month later when *Where We Are* debuted at number two in the album chart. It was the first sign for us that while Westlife were still clearly major pop players, we would no longer be the shoo-ins for number one that we had been for so many years.

It would be stupid to deny that this was a blow – but at the same time, given my circumstances and after the year I had had, I was just grateful to be in a band that was still in the game and making hit records… because, for me, the alternative did not bear thinking about.

My life by now had acquired a strange dual quality. Half of the time I was living in fear and dread, chasing around Sligo between banks and planning meetings with Finbarr, praying that Shafin's debt mountain would not drag us under.

The other half, I was still a lead singer in one of the biggest boy bands in history, singing to hundreds of thousands of fans, jetting around the globe and glad-handing some of the most important people in the world… including the most important of all.

In November 2009, US President Barack Obama was awarded the Nobel Peace Prize, despite having only been in office for a year. The ceremony took place in the Norwegian capital of Oslo, and Westlife were invited to perform.

We had sung at the Nobel Peace Prize a couple of times before, and while we certainly weren't blasé about it – it was always an honour – this one was different. We were to meet an American president, and a very cool one at that.

When we arrived in Oslo, half of the city was closed off. I had never seen anything like it. Obama apparently had 1,500 CIA and security men with him and Oslo was in lockdown. It is a very laid-back city but there was a mood of quiet hysteria.

The performers were to meet the President briefly before the ceremony and we waited for an hour for Obama to appear 'momentarily', as Americans like to say. Wyclef Jean from The Fugees was there, and then the host for the event came in – Will Smith. Will was really friendly, asking us, 'Hey, what's the story, you guys?' He came over with his wife and kids, who were all co-hosting with him. We were chatting away but in my head, all that I could think was, *Wow: I'm talking to the Fresh Prince of Bel-Air!*

The security guys snapped into action and asked us to stand in line to file in to meet Obama. We edged towards an inner-sanctum room and I felt as excited as I have ever been in my life. There was such a feeling of high drama.

When we got into the room, there was a sea of CIA men, all looking exactly like they do in the movies, scrutinizing every person who came in and muttering into walkie-talkies. And in the middle of this dramatic scene stood President Barack Obama.

Immediately I was even more starstruck. Talk about power and charisma! Obama looked so authoritative, fit, calm and basically cool... he looked a million dollars. We inched along in the queue of people waiting to meet him.

As we reached him, I heard a guy behind him brief him: 'Mr President, sir, this is Westlife, an Irish pop band. They will be performing tonight.' He gave us a welcoming smile and extended a hand for shaking.

'Hey, you guys!' the Leader of the Free World said to us. 'I'm quarter-Irish, you know. How are you guys doing? You want to come over here and we'll get a picture?'

Obama's charm and people skills were extraordinary. I was utterly seduced. I don't say these words lightly, but I think he may be an even greater politician than Simon Cowell.

As we all gathered around him for the official photographer, the President of the United States bantered away: 'Wow, now I hear these Irish accents, I want a pint of Guinness! Let's go get one!' He never stopped smiling. I was speechless.

Then my life went from the sublime to the ridiculous. As soon as I flew back to Sligo, Finbarr and I were back in front of an An Bord Pleanála, officially lodging our proposal to convert the remainder of the residential estate at Dromahair to a 50-bed nursing home.

At the same time, Sligo council approved our application to do the same thing to the site at Orchard Lane. Finbarr and I could hardly believe it – yet were also grimly resigned to it – when the residents' committee from the estate next door objected to it again.

How could they object to a nursing home and a retirement village? We couldn't understand it. There was said to be fear that we might turn it into a B & B or even a homeless shelter – but this was not a likely way for us to spend €10m. So we went back to An Bord Pleanála. Yet again. It was like *Groundhog Day* remade as a tragedy – or a horror movie.

Unsurprisingly, Christmas 2009 was even tenser than the previous year had been. More than ever, I felt the financial rug was being pulled out from beneath me and it was getting impossible to keep my balance. I had had to remortgage the house after Ulster Bank pulled the plug on us.

Plus, of course, Gillian was eight months pregnant by Christmas – and on 22 January 2010 she gave birth to our second son, Shane Peter.

We called him Shane because my parents had given their second son, Peter, his dad's name, and we thought it would be nice to do the same. Maybe it can become a Filan family tradition! In any case, I really wanted to call a son Shane. Shane Peter was the perfect name, and our new arrival was gorgeous.

He was also a very welcome distraction from the tsunami of financial woe that was by then engulfing Shafin. Having done a 180-degree turn on backing us, Ulster Bank were pressurizing us big time to repay the loans they'd given us. Meanwhile, Anglo-Irish Bank, who were funding our Dromahair centre development, had their own problems.

Our one bright spot was that Bank of Ireland in Sligo were still being really supportive and even facilitating us to buy more sites. They said they wanted us to have a 'war chest' so we could just buy any property we liked without having to go through tiresome application procedures every time.

They seemed to have total trust in us. My brother Liam had a horse business by the site at Carraroe. He needed to move, and a farm came up for sale. Bank of Ireland paid for it in full, instantly, including the stamp duty. Effectively, they gave us a 110 per cent loan.

It was all so easy. Was it too easy…? It was certainly a crazy contrast from Ulster Bank.

Finbarr and I still felt that one of our best escape routes from our mess was to find a site, get planning permission and sell it to Tesco, and Tesco had given us their blessing to do this. We bought a site at Ballina, again 100 per cent financed upfront by Bank of Ireland.

Tesco also seemed keen on a site that we found in Finisklin next to the Sligo docks. It had seven businesses on it. The biggest was the Bruss car-parts factory, which employed 400 people, and there were also six smaller companies based in warehouse units.

Another developer had assembled the site and managed to secure full planning permission for mixed residential, retail and office use – but now, like so many developers in Ireland, he was under financial pressure and had no money to put his plans into operation.

Could this be the answer to our prayers? The Bank of Ireland certainly thought so, and urged us to press ahead.

Finbarr had a personal contact at Bruss who told him they would be delighted to make way for Tesco, if we could buy the site and help them build a factory elsewhere. We also secured agreements with four of the other six landowners.

Two of them were tough negotiators. One of them clearly saw a major financial opportunity when a pop star asked to buy his land, and asked for around €2m for his quarter-acre of land. *What?* The bank said it was small change next to the overall value of the site. We agreed, subject to us getting the planning permission.

The other guy, whom I shall call Mr Hawkins, drove an even harder bargain.

Unlike the other tenants, Mr Hawkins insisted that we lease his unit from him while we assembled the site, as well as buying it once we'd got planning permission for Tesco. He wanted a pretty hefty rent, too. He was the sole remaining obstacle to beginning work, so we agreed.

Looking back, I shake my head that we got into all this even as the Irish economy was collapsing around our ears. But by now we were so desperate to retrieve the situation that we were trying to spend our way out of debt. We were willing to try just about anything.

Bank of Ireland in Sligo were still showering us with praise and were incredibly excited about this Sligo docks project. They asked Finbarr and I to put together a proposal covering all of Shafin's plans for them to send to their national bosses to get rubber-stamped. We started working on that.

That April of 2010 we were granted planning permission to begin work on the residential nursing home on our first site at Dromahair. If only we could. It would cost us £4m to build and would employ fifty nurses and carers – but by now, of course, our financiers on that project, Ulster Bank, had pulled out. We began looking for alternative sources of funding.

It became clear that the Bruss site in the docks was not going to work for Tesco, and we began examining a site right next to it instead. Mr Hawkins insisted that we continue to pay him his rent, which we did, even though we were not personally legally obliged to. It seemed the right thing to do for the project.

While this was all going on, my escape from it all was that Westlife were rehearsing in Dublin for the *Where We Are* tour. After our year's break, it would be our first major tour in two years, and we were all up for it and raring to go.

Mark, Kian and Nicky were on grand form, it was good to see Priscilla again and we had a real buzz in the rehearsals. Our agents, John Giddings and Sarah Sherlock at Solo, had lined up a huge tour for us, and it had pretty much sold out straight away.

Phew! After our year off, we were all relieved that people still cared.

The spirit in the band was great as we performed multiple nights at all of our usual arena haunts in Britain. Our medley was good fun on that tour: we were covering the Black Eyed Peas' 'I Got a Feeling' and Kings of Leon's 'Sex on Fire'.

We had a couple of big outdoor Irish dates booked too. We did Croke Park again and it was almost more fun than the first gig there. This time, we weren't all so hyped up and fixated on remembering every second of it, and were far more able to relax and enjoy the day.

The second outdoor Irish gig probably meant even more to us. We headlined a festival at Lissadell House, a lovely old country mansion where W. B. Yeats used to holiday, which overlooks the picturesque Drumcliff Bay to the north of Sligo. Leonard Cohen played the other two nights.

Westlife had not played Sligo for many years and that balmy evening we were acclaimed like returning local heroes. I felt my relationship with Sligo was a little damaged by the Shafin shenanigans, but that night it hardly mattered as we belted out our hits with the mountain of Benulben in our sights. It was a special night.

Halfway through the *Where We Are* tour, Shafin got the final, appeal-proof permission to build the nursing home at the

Orchard Lane site. The development was by now a care home and retirement village that would provide eighty beds and around a hundred jobs.

Yet, as with Dromahair, we now had planning permission – but no money to build. The Bank of Ireland in Sligo still loved all our plans, but they could not give us funding until the bank's national directors approved the proposal we had been asked to write, setting out all of Shafin's ongoing projects.

Finbarr worked on this crucial document 24/7 and I helped in my downtime from the band. We were in and out of Bank of Ireland in Sligo as we finessed it. We noticed a definite trend emerge. If I was in the meeting, everything was grand and wonderful. If it was just Finbarr, the bank were always finding problems and asking for rewrites.

It was almost like they were treating me differently simply because I was in Westlife. It would have been comical had it not been so serious, but we persevered with them: we had no choice. They were our only hope.

By now my financial situation was beyond desperate. I still had money coming in from Westlife, thankfully, but it would hardly touch the sides of my account before being snatched out to meet bank loan repayments or interest charges.

I had even missed a couple of mortgage payments and ended up having to remortgage Castledale again just to get some money to live. Westlife was keeping us afloat, just, but we desperately needed that money from Bank of Ireland.

The second leg of the *Where We Are* tour ran later than most of our tours, right up until the end of August 2010, and so we were having our usual discussions about the end-of-year Westlife album while we were still on the road. To my horror, there were mixed opinions about our next move.

When Westlife had reconvened after the year off, we had all been excited and full of fighting talk about being bigger and better than ever and going on for another decade, like Take That. A year into our comeback, that positivity and spirit was starting to wobble.

The tour had been great craic, they always were, but were we really getting bigger and better? *Where We Are* had sold less than our other albums. We weren't unique in that, of course – downloads and piracy meant that album sales were down for everybody.

Our live ticket sales had held up incredibly well and our gigs were still a major draw. However, the most worrying sign was that our relationships were fracturing. We appeared to be drifting apart.

Westlife had been going for nearly twelve years now. OK, we had had a short break, but now here we were, back on the same old treadmill yet again. We were about to go straight from a huge tour into a studio to make our second album inside a year. So what had changed, exactly?

The fans and the shows were still brilliant, but as the *Where We Are* tour came to an end, the band was already starting to feel a little tired and stale again.

We had a lot of conversations on the road. Do we keep going, or do we call it a day?

Is this it?

The interesting thing was that it wasn't one member pushing for it and others against. Mark, Kian and Nicky were all on the same page, looking for clues as to what to do next. We reminisced about how we had always said Westlife should go out at the top, before we started to decline: was now the time?

Mark didn't know. Kian didn't know. Nicky didn't know. Nobody was actually saying we should split right now – so we decided to go to Los Angeles to make the next album.

The conversations about the band ending were torture for me. Mark, Kian and Nicky were all financially secure and had the luxury of deciding whether to go on with Westlife or not. I knew that without it, I was dead in the water.

The other lads didn't have the first idea about this, of course, and I felt like I had a dirty secret that I could never tell them. I was closest to Nicky at that stage, and once or twice I came near to confessing to him just how financially f**ked I was... but I didn't. I just couldn't.

So, in the absence of any decision to the contrary, we flew to Los Angeles to make the *Gravity* album.

Simon and Sonny had fixed us up to make the whole album with John Shanks, who was a US producer who had made both of Take That's enormous comeback albums, *Beautiful World* and *The Circus*. It was painfully obvious that Simon was hoping that John could 'do a Take That' with Westlife.

John was a really cool guy and we spent a lot of time hanging out in his house as well as in the studio. The band were even writing songs again, for the first time since our third album: I contributed to two tracks, 'Closer' and 'Too Hard to Say Goodbye'.

The band vibe was basically good during the sessions. It is always great to be in California, and we were all happy with the way that *Gravity* was going. As we finished off the album in

St John's Wood in London, I think we all felt confident that we had made a better record than *Where We Are*.

After being away from home for so long, on the road and then making the album, it felt wonderful to have some time to spend with Gillian and the kids in Castledale. Yet going back to Sligo also meant returning to the angst of Shafin. All of our main sites now had planning permission but were standing idle, awaiting funds.

We desperately needed to get our overall plan approved by Bank of Ireland HQ, and we took it into the Sligo office that October of 2010. We knew it was really strong. But the bank asked if we could add a few modifications and clarifications and take it back in December.

It was like they were trying to fob us off. Something didn't feel right.

The Westlife machine was ready to roll with *Gravity*. There was talk of the lead-off single being 'I Will Reach You', which Mark had co-written, but Simon went with 'Safe', a big ballad written by John Shanks. We weren't 100 per cent sure that it was a single but we trusted Simon's instincts.

The week of its release, in November 2010, we launched it on *The X Factor*. Simon was doing a boy-band special, and we were on the show alongside JLS and Take That.

It was a programme that was to confirm to us that Westlife was very much a band, and a brand, in decline. Whichever way you sliced it, we were in third place that weekend.

JLS had had an amazing year with their debut album selling like mad and they were just about to release the follow-up. They were the hot new boy band that the teenagers and kids were going crazy for. They were so young and had so much energy – they reminded me of Westlife as we went from our first album into *Coast to Coast*.

Take That were at the other end of the age scale but they were so massive that you couldn't imagine a pop band being any bigger. Robbie Williams had just rejoined, their albums were all going multi-platinum and they had announced a thirty-date stadium tour that included five at Wembley Stadium. It had sold out immediately.

Were we envious? Of course we were! I have to admit we looked at Take That on that TV show and we thought, *Now* that's *the way you do a comeback*.

So we sang 'Safe' on *The X Factor* and we did a good version and it went down well, but we looked at Take That and JLS and there was hysteria surrounding them both. Westlife had always had that – but we couldn't feel it that night.

Our song just wasn't strong enough. It was safe in more ways than one.

There was a telling moment after the show. We were in a Winnebago outside the studio with Simon and Sonny and a laptop, looking at iTunes, where it tracks singles sales as they happen. The music-industry execs were expecting a spike in all of the bands' sales as soon as the broadcast finished. Simon said JLS were a cert for number one, and they were streets ahead at the top, but 'Safe' was hardly moving at all.

Simon and Sonny could see we were down about it and were telling us not to worry and that a top-three single wasn't the be-all and end-all, but it felt like a significant and worrying moment for us. And it felt even worse when the chart was announced and 'Safe' was number ten.

Number ten. For the first single off an album. Now we knew for sure: this just was not good enough. We felt like it might as well have been number fifty.

The following week, *Gravity* came out and was number three – behind Take That and JLS. It confirmed everything that we had feared on *The X Factor*.

What was worse, we thought that was where we should be.

The *Gravity* tour for the next year was still selling out so we could still shift gig tickets, but we no longer had the kind of devoted fans who would run out and buy a single the day it came out; the kind that JLS had now, and the kind that Take That had managed to hold on to.

We had been incredibly lucky and spoilt for years, there was no question about that. We had started taking it for granted that album after album would go straight to number one. Now that it wasn't happening any more, it was hurting us.

If we were all still loving being in the band, we could have probably dealt with it. But by now we weren't. It posed the question: if we weren't having number-one records, and we weren't enjoying it, what was the point of it?

As we went into Christmas 2010, even I was wondering if Westlife should call it a day. I knew that it would leave my future looking even more dire than it already did, but this band that had been great to be in for more than a decade suddenly felt negative, frustrated and angry.

What did we have to look forward to next year? Westlife was feeling like shite now. The *Gravity* tour would be brilliant, because we always loved our tours, but as soon as the tour was over and we had to think about making another record, we would start feeling shite again.

Really, apart from keeping me from financial catastrophe, what was the point?

For selfish reasons, I was still praying that Westlife would not split – but it was looking more and more inevitable.

For the first time, I started trying to imagine a future without Westlife. Shafin had still got planning in place for all of its sites – maybe when we got the go-ahead on funding from the Bank of Ireland directors, we could turn things around, pay off our debts and even make some profits on our five years of blood, sweat and (many) tears.

The Bank of Ireland in Sligo had finally sent our proposal to their head office just before Christmas. They didn't take long to consider it. Early in January 2011, they rejected all of our plans outright and told us there would be no future funding. Straight away, Finbarr's bank card stopped working.

Now the really bad shit was about to start.

# 13

# LOSING THE MEANING
# OF 'LIFE

Although Shafin Developments was the most frustrating and frightening experience I had ever been through, Finbarr and I had always had a plan to turn it around. We would be OK once we got the planning permissions; we would be OK once we were building and selling properties; we would be OK once the Bank of Ireland mega-loan came through.

Now Bank of Ireland had slammed the door on us, for the first time we couldn't see a way out of the mess. We were millions in debt and we had no way even to begin to repay any of it.

But Bank of Ireland hadn't just stopped trying to help Shafin. They wanted their money back – yesterday. Their head office sidelined the Sligo branch and appointed a senior guy from their Athlone office to deal with us.

He came out to Sligo and talked to Finbarr and me as if we were halfway between idiots and criminals. He told us all of our plans were rubbish, everything was wrong and we had to sell all of the sites immediately.

One of the Sligo bank managers who had given us the loans – and urged us to have more – sat meekly in the same meeting and hardly said a word. I kept looking at him, and thinking, *Isn't this where you explain what has happened?*

Instead, he just kept his head down as the guy from Athlone with the bad attitude tore into Finbar and me. This charmer left, threatening us with legal action if we didn't get repaying – and fast.

Financially, my life became even more of a nightmare. Every day brought more enormous bills; more repayment demands; more threats to take us to court. Back in the heady early days, I had made myself personally liable for the majority of Shafin's loans. I couldn't believe I had been so stupid.

Shafin had lost €2.4m in 2009. In 2010 it was €2.6m. By now I was paying out €70,000 per month just in interest on our loans. Some months, I would not have enough in my account to do it.

Fridays were the worst. Every Friday I would get emails from one or more of the banks.

'You have missed a further mortgage payment. Can you please pay €356,000 by end of business on Monday.'

'You are in arrears with your repayment of our loan. Can you please transfer €3.4m by the end of the month.'

Crazy, crazy shit like that. If I could have paid them, I would. But it was getting to the stage that I hardly had a penny.

I would go in for meetings with the banks. At one point, I was virtually pleading with one guy, asking how I could be expected to repay the vast sums he wanted. He raised a cold, cynical eyebrow: 'You can sing can't you?'

Finbarr and I hadn't totally given up. We started to try to raise private funding to finance the projects, both in Ireland and abroad. Yet the global crash, the financial basket case that Ireland had become and plummeting property prices meant 'development in Sligo' had become dirty words.

It was a bleak, depressing time – I was truly desperate. For the first time, the awful truth hit me between the eyes: that I could lose my beloved Castledale, all of the development sites, everything. There might be no way back from this.

I didn't hold anything back from Gillian, and we talked long and hard into the night about what might happen. I loved that woman more than ever. She was a complete rock and would just remind me: 'Look, whatever happens, we have got each other and the kids. Nobody can take that away.'

It was true – but they were the only things that they couldn't take.

It was a blessed relief to get away on the road on the *Gravity* tour. Even though, by now, being in Westlife was little more than an endurance test: how much longer could we bear it?

The shows were still fantastic, though. At this stage the gigs were the only enjoyable part of being in the band, and the glue that was still – just about – holding us together. Every night without fail, we would be buzzing, and grin at each other as the fans went wild, and I would think: *Isn't this still the best job in the world?*

Yet as soon as we walked offstage we were back to reality. We just were not enjoying being in Westlife any more. We seemed to be taking it in turns to choose petty things to row and fall out about. There were tensions between all of us. Some days, it even felt like we were no longer friends.

When we did go out for dinner or a drink, it felt wrong, like we were faking our closeness. Inevitably, we'd end up talking about the band, how depressing it had become, and how the fallings-out and petty shite were dragging us down.

I was closest to Nicky now, and Mark and Kian would hang out together, but it wasn't as if the band had divided in two. We were all divided from each other. Where once Louis had made us into a proper gang, now we were four very distant individuals. How had this happened?

We were resentful, discontented, and not nice to be around. We had always been a pretty easy-going, low-maintenance group on the road. Suddenly, we were going through tour managers at a rate of knots. We were not a happy bunch.

We were even falling out with our label. After 'Safe' had been a flop, by our standards, we wanted to put things right with a second single from the *Gravity* album. We were pushing for Mark's song, 'I Will Reach You'.

The message coming back to us from Simon's office via Sonny and Louis was that there was no point in doing this because it would not affect the sales of the album. The label refused even to release a second single.

We were seriously pissed off with this, and with the idea that we were reduced to the kind of band who only gets to put out one single from an album. What was happening here? It angered us so much that we asked to be moved from Simon's label, Syco, onto another Sony imprint, RCA.

Although there were specific frustrations between us, mostly we were angry at the band and our situation. We were angry that we weren't the force we had been; that we were now just another band, and no longer dominating the pop world. Shit, we were just angry all round.

It's amazing in the circumstances that the gigs were as good as they were, but the first half of the *Gravity* tour, playing twenty-five British and Irish arena dates in the spring of 2011, was a riot. The stage was the only place we were happy. The Point Depot had by now been reborn as the newly refurbished O2 and we ended with five nights there, which were incredible.

If only we could just perform, and never do anything else! But, sadly, this wasn't possible.

We were still having amazing adventures. At the end of the tour's first leg, we did a couple of Middle East gigs, in Oman and Dubai, and then featured in two major historic events in Dublin in quick succession.

In May 2011, the Queen made a state visit to Ireland. Because of Britain and Ireland's fiery history, and the Troubles, it was the first time she had ever been to our country – in fact, it was the first visit to Ireland by a British monarch since King George V, her granddad, exactly 100 years earlier.

It was obviously a massive happening and crowds turned out to see her. Westlife were invited to entertain her at a big gala performance at the National Convention Centre, along with The Chieftains and the cast and orchestra from *Riverdance*.

We sang 'You Raise Me Up' and I was pretty nervous, as the Queen was right in front of me in my eye-line. We nailed it, and then at the end we lined up with the other performers as the Queen came up onstage to greet us. It was being shown live on TV.

The Queen passed along the line shaking hands and saying, 'Hello,' and then stopped when she came to me. Ah, we were going to have another of our heart-to-hearts! She leaned forward and said something to me… and I didn't hear it.

My heart was beating fast and my blood ran cold. I was live on TV talking to the Queen and I hadn't got a clue what she had just said. I couldn't exactly say, 'You wot?' What came out, I think, was 'Excuse me, ma'am?' I heard Mark giggle next to me.

'Are you on tour at the moment?' the Queen asked me.

'Ah, your Majesty, we've just finished a tour, and we're about to go on tour again,' I told her.

'Splendid,' she said, and moved on.

The Duke of Edinburgh was accompanying her and followed her down the line. As he shook Kian's hand, Kian asked him, 'Are you enjoying your visit to Ireland, sir?'

Prince Philip stopped dead and glared at him. 'Well, of course I am. What do you expect me to say?' he said, and walked on without waiting for a reply. Poor Kian went white. He had messed with the wrong duke.

Four days later, Westlife were renewing our acquaintance with President Barack Obama.

Obama was also in Ireland on a state visit and was to give an open-air speech from a stage erected next to Trinity College in Dublin. A few Irish actors and artists were to warm up the crowd beforehand, and Westlife were asked to perform three songs.

The shades-wearing, walkie-talkie-carrying CIA and security men were out in force again. We sang 'What About Now?', 'Flying Without Wings' and 'You Raise Me Up' and Liam Neeson and Brendan Gleeson made speeches, then a loud roar rent the sky as Obama flew in from a function in Cork in his huge Marine One helicopter. It literally landed in the street behind the college and a blacked-out car took him 50 yards to the stage.

Obama gave a fantastic speech, and then hung out for a while with the artists and performers in a room at the college. It was far less formal than the Nobel Peace Prize, and he was mingling and chatting to people like Daniel Day-Lewis and the golfer Padraig Harrington.

We were reintroduced to him and a flicker of recognition ran across his face: 'Hey, haven't I seen you guys before?' But we were quickly eclipsed by one of the most momentous events in Barack Obama's life – as he met Jedward.

We already knew singing identical twins John and Edward Grimes pretty well, as Louis had become their manager after mentoring them on *The X Factor*. However, I think it is accurate to say that their fame had not stretched across the ocean to Washington, DC.

President Obama was thus somewhat nonplussed suddenly to find himself flanked by two grinning, gabbling forces of nature in glittery red Michael Jackson-style jackets and starched two-feet-high skyscrapers of hair.

Jedward were excited and hyper and yelling at him in fake American accents: 'Hey, Mr President! Hey, Mr President!'

Obama responded by burying his fingers in their towering quiffs: 'My God, you guys have got some hair on you!'

It was hard to imagine a more unlikely encounter. We were all pissing ourselves laughing, but I don't think that Obama minded – because he was doing the same thing.

Westlife also did one more thing of note during the break from the *Gravity* tour.

We decided to split up.

We took the decision in a hotel suite in Switzerland, overlooking Lake Geneva. We were about to play a private corporate gig, and we were having a band meeting before the show.

It was probably the thirtieth time that year we had sat down for a heart-to-heart about our future, and normally they ended inconclusively with us muttering, 'Let's give it a bit longer.' This time was different. This time we saw it through.

We all spoke in turn and we found it in ourselves to tell the truth – that we just weren't enjoying the band any more, and what had once been a mission and a passion had become a chore and heartache. We admitted that we had been drifting apart and, if we were honest, the thrill had gone.

It was an incredibly emotional moment as we talked and stared out over the profound, picturesque lake. We reminisced about the adventures we'd had; the incredible experiences that we had been so lucky to enjoy. And we agreed that we should bow out before we spoiled the band's legacy.

It was also a turning point for me. I was still petrified by the prospect of the band splitting, and I knew it would leave me even further up shit creek without a paddle. Yet for the first time I thought it was the right decision for everybody – even for me.

Whatever happened to me next with my money woes, I still needed to be happy in my life – and Westlife was no longer a happy place to be.

By the end of the meeting, we were all agreed, and laughing and hugging each other. We were quite teary-eyed at what had just happened and what we had resolved to do, but the main feeling was one of mass relief, as if we had finally taken a deep breath and faced up to the inevitable.

We decided not to announce the news right away. We didn't even tell Louis at this point. We had the outdoor British and Irish dates to play and then an Asian tour into October, and we decided to put out a statement at the end of that.

Even the timing seemed right. We had a second Greatest Hits album, imaginatively titled *Greatest Hits*, due out that Christmas. It seemed a fitting bookend to our career. We could release *Greatest Hits*, play one last big farewell tour, then go our separate ways.

That night we played a great gig. It was a funny one – it was the AGM of some big multinational corporation, and a lot of the people in the audience clearly hadn't got a clue who we were. But we played a blinder, and it was a very emotional one for us; we were doing a lot of hugging onstage.

There was a real sadness mixed with the relief. We had so much and now we were ending it. We had decided to walk away from the life we had loved – living our dream, being pop stars, having total security. Why would anybody ever want to stop doing that?

And yet we did. And we knew we had made the right decision.

Even so, I knew that if my private life had been a living hell for the last two or three years, even worse lay ahead. We had a couple of beers after the show and then I went to my hotel room, walked into the bathroom, closed the door, stared in the mirror and exhaled slowly.

'Jesus Christ.' I told myself. 'This is it.'

I didn't sleep a wink that night. And I felt certain there would be many more sleepless nights ahead.

\*\*\*

Back in Sligo, I was still attempting the impossible task of placating the banks who were queuing up to apply the thumbscrews. I would get some Westlife money in, put some to one side to buy food and pay bills for the family, and give the rest to the banks.

I was selling off all of the top-of-the-range cars I had bought when money was no object. I had once spent £180,000 on a James Bond-style Aston Martin DB5. Its value had soared and I sold it for £320,000.

Yet it was like trying to put a sticking plaster on a gaping wound. I wasn't earning remotely enough to service what I owed. I felt – I *knew* – that Gillian, the kids and I were living in the shadow of impending disaster.

Amidst the impossible demands for millions of euros from Ulster Bank and the Bank of Ireland, there were other, smaller creditors such as architects and estate agents. And, there was Mr Hawkins.

Finbarr and I had continued to pay rent on his warehouse unit on the Sligo docks site, even after we had decided not to pursue the site for the development. Now Shafin appeared to be going to the wall, we had to bring this arrangement to an end.

When Finbarr broke the news to Mr Hawkins, he went crazy and wouldn't accept it. He took out a court injunction for back rent, although we told him that the banks had pulled the plug on the company's funding.

Then again, this was not the worst thing that he was to do...

Luckily, I had one invaluable release from all of this pressure – now we had decided to split, Westlife were enjoying being a band again.

We played a series of outdoor British and Irish high-summer shows and they were a joy. Then we went out to LA to record four new songs for the *Greatest Hits* album with John Shanks.

John and Gary Barlow co-wrote 'Lighthouse' for us, and Mark co-wrote a cool song called 'Beautiful World'. Nicky and I collaborated with two songwriters on what was to be the final track on our final album, fittingly called 'Last Mile of the Way'.

Around this time, ironically, our record label tried to extend our contract. A new head guy had arrived at RCA and called us in for a meeting, where he offered us a couple of million quid to sign a two-album extension.

It was flattering but we weren't tempted. When they put the contract in front of us, it seemed a good time to tell Louis and the label that we had decided to split. Louis was upset – he would have liked Westlife to go on for ninety years. But he and the new RCA boss could see we had made our minds up and didn't try to talk us round.

As the *Gravity* tour picked up again, we headed for Namibia and South Africa, where we did a great photo shoot for the cover of *Greatest Hits*. The band leaned against a fence and stared meaningfully into the middle distance (which, give us credit, was something we always did very well).

The last leg of the tour was in China and Southeast Asia and the gigs were some of the most enjoyable dates we had played in two years. We were in Asia for almost three weeks and, in that time, we became the best of friends again.

The tension and the sadness had gone. The four of us partied after the shows every single night. It was bitterly ironic that we had had to split up to rediscover our band spirit, but suddenly we were a gang once more.

We rolled through Hong Kong, the Philippines, Vietnam and Singapore to the familiar scenes of hysteria we had excited in that part of the world since day one. We were loving singing again, we were playing stadiums, and it emphasized to us that we may have lost our way at times but, yes, Westlife *were* going out at the top.

We flew back to Ireland and pondered how to break our big news to the world. We decided not to do a press conference like Take That had done when they had split or as we had when Brian had quit. Instead, we wrote a statement to go on the band website:

After fourteen years, twenty-six top-ten hits including fourteen number-one singles, eleven top-five albums, seven of which hit the top spot and have collectively sold over 44 million copies around the world, ten sell-out tours and countless memories that we will forever cherish, we today announce our plan to go our separate ways after a Greatest Hits collection this Christmas and a farewell tour next year.

The decision is entirely amicable and after spending all of our adult life together so far, we want to have a well-earned break and look at new ventures. We see the Greatest Hits collection and the farewell tour as the perfect way to celebrate our incredible career along with our fans. We are really looking forward to getting out on the tour and seeing our fans one last time.

Over the years, Westlife has become so much more to us than just a band. Westlife are a family. We would like to thank our fans who have been with us on this amazing journey and are part of our family, too. We never imagined, when we started out in 1998, that fourteen years later we would still be recording, touring and having hits together. It has been a dream come true for all of us.

Kian, Mark, Nicky and Shane

We were going to leave it for a couple of days before we put it out, but then we brought the announcement forward twenty-four hours. The day that our statement was getting released, and Joanne Byrne was contacting the media, we all called each other up. We were sad, excited and nervous all at once.

I was saying to Mark, Nicky and Kian: 'Jesus, it is about to come out! Are you OK?'

We all were – sort of.

Joanne put our statement out and I sat with Gillian in Castledale and watched it hit the TV. *Sky News* had a flashing banner proclaiming 'Breaking News' and newsreader Jeremy Thompson, in his most serious mode, intoned: 'News just in – Irish boy band Westlife have decided to call it a day.'

I recorded it on my phone. I still have it today.

I experienced every emotion you can imagine as I sat in Castledale and watched the coverage unfold. The next day, we were on every newspaper front page in Ireland, and most of them in England.

Westlife's split seemed to be a seriously major news story. The strange thing was, the day it broke, Colonel Gaddafi was killed in Libya and his execution dominated every front page the following morning. Had we put out our news a day later, as we had initially planned, the papers would have all buried us at the bottom of page seven.

I was glad that never happened. Westlife deserved to go out with a bang, not a whimper.

# 14

# 'I'M SORRY, SHANE,
# THEY SAID NO'

When the thing that you love, and that has defined you for your entire adult life, suddenly isn't there any more... How do you process that? How are you supposed to feel?

Mark, Nicky, Kian and I knew that Westlife had to end, and we felt relief now that we had finally bitten the bullet, but we also felt bemused and disoriented. What is that saying again? Be careful what you wish for, because it might just come true. We had been emotional when we made the decision to split and we were confused and upset as it got made public. The four of us agreed not to do any media interviews or even discuss it on Twitter while we laid low and sorted our heads out.

It made sense to stay in 'no comment' mode while we were still trying to let the news sink in ourselves. However, it was impossible not to wonder what others were saying, and for a couple of days I was avidly reading fan websites and visiting Twitter.

Some of what I saw made me feel terrible and even, in a weird way, guilty. Fans from all over the world were saying that they were distraught; they were devastated; they could hardly see to type their messages through floods of tears.

'Why?' They kept asking. 'Why? Why are Westlife doing this? Why can't they just go on as they are?'

It made me wonder: how would I answer that question, if these girls were here now and asking me in person? And I realized: all I would be able to say is that nothing goes on forever. All good things must come to an end.

Some fans were finding comfort in humour and saying that they would be crying so much at the farewell tour that they would have to take extra tissues to mop up all the running mascara. They began calling it the tissue tour. It trended on Twitter for quite a while: *#tissuetour*.

The media world also seemed to see it as a big story and a lot of newspapers and magazines produced retrospective special features and career histories. ITV asked Louis if we would film a one-off TV special to say goodbye: *Westlife for the Last Time*. We agreed to that.

Brian, who was by now living in Australia, obviously saw our news and he did one or two interviews in which he said he'd love to rejoin the band for the farewell tour. Our label even came to us and asked if we would be interested in doing this.

The answer was simple: no. No way. We had no malice at all towards Brian, not after all this time, but he had still walked out on us on the eve of a tour, with no warning. We had had to get through that, and we had survived and prospered and been a different band without him for the last eight years.

So, no, Westlife would go out being Westlife – just the four of us. There was talk of Brian maybe joining us for one song on the TV special, and we hemmed and hawed about that, but it never happened.

We had a short lull before the release of *Greatest Hits* in November 2011, and Finbarr and I tried desperately to breathe some life into Shafin Developments. We were still trying to raise private funds to finance at least one of our projects but the crash was in full swing and we were getting nowhere.

We did manage to put together a small group of investors who were willing to help finance the first stage of the docks development, which would have let us build the Tesco and a couple of other retail outlets and start getting some money in. But one of the retailers went into receivership twice as we put it all together, and our consortium got cold feet and pulled out.

Finbarr and I were doing our best but the bank demands and legal threats were getting ever more insistent. Every day my inbox was crammed with people demanding payment from a fortune that I no longer had.

Our main architect tried to take us to court for €500,000 he claimed we owed him. It was a pity – our contract with him had made it clear he got half of his money when we started work, and half when the development went ahead, which it no longer would.

Finbarr and I had given him his first payment in full. He had made €500,000 more than either of us had from the project.

People went to extraordinary lengths to serve court papers on us. One day a big flowery lavender box arrived at Castledale, dressed up to look like a present from a Westlife fan. Nicole saw it and was excited: 'What is in the box, Daddy?'

It was a summons.

A few people were decent. When one project fell through we had to default on a €4,000 payment to an engineer. He called me up and simply said: 'These things happen. You have paid me a lot. I hope you get it all sorted – good luck to you.'

Yet he was the exception to the rule. Far more typical was the creditor who knocked on Finbarr's door and thrust a summons into the hands of his bemused sixteen-year-old son, Killian. It was a shitty trick – and it wasn't even legal.

The bad news kept coming, thick and fast. The net was closing in.

We had to start thinking the unthinkable. After the kids had gone to bed, Gillian and I would sit downstairs and try to work out what we would do if, or when, we lost our home.

I had realized that I could go bankrupt. I was determined not to let it happen, and I still had a desperate, unfounded optimism that something would turn up to save the day. But at the same time, I had to look at the cold, hard facts.

I had debts of €23m, all to banks. I had no money and was selling anything I could lay my hands on to survive. And my sole source of income – Westlife – were calling it a day.

Talk about a perfect storm. As far as I was concerned, bankruptcy was not an option. It was too shaming; too disgraceful; too awful. But at the same time, as the storm clouds gathered around me, I knew I had to plan for the worst-case scenario.

My lawyers began putting together a plan for me to try to agree an Individual Voluntary Agreement, or IVA, with my creditors. Basically, I would offer to pay a certain monthly sum, or an agreed percentage of my earnings, over an agreed time frame.

It would be an alternative to bankruptcy. If the creditors all agreed, it would mean I could work like crazy to pay them as much as I could. I even dared to dream that we might miraculously be able to hold on to Castledale, although cold, hard logic told me it was impossible.

My creditors might be open to an IVA or they might not. It all depended if they wanted to work with me, or to drive me into the dirt. But as my legal team began to put it together, the lawyers had some serious advice for me.

They said that if we failed and I had to go bankrupt, it would be far better for me to be living in England than in Ireland. At the time in Ireland, anybody who went bankrupt had to surrender their income to their creditors for the next twelve years.

Twelve years! It sounded like a life sentence. In England, it was twelve months.

Aside from the emotional wrench of leaving Castledale, it would not be too hard to go. Gillian and I had had the house in Cobham, in Surrey, for eight years now; some years we spent almost as much time there as we did in Sligo.

There was also another good reason to relocate to England. If I had any chance of making an IVA work, I would have to be earning money after Westlife had split. There was only one thing that I knew I was any good at.

I was going to have to do the thing that I had thought I would never do, that had never held the slightest attraction for me, and that I had turned down vehemently when I was offered it in Westlife.

I was going to have to launch a solo singing career.

I had already tentatively discussed the idea with Louis after Westlife announced we were splitting. Ever Mr Positive, Louis eagerly assured me that I could do it, that he would love to carry on managing me, and that he would get me a deal.

He also said that it would be a lot simpler if I were living in London rather than Sligo. It would make all of the chasing around record labels, TV shows and interviews easier, and show a proper commitment to starting a new career.

At this time, Louis still knew nothing about my impending financial meltdown: his advice was purely professional and practical. Suddenly, everything seemed to be pointing towards a move to England.

So in October 2011, not long after the announcement that Westlife had split, Gillian, Nicole, Patrick, Shane and I all packed up and left Sligo to make Cobham our main home. The move was made harder by the fact that Gillian's mum, Rosaleen, was diagnosed with breast cancer just as we moved and we felt that we should be there by her side.

Luckily, Rosaleen's treatment was totally successful, and in many other ways, it made sense to be out of Sligo – because it was getting to be not a nice place for us to be.

Mr Hawkins from the docks reappeared, still demanding his monthly payment. Finbarr explained one more time: the development had not happened. The banks had turned off the taps. Shafin had no money. We were sorry, but we couldn't give him what we didn't have.

It would be fair to say that Mr Hawkins was not satisfied by this response. He seemed to think 'yer man is a pop star in his mansion, he must have loads of money'. And he had had an idea.

Mr Hawkins sent us handwritten letters. If we didn't pay him, he threatened, he would decorate the outside of his van with photographs of me, Gillian, Finbarr and Finbarr's wife, Geraldine.

Hawkins said he would rig up the van with a loudspeaker so that as he drove around Sligo, he could tell the town how he felt about the situation. To emphasize the point, he emailed Finbarr a photo of what the van would look like. It carried a charming message:

ALL FLASH BUT NO CASH

I could not believe it. Nicole was now six years old: did he really feel it fair to put pictures of her mum and dad on a van and drive around town slagging them off? It was low and vicious.

Finbarr had by now opened a supermarket where we had grown up, in the old Carlton Café premises, and he decided to give Hawkins €200 per week from the shop takings not to do his van scheme. The low, vicious blackmail had worked. I was furious that anybody could stoop so low.

As the release of *Greatest Hits* neared, Westlife were back on the promotional treadmill with a vengeance. One November day alone we did *BBC Breakfast*, *Loose Women*, QVC and a Christmas special for Bliss TV. It was quite a schedule.

Yet when the 'Lighthouse' single was released, it only went into the chart at number thirty-two. Thirty-two! It was the only song we had ever released that Louis had absolutely hated. Clearly, we should have listened to him.

*Greatest Hits* came out the following week and charted at number four (although at least it was a number one in Ireland). This was our new sales pattern – good, but not great. It all seemed to confirm our decision to split.

The kids adapted to life in Cobham quickly, but at Christmas Gillian and I really felt the wrench of being away from Castledale. We felt like we were in exile. As usual, I tried to stay upbeat. It's only a temporary thing.

It's just while we sort ourselves out.

*Something will come up.*

Thankfully, something very exciting was about to come up for Westlife. We were to kick off the *Greatest Hits* tour, the *#tissuetour*, with ten days in China in the spring of 2012.

We played seven dates in the country, in Beijing, Hangzhou, Shanghai, Shenzhen, Wuhan, Chengdu and Guangzhou, and every night was hysteria. Every single venue was the size of the O2 in London, and every one was sold out.

Because China had been closed off to the West until late in Westlife's career, we had never had the chance to play there regularly, as we had in the rest of Southeast Asia, but now it was clear that we were massive there. What a shame that we had only found out as we came to say goodbye!

It was a brilliant start to what we were dubbing the *Farewell* tour; and what was even better was that Westlife had retained that closeness we'd found towards the end of the *Gravity* tour. We were the best of friends again.

As we had discovered on our previous jaunt, deciding to split had dissipated all the tensions and the bad feelings between us. On the *Farewell* tour, we were proper mates again. Every night we went out after the show, and nearly always ended up in McDonald's at 3 a.m.

We had taken a camera crew with us, and they shot some amazing footage of Westlife in China, having the time of our lives, partying and being a gang again. That film has never been seen. I hope it is one day – because we looked on top of the world.

Nicky, Mark and Kian knew I had a lot of property in Ireland and they obviously knew the economy was going down the toilet. In China, they asked me, 'Are you covered? Are you OK?' I told them I had a few problems but was working hard and should be able to sort them out. Yeah, I was sound.

I was lying, but it was a white lie. It was the last time I would be able to use Westlife to escape from my woes and forget what I was going through. The band was having a great time right then. I didn't want to drag us down.

Those Chinese dates were the happiest Westlife had played in three years. As they came to an end, our Asian promoter Michael told us that he could get us twenty more dates straight away. Could we stay and play them? They would be worth millions to us.

We couldn't... because Kian had just taken a TV job as a judge on *The Voice of Ireland*.

It was so funny. It reminded me of all the times that we got offered silly money for corporate gigs and ended up turning them down because somebody had some lame excuse. It had bugged the hell out of me then. Now, it was just comedic.

I remember us four in a Chinese taxi, laughing our heads off and saying, 'For f**k's sake, Kian! We could do twenty more gigs here if you weren't doing your telly show!' Kian was smiling, saying, 'Sorry, lads – I had no idea.' And he hadn't.

We were past resenting and begrudging stuff like that. It was nobody's fault. Life is too short. The important thing was that as we entered our last lap, Westlife was fun again.

When I got back to Cobham, Louis began arranging meetings for me with record labels. He and I went to see a stream of A & R chiefs and executives who were hugely encouraging about the possibility of a solo deal. I was still dead nervous about the idea of going solo – but it was looking positive.

At the same time, I went straight into a series of meetings with the lawyers who were looking to negotiate the IVA with the banks on my behalf. The Chinese trip had lifted my mood and I had rediscovered some of my usual fighting spirit and optimism.

*There is no way I will go bankrupt*, I told myself. *We will find a way through this. I'll explain to the banks that I want to work together with them to put this right, and we'll come to an agreement that suits all of us.*

We were all grown adults, after all. It shouldn't be beyond us.

Bank of Ireland had just served court papers on me to try to get their money back and the newspapers were starting to run speculative stories about my financial position, but even so I remained optimistic that the bank would drop the court case when we got around the table to talk. We would sort it out between us.

My legal meetings were long and arduous. My team had to prepare documents itemizing all of my personal assets and debits. Castledale topped the list in both of the categories. I had by now remortgaged it three times to pay my bills, and its mortgage ran to €3.7m.

I went over and over everything with my legal team, right down to the value of my wedding ring. When they were finally happy with the accounts, they sealed them in an envelope to be lodged with the local court.

A few days later, I heard from the lawyers that there was to be a big meeting with all of my major bank creditors at the end of April 2012. It was to be held in Dublin, where I would by then be rehearsing with Westlife for the rest of the #*tissuetour* dates. Perfect!

First, I had a couple of weeks to chill out and relax with my family in Cobham. This included Easter weekend at the start of April. I had dropped Nicole off at a friend's house for an Irish dancing class, then headed back an hour later to pick her up. I had just pulled up outside the house when my phone rang.

It was Joanne, my Irish PR. The news that she had could not have been any worse.

'Shane, there is going to be a big story tomorrow in the *Mail on Sunday*,' she began. 'They have got hold of all of your financial information from your IVA court application.'

I sat in my car and my jaw dropped open like a bad actor. I could not believe what I was hearing.

'What…? No! How can they? The papers were sealed to go to the court… What the…? They can't… Oh, holy f**k!'

I broke out in a cold sweat as Joanne talked to me. A *Mail on Sunday* journalist had called her. They had the entire document my legal team had drawn up. They knew every single thing about my finances. And they were running a story the next day – a very big story.

Joanne has always been a very sharp and cool-headed PR and she outlined our immediate strategy. We would say nothing for now. No comment. We didn't know how this would go and we had nothing to gain from talking.

'I'm sorry,' she said, and hung up.

I sat in the car. I felt like sobbing.

This was it.

This was the end of the world.

Until now, I had managed to keep the extent of Shafin's problems secret. There had been a few press stories, but nothing too dreadful. Gillian had known how bad things were, as had my parents, but I had figured it was my private business. I would resolve it with the banks, privately.

Now, as of tomorrow morning, the whole world would see that I was financially f\*\*ked, destitute and heading towards skid row. My big dirty secret would be on headline boards outside every newsagent's shop in Ireland.

The rest of the band would know. Louis would know. Simon would know. The fans would know. *The whole world would know.*

Jesus Christ! How had this happened?

It was twenty minutes before I could bring myself to knock on the door and pick up Nicole from her friend's house. In the car she chattered about her day all the way home and I never heard a word. All I could think was that my world was about to fall apart... and if mine was, then so was hers.

I told Gillian as soon as I could take her to one side, away from the kids. We hardly slept that night. I kept going to the *Mail on Sunday*'s website. Eventually, in the early hours, there it was:

SHANE 'FACING BANKRUPTCY OVER HIS DEBTS'
*Westlife's Shane Filan could be forced into bankruptcy if his creditors refuse to accept a proposed repayment scheme that he put before the courts in Britain last week.*

\* \* \*

The *Sunday World* also had the story and went for the more direct approach. 'SKINT SHANE'S €23M BOMBSHELL' their headline screamed, before listing the debts of my 'property nightmare portfolio' in full.

As soon as my solicitors' office opened on Monday morning I rang to ask how the f**k the leak had happened. They were truly shocked and apologetic but assured me it was nobody on their side; somebody at the court must have seen my name on the envelope, copied the documents and flogged them to the tabloids.

I never did find out who did it, and it hardly mattered. The point was, my secret was out – and it opened the floodgates.

For the next few days, it seemed the most important topic for every newspaper, TV show and website in Ireland was Shane Filan's finances. They chewed over the info, tut-tutted, second-guessed what had gone wrong and generally made themselves judge, jury and executioner.

It was a horrible, hideous, humiliating time. I stuck rigidly to Joanne's say-nothing policy, although it was aggravating not to give my side of the story. But she was right. I was so angry that if I had spoken to the papers then, f**k knows what I would have said.

Nicky sent me a cool text the day the *Mail* story appeared. It just said, 'Keep your head up.' And Louis Walsh, as he always is in a crisis, was amazing.

He called me up, flabbergasted. 'How the f**k did you keep all that secret?' he asked me. 'How the hell did you keep it from us? And why the f**k didn't you tell me and ask me to help you?' Then he went out to bat for me.

'Shane is wiping the slate clean and starting over,' Louis told the Irish papers. 'He will be fine. He has a massive solo deal in the pipeline and is going to be a massive, massive star.

'I am 100 per cent sticking by him through this. He is facing up to it and doing it in a very honourable and honest way. You have to respect him for that.'

Yet Louis's wasn't the angle that the media took. There was no shortage of columnists and opinion pieces happy to declare that I had been plain greedy, got above myself and deserved everything that was coming to me.

The fact they didn't have the slightest idea what they were talking about didn't seem to bother them. *Schadenfreude* was heavy in the air... and the worst offender was the *Sligo Champion*.

We had always supported our local paper. They had always got access to me and to Westlife for interviews. Gillian even judged a fashion show with them three years in a row. We supported their charity.

In the early days of Shafin, the *Champion* had run supportive pieces about our planned developments and how many jobs they would create for local people. Now it was very different. They had a good juicy story to get their teeth into now that it had all gone wrong.

For five or six consecutive weeks, Gillian and I made the *Champion*'s front cover. They honed in on the sensationalist aspects of the story: the fact that we could lose our home; the move to Cobham; the value of my wedding ring.

The newspaper's headlines included 'FIRE SALE' and 'THROUGH THE KEYHOLE'. One week we dominated the entire first four pages of the paper. There was no other news in Sligo that week.

It got to the stage, I am sure, that even people in Sligo were sick of reading about it. It was all too much. It was a media feeding frenzy – and we were trapped at the centre of it.

It cut me to the quick. I was expecting to get slagged off by the red-top tabloids: that is what they do. But I had hoped for better from the media in Sligo, the hometown I had travelled the world talking about. I never expected them to turn on me so viciously.

It was bad for Gillian and me, reading the headlines online in England, but it must have been worse for my family. We were mortified to think of our poor parents, still in Sligo, walking around town with everyone reading this stuff.

We sat and stewed in Cobham – and then I had to get on a plane to Dublin.

I was meeting Westlife to rehearse for the main body of the *Greatest Hits/Farewell* tour, but first there was the little matter of my IVA meeting with all the banks that I owed money to.

This meeting was a big deal. It would basically show me if the banks were willing to negotiate an arrangement with me – or if they were intent on the nuclear option of driving me under and making me bankrupt.

I was still desperate to avoid bankruptcy. I didn't want it in my life or touching my family or the band. I didn't want to be known as 'Shane Filan, the bankrupt pop star'. I knew that I was heading for an incredibly tough meeting but I tried to be optimistic. Surely there was a better solution?

Gillian and the solicitor who was looking to negotiate the IVA came with me. Ever since my papers had been leaked to the

*Mail on Sunday* it was open house on my private affairs, and the newspapers that morning were all talking about the meeting.

This bugged me because I knew having the media all over my case and making it high profile would put pressure on the banks not to be soft on me. I thought it could affect how things worked out. And, to be honest, I think it did.

The IVA meeting was horrible, one of the worst days of my life. Gillian and I were put to wait in an anteroom while my solicitor went in to talk to the bankers. We had expected to be there about fifteen minutes; instead, it was a very, very long hour and a half.

When we finally got into the room, there were seven or eight executives around the table, representing the five banks that I by now owed money to. What was noticeable straight away was that there was not a familiar face among them.

These were senior figures from the banks, most of whom had flown in from London. There were more English than Irish accents in the room. Not one of them was a person who had actually sat down with Finbarr and me, talked through our plans and then loaned us money.

I'm sure the local managers had briefed them, in a report or an email, but they didn't know me personally and they had no idea what had really gone on. They may have never been to Sligo. As far as they were concerned, I was just one more Irish failure who had overreached himself.

And not only that – I was an uppity pop star to boot! Maybe the sort of person who needed to be taught a lesson...

I spoke first in the meeting. I thanked them for coming and said that I wanted to work with them to repair the situation as best I could. I wanted to negotiate an IVA that was fair and made sense for all of us.

I stressed that I wanted to fix things together. It wasn't that I didn't care that I had a mountain of debt: I did, and that was why I was trying to do an IVA rather than taking the easy option of declaring myself bankrupt and writing off the debt.

I told them I would work with them and earn as much as I could. I would work hard to support my wife and kids and then a lot of the money left over would be going to them towards my debts. I guess I was saying that I wanted to be honourable.

When I finished talking, one of the bankers fixed me with a steely glare. 'Are you going to hand over the keys to your house?' he asked me.

So that was the way it was going to go.

'Yes,' I said. 'If that is part of the agreement, of course I will. I'm not expecting to keep it.'

We had quietly hoped for a miracle, but in our hearts Gillian and I had known for a while that we would lose Castledale, the dream home we had built from nothing. Yet I was taken aback at the tone of this very first comment. There was a lot of anger and resentment in the men ranged against me in that room.

The mood was that I had done wrong and must be punished. None of the bankers seemed to feel they had done anything even slightly questionable – except one.

The man from Ulster Bank gave a little speech during which he acknowledged that we had all made this mess and we all had to clean it up. I looked around the room.

*Well, yeah!* I thought. *You're the men whose banks were happy throwing millions of euros at a twenty-five-year-old pop* *star with no experience of property, and encouraging him to buy and build more and more! Too f\*\*king right you helped to make this mess!*

Perhaps wisely, I left this unsaid.

The task of the meeting was to work out a formula for the IVA. We could either agree that I would give them a lump sum over however long it would take me to earn it, or that I would give them a fixed percentage of my income over the next few years.

They went into my plans in depth. I explained that I was looking for a solo deal after Westlife, that I had already had a lot of meetings with record labels and my manager was very confident it would be a good deal. I wouldn't have a record out that year, but I should have one the following year.

Over two hours, various proposals went back and forth between the bankers and my solicitor. Our first proposition was that the banks should take 50 per cent of my earnings, after my living expenses, for the next three and a half years.

I sensed that they wanted a lot more; possibly, that they wanted blood. The mood was not good. The meeting was inconclusive, and broke up with the promise to keep working towards a deal. Legally, we had a month from the date of the meeting to make it happen.

If we didn't, I would be bankrupt.

I went straight from the meeting to meet Westlife at tour rehearsals.

It was the first time I had seen Nicky, Mark and Kian since my money troubles had exploded all over the media. They were concerned and sympathetic, and asked me, 'Jeez, are you OK,

Shane?'

I told them I was fine – ever the in-denial optimist! – and explained about the meeting I had just been in, and that I was trying to negotiate a settlement. They nodded and didn't intrude any further. We got back to our dancing.

A week before the *Greatest Hits/Farewell* tour began, Shafin Developments finally went bust. Ulster Bank appointed a receiver: we owed them €5.5m. We had known that it was coming but it was still a sad day, and excited another wave of media coverage. Some of it appeared to verge on gloating.

In the midst of all my financial grief and turmoil, it was good to get back on the road and do what I did best, for the very last time – singing with Westlife.

Inevitably, we had mixed emotions on the *Farewell* tour. It was a huge jaunt, with multiple arena shows in all of the major cities, thirty gigs in all, before we ended our career at the scene of one of our greatest triumphs: Croke Park. We were doing two dates there – amazing!

It was also a fantastic production. We'd gone the extra mile with the staging and in rehearsals with Priscilla, and we knew the #*tissuetour* was one our moist-eyed fans would never forget. After fourteen years, we wanted to make sure that Westlife went out with a bang.

Yet there was also a very hardcore, profound sadness underlining it all. Because: *it was the last time*. We had spent our whole adult lives jumping onstage, singing and dancing with Westlife, and after this tour we would never do it again.

It was impossible not to feel melancholy. Every night was a goodbye. We would sit in someone's dressing room before the show and say, 'Ah, just think, 10,000 people here, and it is the last time any of them will see us!' We fixated on this point so much it became morbid.

We couldn't miss the fans' sadness, either. Every night, the women and girls who had pushed their way to be right at the front by the stage were looking up at us and crying. Quite often they would be mouthing, 'Why?' Because when it came down to it, we were the ones who had made them cry.

At the end of the set each night, we all made a short farewell speech, reminiscing on our many, many good times and thanking the fans for everything, before we went into 'You Raise Me Up'. It was all I could do to get through it without bawling myself. #tissuetour indeed.

So that was what was happening onstage on the *Farewell* tour. Offstage was a different story entirely.

During the days of the tour, I was hardly off the phone from my solicitor, frantically trying to negotiate the IVA with the banks. I was offering higher and higher percentages of my income, but the bankers weren't biting. They were playing hardball.

It didn't help that my dilemma was being played out every day in the pages of the press as if it were a soap opera.

'WILL WESTLIFE SHANE GO BANKRUPT?'

'CAN SHANE GET AN IVA?'

Some of the stories had the implication that the banks would be going soft and letting me off lightly if we came to a deal. It must have affected the bankers we were dealing with, who were reading this crap over their breakfasts.

It came to a head in Belfast, a city that had always loved us. We did five nights on the #tissuetour at the Belfast Odyssey

Arena, a place that Westlife played no fewer than sixty times in our career. At our last gig there, Peter Aikens, the promoter for every single Northern Irish Westlife show, even gave us a plaque to commemorate it.

Down in Dublin, my solicitor had another IVA meeting with the bankers that day. I was praying this one would produce a breakthrough. We had agreed that she would offer them 60 per cent of my income over the next three and a half years. It was a big leap from our last offer.

I told Nicky about the offer as we hung out in his dressing room right before the show. We could hear the fans going mental in the arena. 'So what's the craic?' Nicky asked me. 'Do you think you're going to get it sorted?'

'Aye, I think so,' I said. 'They've turned down a lot but I think it's looking good this time. I've got a feeling.'

He smiled. The tour manager appeared in the doorway. 'OK, guys, you're on!' he told us, and headed towards the stage. Nicky and I got up to follow him, but as I got to the door, my phone rang. I ran back and grabbed it.

It was my solicitor. 'Shane, it's a no. They're not accepting it.'

F**k! What the... I suddenly felt faint, as if I might actually pass out. What more did they want? What was I supposed to do?

'They're saying 60 per cent is not enough and they don't like the three and a half years.'

I could hear an impatient crowd stamping their feet. 'WEST-LIFE! WEST-LIFE!' The tour manager reappeared in the doorway: 'C'mon Shane, mate, we're on!' He was looking anxious.

He wasn't as anxious as me. We had just over a week to go before the deadline, after which I would be declared bankrupt.

So now what?

There was only one thing for it.

'Offer them 70 per cent,' I told her. 'Do you think they'll go for that?'

'I think there's a good chance,' she replied.

By now the tour manager was pulling at my arm. 'Shane! Now!'

We ran down a backstage corridor. My head was in turmoil. I had always assumed that negotiation and common sense would win the day, but now... Now, I was really thinking that in ten days I could be bankrupt. Jesus!

Fifteen seconds later, the curtain dropped and I was singing the first line of 'What About Now'.

It was the first time in my life that I had ever not enjoyed singing with Westlife. The first few songs were horrendous, and I really didn't want to be there. Then the music and the screams and the adrenaline kicked in, as usual, and I got a bit more into it. After all, it was Belfast.

Even so, for the first time a penny was dropping on exactly what I was dealing with. For the first time, I thought, *The banks don't want to work with me. They don't want to do a deal.*

*They want me to go bankrupt.*

It was a chilling moment.

The next morning, my normal positivity kicked in again and I was back on the phone with my solicitor, finalizing the small print of our 70 per cent offer. She confirmed to me that it was a fair one, a good one: we were definitely going the extra mile here.

The #tissuetour rolled on, with return visits to Birmingham, Nottingham, London and Manchester. Yet for once, Westlife shows were not doing much to lift my spirits. In fact, we all felt like we were heading towards a funeral.

Every night was a sea of tearful faces, sorrowful fans and heart-rending signs in the crowd. Every night our farewell speeches got more intense and more moving. We began to get obsessed with counting down to the final, Croke Park shows: 'Jesus, only eighteen days to go!'

'Seventeen...'

'Sixteen...'

Two weeks before the end of the tour, we had a day off. It was 10 June 2012.

This date had been in my head for the last month. It was the legal deadline to secure an IVA before I would otherwise be declared bankrupt. It was a Sunday, but even so, my lawyer was meeting with the bankers one last time.

I was going spare with worry waiting for news in Cobham, so Gillian and I decided to go to the cinema. Well, what can lift your spirits better than a good comedy? We'd loved Sacha Baron Cohen doing Ali G, Borat and Brüno, so we went to see his new movie, *The Dictator*.

It was funny but I was not in the mood for laughing. I didn't see it all, anyway. Halfway through the film, my solicitor called me from outside the IVA meeting. The bankers had some further queries. I spent thirty minutes on my mobile in the cinema foyer.

*The Dictator* ended and Gillian and I drove home. I was still mad with anxiety – but the phone call had encouraged me.

It meant that the bankers were seriously considering the proposal, right? They were thinking about it? And now they were still talking, into the evening – they wouldn't do that if they were just going to kick it out!

I was offering them a great deal that included 70 per cent of everything I would earn over the next few years – why would they turn that down?

I talked myself into it. F\*\*k, yeah! They were going to accept!

*Great!* I thought. *I don't even care that I'm paying them such a big share of my earnings. Gillian and I can keep the house, and I can leave Westlife with my head held high. We can shake hands, sort this out together, and then I can move on.*

They were definitely accepting... or were they? It had got dark by now and I was pacing around the house, going back and forth between elation and despair. It was after eleven o'clock at night when my phone finally rang.

It was the solicitor.

'Shane, they said no.'

*They said no.*

'No?' It was all I could say.

'They said no. I really thought that they would accept it. I'm shocked that they didn't. I'm so, so sorry.'

*I am bankrupt.*

I thanked my solicitor for her efforts, hung up the phone, and burst into tears.

*I am bankrupt.*

My whole life flashed before my eyes. It felt as if somebody had died. My kids were upstairs fast asleep in their beds. For them, everything was great; life was great; Daddy is a pop star. They didn't know everything had just vanished beneath them.

*I am bankrupt.*

Everything I had worked for since Westlife had started was

gone. Everything. Castledale, the cars, all of our money: all gone. The world would know tomorrow just what a failure I had been and how I had f**ked everything up.

*I am bankrupt.*

I sobbed inconsolably. Everything I had kept held in since Shafin started going wrong came pouring out. This was it. This was the bottom of the barrel. I had never felt worse in my life.

*I. Am. Bankrupt.*

It should not have come to this.

It had come to this.

*Bankrupt.*

# 15

# A CITY OF TWINKLING LIGHTS

It was an hour before I could calm down from the news. I was bawling and raging; angry, confused and scared. I had never thought it would happen. Right up until the eleventh hour, I had thought something would save me. Now, I had to face up to a new life.

A life as a bankrupt.

All the while I was howling and panicking, Gillian was right next to me. She was listening, talking, coaxing me down and telling me everything was going to be OK. She was upset, too – but she was so much calmer and more rational than me.

Eventually, I fell into silence. It was midnight. We had a cup of tea.

'Look, you couldn't have tried any harder,' Gillian tried to console me. 'You did your best. There is no more you can do. You still have me, Nicole, Patrick and Shane. What more do you need?'

We went up to bed. I lay staring at the ceiling, as the whole grisly last five years replayed in my head like a bad dream. Where, exactly, did it start going wrong? When should I have said, 'Enough'? Why had it ended this way? Why?

Eventually, I fell into a shallow, troubled sleep. The morning came quickly, and with a start, but as I woke up I found that my nightmare was continuing.

*I am bankrupt.*

Bang! The bedroom door flew open. The kids came running in and jumped all over me as I lay there like a zombie. They were so innocent, so happy, and it upset me so much that I had to jump up and run to the toilet so I didn't start crying in front of them.

*They are too young to see me like this. I have to worry for them; not them for me.*

That morning I moped around the house. Then I got on a bus and went to Cardiff to play a pop concert.

I heard the air brakes screech on the big fancy tour bus as it pulled up outside my gates in Cobham. I wandered out to get on it in a bit of a daze. Nicky, Mark and Kian were all making their way to the show separately, so at least I had time to collect my thoughts on the drive to Wales.

I called Louis from the bus. He was as brilliant as ever. He gave me the same pep talk as Gillian, 'Look: you have your wife; you have your kids; you have your health. Nobody can take those away from you.'

It was exactly what I needed to hear. So was the next thing that he said to me.

'And you have your voice. I'll get you a deal. We're close to it already. You can start over.'

My bankruptcy wasn't yet all over the news and Twitter, but I knew it was only a matter of hours. Luckily, it gave me time to tell the other lads myself. I wanted them to hear it from me, not from anybody else.

I couldn't have timed it better. Westlife were doing a meet-and-greet before the Cardiff show, signing autographs and having our photos taken with fans. We all lined up and, just as it was about to start, I dropped my bombshell.

'Lads, I want to tell you something. I didn't get my IVA. I'm bankrupt.'

I did it like that because I didn't want it to be a big scene. It worked. Three heads swivelled my way; three jaws dropped as one. Nicky, Mark and Kian all went to speak... and the first wave of fans was upon us.

'Can you sign this, please?'

'Can I have a photo?'

'Why are you splitting up?'

'We'll talk about it later,' I whispered to the lads, and we got down to the serious business of writing our names. When we were finished and had gone backstage, they asked me a string of questions. Mostly, they wanted to know if I was OK.

'I'm fine,' I said. 'I'm all right. I've got nothing, it's all gone, but I'm happy. I'm going out to sing tonight and I'm going to enjoy it.'

The weird thing was – it was true. I got up onstage in Cardiff that night and I loved every second of it. I knew I wouldn't get any money from the show, or any of the rest of the tour, because it would go straight to my trustee.

But I didn't care. I felt happy again.

In a strange way, it reminded me of what it had been like right at the start of the band, when we weren't getting any money and we were just doing it for the joy of singing. It was all about singing again, all about being a pop star, and none of the other shit.

The worst thing in the world had happened to me, and I was still alive. I still had my voice. The fear had gone: it felt like I had had a skyscraper lifted off my chest. It was the first gig I had properly enjoyed, without having anxiety at the back of my mind, for a long, long time.

When the tour bus dropped me at my house again in the early hours, Gillian was waiting up.

'How was the show?' she asked me.

'It was amazing!' I said. And I meant it.

It set the tone for the rest of the *Farewell* tour. I cocooned myself off with the band, didn't do any interviews and didn't even look at Twitter. My bankruptcy was all over the papers by now, yet I didn't want to get distracted by crap like that.

These were my last two weeks in Westlife. I wanted to savour and appreciate every minute. Every arena we played, I looked out and thought: *I may never be here again.* I was going to sing solo, sure, but it would be in places a lot smaller than this. It was so bittersweet.

The fans were all saying the same thing to me at the meet-and-greets: 'Are you OK, Shane? Are you going to be OK?' 'Sure,' I assured them, every time. 'Forget all the business stuff now. Tonight is all about singing.'

There was a heartbreaking occurrence as the tour neared its end. Gillian and I had started following the Twitter account of two parents whose little girl, Niamh, had neuroblastoma a form of childhood cancer. We spoke to them, and they told us Niamh was a big Westlife fan.

We arranged for our tour bus to call at her hospital on the way to a gig, but the bus turned up late and we had no time to do it. We were to rearrange it – but two days later, little Niamh died. When Gillian and I got the call telling us the news, we broke down in tears on the tour bus.

Her parents didn't think that she would die. They were busy raising funds to get her treated in America. It was so sad, and I became a patron of her charity, Niamh's Next Step.

It certainly gave me some perspective. So I had money troubles – so what? There was *real* pain and suffering.

As the tour went into its last week, we played the Metro Radio Arena in Newcastle. It had a different sponsor's name now, but it was the same place Westlife had played our first big headline show, more than eleven years earlier.

Wow. Talk about memories…

At the pre-show meet-and-greet, a woman about ten years older than me, who had clearly been into Westlife from the start, came up to me. Shyly, apologetically, she handed me a £20 note.

'Here you go, love,' she said, quietly. 'Get something nice for your kids.'

It was like she was giving a child a fiver to go and buy some sweets. It was such a kind gesture, and so touching. 'Thank you,' I told her, and meant it. 'But I'm not going to take your twenty quid.'

'Oh, please, please…' she begged me.

'No, but I'll sign it,' I said, doing exactly that. 'You keep it, and you will always remember the day you offered it to me.'

I gave it back to her, and she went away happy. It was the sort of moment that restores your faith in human nature.

'Jesus, Shane, you should have taken it!' said Nicky, as Mark and Kian nodded and creased up behind him.

I laughed as well. It was nice to laugh again.

After Newcastle, we had just Glasgow, Belfast and Dublin left. They were three heartlands for Westlife: three great Celtic cities where we had always gone down amazingly.

The three shows in Glasgow were stunning, and Belfast was a brilliant chance to erase the thought of my appearance there a few weeks earlier, when I'd taken that terrifying phone call just before I went onstage. It was nice to be able to leave the city with happy memories instead.

Now Westlife just had two *#tissuetour* shows left – the small matter of two sold-out gigs at Croke Park, on 22 and 23 June.

These shows were such a rollercoaster of emotion for me. I think I felt every human feeling known to man, and a few more besides. Just like the first time we had played there, every family member and friend we had in Ireland seemed to be there.

Yet this time felt different.

We were so proud that we had sold out 170,000 tickets for this huge, final farewell, but at the same time it was tinged with an almost unbearable sadness. It was spectacular, and amazing, but we would never do it again.

This really was it. After a truly incredible, unforgettable fourteen years, it was goodbye to Westlife. Not *au revoir*. Goodbye.

At the end of the second show, I walked out alone along the enormous walkway that led into the crowd to bid everybody farewell for the very last time. The mobile phones, cameras and lighters twinkled around me in the teeming rain like a city at night.

'People always ask us, "What's your favourite memory of Westlife?"' I said. 'Well, tonight is my favourite memory of

Westlife. Right now.' The tidal wave of applause nearly knocked me over.

'It doesn't get any bigger than this. We started off in Sligo fourteen years ago when twenty or thirty people came to our gigs. Now we've got 85,000!' I think this time the clapping was even louder.

'I want to thank the three boys behind me. My three best friends for the last fourteen years. We've travelled the whole world, we've broken all the records – we've done everything we could have wished for.

'This was all we wanted to be when we were younger – we wanted to be pop stars, like the Backstreet Boys. We got to do it, for fourteen years, and that's all thanks to every single person in here tonight.'

Everybody was cheering. My eyes were watering in the rain.

I thanked our Irish promoter, Caroline Downey from MCD, who along with Dennis Desmond had put on every single Westlife gig in Ireland since we started. There had been a lot of them. I said hi to all my family and friends from Sligo. I had no script; I was just talking from the heart.

'I want to give a big shout-out to our manager, Louis Walsh. I remember saying to Louis years ago, when we were supporting Boyzone at the Point Depot, "Do you ever think we'll play this place?" He said, "Yeah, definitely!"' (I did Louis's words in his voice – and got a laugh. I do a very good Louis Walsh impersonation, even if I say so myself.)

'Well, we got to play it seventy-three times! We got to play Croke Park four times in the last four years!' The applause ratcheted up even further.

Now, it was time for the super-important stuff.

'I want to say a massive thank you to my mum and dad. I'm so proud to be your son. Thank you so much for everything. I love you so much. You know that.' By now I was tearing up – but I was never going to get through this one without crying.

'The most important person in this stadium tonight is my beautiful wife, Gillian.'

There were 85,000 people around me in Croke Park, but for the next few seconds, I was talking to only one of them.

'Gillian, I've loved you since the day I saw you for the very first time. We were only twelve years old. It took me a long time to get you initially, but I got you.'

People laughed and said, 'Ah…' but I could not have meant it more.

'You've stuck by me so well. I can't describe how much I love you. You've kept me focused on the job in hand; you've kept me going, every time. I love you so much, baby. You've given me three beautiful, lovely children, and that's all we need, babe. That's all we need. I love you.'

I blew her a kiss.

And then it was time for the big finale. The last ever Westlife moment, and one that took me right back to where it had all started for me.

'I want you all to do me a favour now! If you've got a mobile phone, I want you to turn on your little flashlight app and hold it up high while I tell you a quick little story.'

Suddenly, every light in this strange, temporary city around me was burning bright. There it was. That city of twinkling lights I had seen on the Michael Jackson video, all those years ago.

'I remember when I was eight years old, I was watching a video of Michael Jackson and all I saw on the telly was this...' I gestured out at the flickering digital lights surrounding me.

'I said to my mum, "That is going to be me some day!"'

'Well, Mum: the dream has come true.

'Thank you all so much.'

Miraculously, the rain had suddenly stopped.

'I want to dedicate this last song to my mum and dad – to all our mums and dads. Nicky [Nicky's dad] and Kevin [Kian's dad] who are looking down – thanks for stopping the rain for us! I want everyone to sing this really loud, OK?'

By now, Mark, Kian and Nicky had joined me at the end of the walkway.

'This is our last memory of Westlife, so make it a good one. This is "You Raise Me Up".'

What followed were the most emotional three minutes of my career – maybe of my life. There was an encore of 'World of Our Own', and of the song that made us: 'Flying Without Wings'. And then it was over.

Westlife was no more.

The aftershow party was bizarre. I felt exhilarated, but also numb. It felt like too much had been happening to me in the last few weeks, both crazy highs and lows. You can only feel so much emotion before you explode, or shut down. I was getting dangerously near to that point.

The next morning, I woke up in the Four Seasons. I was a bankrupt, and there was no more band. So what did I do?

I went to the pub.

Westlife went together, all four of us, to Kehoe's in the heart of Dublin, my favourite pub in the whole of Ireland. We had great craic for hours.

Well, could you think of a better way to go out?

\* \* \*

Before too long, it was time to fly back to England – and to a new, very different existence. It was time to come to terms with my new life.

Time to learn what being bankrupt really meant.

The court had now appointed a trustee to sort out my estate, and to work both with me and with the banks to try to get the best outcome for everyone. It was to be a difficult and quite often depressing process, but he was at least pretty even-handed and fair to deal with.

The trustee was to take half of the money I earned for the next three years. My personal living expenses were all to come out of the half I kept. Castledale obviously had to go, as did every asset I owned except for the family home in Cobham, which I was left with as part of the agreement with the trustee.

The trustee worked closely with my business manager, Alan, who had done Westlife's accounts right from the start. Alan had no obligation to step into the car crash of my life, but he went the extra mile and then some.

He was amazing – because I could not have had the conversations he was having on my behalf without dissolving into tears.

Everything changed. Gillian and I began living hand to mouth, day by day. Suddenly, I had no regular income, especially as my solo record deal had yet to materialize.

For the first time since Westlife got huge when I was twenty, I really had to think about money and what I could afford. The days of see it, want it, buy it had gone. There were to be no family holidays or fancy cars. We could take absolutely nothing for granted any more.

I have always been a strong person but the first few weeks of bankruptcy were unbearable. I was worried sick every second of the day. Questions buzzed around my head: would I have enough money to get through the week?

Some nights, I would put the kids to bed, come down to join Gillian in the sitting room, and burst into tears. The fear and the anxiety were overwhelming. Never in a million years had I ever thought I would feel – I would *be* – like this.

But this was my new reality. This was my life.

I felt so, so guilty that I had brought us to this. It was all down to me. If I had just stuck to singing and never gone near property, none of this would have happened. What the hell had I been thinking of?

Of course, every TV reality show going wanted me. *I'm a Celebrity… Get Me Out of Here*, *Celebrity Big Brother*, *Strictly Come Dancing*, *Dancing on Ice…* the lot. A couple of them, particularly *Celebrity Big Brother*, were six-figure sums.

I wasn't tempted by any of them. I knew they all just wanted me to go on and talk about my bankruptcy and my personal life, and I was not about to do that. Louis hated the idea and I knew it wasn't right for my career.

So for weeks, I did virtually nothing. Louis arranged a few more record-label meetings. I played a bit of golf, but I was so unhappy and stressed out that I couldn't enjoy it. It felt like everything I touched turned to shit.

And then I had to go back to Sligo to see my family.

I had never been away from my hometown for so long before. Even at the height of Westlife's superstardom, the longest I had ever been away from Sligo was five weeks. Now I was about to return for the first time in seven months.

As Gillian and I drove there from Dublin, I felt like my every memory of Sligo was flashing before me. I felt nervous and apprehensive. So much had changed in my relationship with the town. For the first time in my life, I didn't feel welcome.

Going to Castledale was heartbreaking. Gillian and I didn't let on to the kids that we were about to lose it and they just loved being there again.

It was great to see my parents again, but even this had a dark side. Nothing that had happened had been my mum and dad's fault, yet they had suffered through me and been exposed to all the scandal and gossip surrounding my fall from grace.

It made me feel guilty, and angry – emotions that I was getting very used to.

The first day or two Gillian and I were in Sligo, we hardly went into town, but then we thought, *Why shouldn't we?* It was our home; why should we have to skulk around? We decided to go out for lunch.

We left Nicole, Patrick and Shane with their grandparents and went to a great little restaurant on the outskirts of town. We had always loved going there when we lived in Sligo. We sat down, got a drink, placed our orders – and then a man approached our table.

It was Mr Hawkins, the guy whose last contact with us had been to threaten to plaster our pictures all over his van and drive around Sligo with a loudspeaker.

'Hi,' he said. 'Can I talk to you for a second?' 'Of course you can,' I told him. We went outside. I have to give it to Mr Hawkins; he didn't waste time on small talk or social niceties.

'Where is my money?' he asked me.

I couldn't believe my ears. 'What?' I asked him.

Off he went on a rant – but he didn't get far this time. 'How dare you?' I asked him. 'After the letters you sent my family, are you having a laugh?' I was so sick of this. And then it dawned on me. A little voice in my head said: *I don't have to listen to this any more.* And that was the end of that. As I walked away, I said, 'If you have got a problem, take it up with my solicitor.' I never heard from Mr Hawkins or his stupid van again.

I even managed to enjoy the rest of our stay in Sligo, before returning to the reality of life in Cobham. Every day seemed to bring a new reminder of our reduced circumstances; of my downfall.

One particularly bleak moment came a few months after the end of the *Farewell* tour. The Westlife accountants sent through the usual email itemizing the tour payments to the members of the band.

Mark, Nicky and Kian's names were all there as usual, but next to them was a new one: Kevin, my trustee, who was obviously taking my share. It was a seven-figure sum.

How I could have done with that.

It was one of the many things that brought home to me just how grim my plight had become. I wondered what the other lads had thought when they got that email.

It was a dark, dark time, and even somebody as naturally upbeat as me could have gone under – if not for Gillian. She was amazing throughout, and especially during those first bleak weeks when I was wallowing in despair. She saved my sanity and she saved me. She saved us.

Even when I was wracked by anxiety, Gillian was so positive about our future and our family. She didn't seem to have a doubt in her head that we would come through this – and we would come through together.

She would give me almost daily pep talks: 'Shane, we will be fine. We are going to survive. You can still sing, and you will get a new deal. You will have a career, and it doesn't matter if it is big or small. It will be enough.'

When we came out the other side, Gillian confessed that she was often putting on a front and bullshitting, saying the first thing that came into her head – anything that would lift my spirits. Well, it worked and it was incredible. When she could see me falling, she picked me up.

I was lucky to have two miracle-workers in my life – and the other one was Louis Walsh.

Louis did what he said he was going to. He got me a deal. We had thought of talking to Simon at Syco, but I looked at their current roster. They had One Direction, who were now the biggest boy band in the world; they had all the *X Factor* acts; would I *really* be a priority for them?

No, I had loved working with Simon for years, but now it was time to look elsewhere.

And Louis came through. After all of our meetings, we had a few offers on the table, which was nice and a relief, and we chose to go with Universal Records. It just seemed the best fit, and there was a nice symmetry to it – because Westlife had turned them down when we signed to Simon.

By Christmas 2012, I knew that I would be going with Universal, but I couldn't announce it or sign the deal for legal reasons. In any case, Gillian and I had one last, pressing ordeal on our minds: we had to move out of Castledale.

This was the dark cloud that had been hanging over us ever since my bankruptcy. The banks had originally wanted us out of the house straight away, but as my solicitor had explained to them, it wasn't an easy job to pack up a place of that scale.

It was a huge house and it was packed with stuff. It was where we had lived, loved, laughed, brought our children into the world and raised them. It had been our heaven; our haven; *our home*. It had been very, very special.

The banks grudgingly agreed to give us until early January. So that Christmas we flew back to Sligo to spend our last three weeks in the home that Gillian and I had first started planning and dreaming about more than a decade earlier.

It was such a shit, horrible Christmas. It felt precious to have a few last days in the house, but it was so poignant that it was unbearable. We had built Castledale from scratch, and now we had to take it apart before having it ripped away from us.

It was the house we had assumed we would live in for our whole lives, bring up our children in, and then leave it to them. Every room was full of associations; every corner had its memories. It was our spiritual home and now we were leaving it.

Our families helped and we hired a removals firm, but basically Gillian and I emptied Castledale ourselves. We packed everything into boxes. We even watched the snooker table, on which Finbarr and I had scrabbled for loose change, being dismantled.

The kids were too young to know what was going on so we didn't tell them. We simply said there was a problem with the roof and we were moving everything out to get it fixed. Luckily, at that age you believe everything your parents tell you.

On the final day, Gillian and I left the children with their grandparents and walked slowly together from room to room for one last time. It was the moment I had been dreading. Our home was as empty as it had been eight years earlier when we had first moved in.

It was the saddest day of our lives. I know how dramatic this is going to sound, but losing Castledale felt like a member of our family had died. And now we were about to close the coffin lid.

When we got to the top floor, where I had watched so many football matches, sunk so many Guinnesses and played so many games of pool with my friends, I lost it. It was too sad. I slumped on the bar and I cried as hard as I had cried when I'd learned I was being made bankrupt.

It took me a few minutes to collect myself. Gillian and I walked out onto the balcony one final time. The view we had loved across the fields – the fields that had helped to bankrupt me – was as beautiful as ever.

There was no 15-storey hotel towering over it. There was never f\*\*king going to be. For a second, it was too much to bear.

But you move on. You always move on. Gillian and I had a cuddle, hugged each other, took a deep breath, walked down the spiral staircase and closed the door behind us.

We tried not to look back.

We didn't quite manage it.

The next day, we had to hand in the keys – but we couldn't hang around. We had a flight to catch.

I had to get back to London so I could start writing songs for my first solo album.

# 16

# MY LIFE AFTER 'LIFE

When I'd first realized that I was going to launch a solo career, I had become fixated on one topic. Where would I get my songs? Who was going to write them? It was a question that went around and around my head until it began to drive me crazy.

The answer was not what I expected: it was me.

When I signed to Universal, they knew everything that I had been through over the last few years and clearly figured that I might get some decent songs out of it. 'You have a lot to talk about!' they told me. 'Why don't you try writing?'

I agreed, but with reservations. Although I had co-written a few tunes for Westlife over the years, I had never seen it as my major talent. 'I'll try, but I hope you haven't signed me expecting me to write hit songs,' I cautioned. 'I never have and I don't know if I can.'

Universal booked me into a studio to work with a selection of professional songwriters once I came back from clearing out Castledale. The night before my first session, I was dead nervous. I was sitting doing a jigsaw with Nicole in Cobham, but my mind was hardly on it.

The next morning, my head cleared a little as I drove around the M25 to the studio. 'Look, let's just do it!' I told myself. 'Let's give it a go! If it is shite, it is shite, and then nobody will hear it so it won't matter.'

The first writers Universal had picked for me to write with were Nick Atkinson, who had co-written Boyzone's 'Love You Anyway', and Tom Wilding. We talked about what I had gone through recently and they were gobsmacked. They could hardly believe it.

'Well, let's write about what is important to you,' they suggested.

Tom was playing guitar and Nick and I started singing and coming up with lyrics. I remembered doing the jigsaw with Nicole the previous night. I picked up a pen.

If life is like a jigsaw, where would you start?
You think you got the picture, like it's written on your
heart...

Within three or four hours we had written 'Everything to Me', the song that was to become my debut solo single. It was a song totally and wholly about Gillian and the kids; how they were all that mattered to me after all I had gone through; how they were everything to me.

'Cause I don't need the sunlight shining on my face
And I don't need perfection to have the perfect day
I just want to see you happy, a smile on your face
Nothing else matters 'cause you're everything to me, to me,
to me...

\* \* \*

The words poured out of me, and I loved writing it and the fact that it was upbeat, but I didn't know if it was any good or not. I was too close to it – plus I was still in emotional turmoil from moving out of Castledale two days earlier. It was difficult to see anything very clearly.

Nick produced and tweaked it and sent it over to the record label a couple of days later. They came back straight away and said they loved it, it was exactly what I should be doing, and could I do more of the same, please?

It was a major confidence boost. Driving into the next songwriting session, I didn't even feel nervous.

One thing I knew was that I wanted it to be a cheerful album. I had been through so much grief in my life recently that I could easily have made an angry, bitter record. I didn't want that. I wanted it to be positive. I wanted to look forward.

*'Let's write about what is important to you...'*

As the sessions developed and I worked with a whole range of songwriters, there was one theme dominating my lyrics: how much I loved Gillian and my children, and how grateful I was to have a fantastic, happy life with them.

What was it that Gillian had said at the darkest point of the storm, when I could see no way out? 'You still have me, Nicole, Patrick and Shane. What more do you need?'

She was right. Forget all the shite that had gone down in the last few years. I was still a very, very lucky man.

Universal had given me six months to make the album, which felt amazing to me. It could not have been more different from Westlife – in fact, we would probably have made four albums in that time!

Over the months, it all came together. I went to Steve Mac's studio to do a track with him and Wayne Hector. Before we started work, I went to the toilet for a pee. On the wall at eye level was a platinum disc commemorating 36 million sales of Westlife records.

The funny thing was: that disc was out of date. We had actually sold 46 million.

Jesus. No pressure, then! But in a strange way, seeing it was an inspiration to me.

I went back into the studio laughing at what I had just seen. Steve came up with a great melody sitting at the piano and Wayne and I started improvising lyrics. The three of us wrote 'About You', a song for our wives that told them how perfect they were.

As a lyricist, Wayne is a genius. They don't come much better than him and writing with him taught me so much. That week, he and I also wrote the lyrics to 'In the End', a song about love pulling you through the bad times; a topic that I felt I knew a little about.

With two songwriters called Paul Barry and Patrick Mascall, I penned 'All You Need to Know'. It was another tribute to Gillian, a thank you to her, and it is still my favourite song on the album.

Universal sent me out to write some songs in Nashville, too. It was a magical city of music that seemed to have a recording studio in virtually every house. I even managed to sneak in a trip to Memphis to see Elvis's mansion, Graceland, which was pretty freaky.

Out in Texas, with a guy named Brandon Hood, I wrote a song called 'When I Met You', all about the night that I had fallen in love with Gillian in Equinox club in Sligo, and lain awake until dawn wide-eyed and thinking about her. I loved the fact that I could write a good song with one person rather than with a team.

Universal were still liking the songs, and back in Cobham I was playing them to Gillian. She loved them, although she was a bit taken aback that so many were about her. She knew the exact story of where a lot of them came from. It made her emotional – as it did me.

Mostly, though, Gillian was proud of me that I had discovered a passion for songwriting. I had dabbled in it in Westlife, as we all had, but it had not been encouraged, or a big thing.

This was different. This was our future.

The album was so focused on me and Gillian that I knew it could only have one title: *You and Me.*

Getting the finished CD was a strange moment. I had received many, many finished CDs over the years, but this was the first one with my name alone on the front cover.

I felt very proud.

The cover also featured my new haircut: a perky quiff. Ross Williams, who had done my hair for years in Westlife, came up with it and sculpted it into place. He didn't tell me it would take half a bottle of hairspray to keep it up there though!

I did a slew of interviews leading up to the release of the album in November 2013. The elephant in the room was my bankruptcy and fall from grace – would journalists want to ask me about it? Of course they all did. They could hardly believe what I told them.

Nor could I.

For I found that I didn't mind talking about it; in some ways, it even helped me come to terms with it. Plus, if that was the price

I had to pay to talk about my new career, then so be it. I had been through worse.

The *Sligo Champion*, of course, was still keen to remind its readers of my darkest hours. The trustee had put Castledale on the market, and the paper led with a picture of the house and a clever headline:

'GOING FOR A SONG'. We had lost our family home and they were making a bad joke about it. They even put it in red ink. Classy!

But they couldn't hurt me now. I couldn't care less. We were moving forwards.

Old habits die hard, and I was concerned to see how high – or otherwise – the single and album would chart on their release. 'Everything to Me' went into the chart at number fourteen when it was released in late August 2013.

For Westlife, this would have been a disaster, but I was very aware that Westlife rules no longer applied. I just felt proud that I had written this little love song about my wife and people had liked it enough to go out and buy it.

It mattered more to me that the album went top ten, and I was relieved when *You and Me* went to number six in November. Universal seemed pleased, Louis was delighted, and I thought it was not bad for a fella who just six months earlier had been skulking around his house, not even knowing if he could write songs.

One effect of all the changes in my life was that my nerves seemed to have gone. At Christmas that year, Louis got me the biggest TV slot of my solo career to date – the final of *The X Factor*.

It was a show that Westlife had played so many times and I had always gone on feeling anxious, knowing what a huge stage it was. This time was different. It was very different.

I was to duet live on 'Flying Without Wings' with one of the contestants, Nicholas McDonald, and as we walked on, I felt utterly calm. The adrenaline was pumping through my veins but I felt ice-cold and in control.

*This is it*, I thought to myself. *I was born to do this. This is the start of the rest of my career; of the rest of my life.* We absolutely nailed it.

That was a real tipping point for me as a solo artist. Since that night, I have had a quiet but strong faith in my abilities at the very highest level. It made me realize: I have nothing to fear, and I fear nothing.

*'You can sing, can't you?'*

Yes, I can. Bring it on.

And my new-found self-belief helped to set me up for the real acid test: my first solo live tour.

Tickets had already gone on sale and were selling fast. Dublin sold out straight away and we added more dates, which was amazing news for me. It was good to know that, despite the best efforts of the local media, Ireland had not forsaken me.

Of course, journalists were still trying to have a pop. My live agents had told me there was a lot of demand for meet-and greet sessions before the shows, and asked if I wanted to do them.

I said that would be great, as long as the fans got good value for money and weren't just paying for a handshake. We said they could hang out at the venue, see the sound check and spend a little time with me. It would hopefully be a great day for them.

My agents started to advertise the meet-and-greets – and a local Sligo radio station immediately announced that I was demanding that fans pay €300 just to have a photo taken with me!

The station even staged a whole debate on the topic. The implication was clear: greedy old Shane, up to his old tricks again! €300 for a photo!

My Irish PR, Joanne, contacted the network and pointed out that every artist going is doing the same thing nowadays. It is just the way that the music industry works, as artists look for ways to make up for plummeting CD sales. And nobody was being forced to do it.

Once, this story would have hurt me. Now, I couldn't care less. There has been too much water under the bridge. Stuff like that is not on my radar now – and it never will be again.

I certainly wasn't going to let it spoil the tour, which felt to me like my audition to the world. I was obviously going to sing both solo and Westlife material, and I knew exactly what I wanted: people to say I was a great live performer. Being just OK wouldn't do.

Louis fixed me up with a great tour manager, Liam McKenna. He was sharp, funny, smart, efficient and a real piss-taker. As soon as I met him, I knew he would make life on the road as a solo singer a lot easier – and more enjoyable.

The tour kicked off at the Philharmonic Hall in Liverpool. It holds about 2,000 people, which would be a broom cupboard for Westlife but was a big deal for me. Gillian, Nicole and my mum and dad had come to support me, and I was so psyched up before the show. It felt like a moment of truth.

*This is the one. It all starts here!*

The show was quite overwhelming. I had so much nervous energy that I was gabbling away before every song like a madman. I must have thanked everybody I could thank twenty times. I even overran the evening curfew.

After the show, my production manager, Karen, gently took the piss, suggesting that maybe the next night I might try to keep my mouth shut a bit more and maybe we could all get home before dawn?

But I couldn't help it. I was so grateful to be back on a stage, and to every one of the fans that had paid to see me. It felt like I was back.

Performing solo was exciting, but I wasn't used to keeping a whole show together on my own, and I hadn't toured for two years and was out of practice. After the show, the adrenaline oozed out of me like water being wrung from a cloth. I had one can of Guinness and slept for thirteen hours.

The buzz carried me through the next night, in Birmingham, but the night after that, in Reading, I hit a wall. I had to work it really hard and my voice felt knackered. The next day was a day off and I spent the day zapped, lying around my house, drifting in and out of sleep.

I felt bleary, disoriented and half-dead. I was sure that I was getting sick and would have to cancel the rest of the shows. What was happening to me?

Happily, I think it was just my body getting used to a new rhythm; a new reality. I woke up refreshed after my day off and never looked back. The rest of the tour was a real high.

What was great was the mix of fans who were coming to the shows. There were the older Westlife fans who had grown up with me in the band, but also a lot of fans in their mid-teens, probably because the music that I was playing now was a lot more poppy and upbeat.

At my Cardiff show, there were four women in the front row who were in their sixties if they were a day; maybe even seventy. One of them was going totally mental, yelling along to every song with her eyes closed and telling me that she loved me.

She was shaking her booty in front of me as I sang 'Blurred Lines' by Robin Thicke, and I high-fived her at the end. The funny thing was, right behind the four older ladies stood their husbands, arms folded and expressionless; behind them were fifteen-year-old girls. All human life was there.

In London, I played the Hammersmith Apollo for the first time. Westlife had never been there because we had started off at Wembley Arena, but it was a real thrill for me to play such a serious, iconic venue.

For all that I had done with Westlife, I couldn't help but feel excited to stand outside the Apollo and see my name up in lights. A little voice whispered inside my head:

*'Ah, Shane Filan from Sligo – look at him now!'*

I took a photo of it and made it my Twitter page background.

The tour was going grand, and I warned the band to brace themselves for Belfast. It was a city that always went mad for Westlife, and I had a feeling that it might do the same for me. The band all gave me a look that seemed to say, 'Yeah, whatever.'

They can't say that I didn't warn them.

We were playing two nights at the Waterfront, which is a cool hall that can hold maybe 2,500. It had sold out very early. As we walked onstage at the start, the screaming that erupted could have parted your hair.

I saw the band exchange shocked glances. Jesus! It was like the level of noise that Westlife used to get in arenas, packed into a venue a fifth of the size. I couldn't hear myself sing. I couldn't hear anything. The production crew were going spare because they couldn't work the sound. The screaming was so loud it was coming out of my mic.

After the show, I had a raging migraine from the din.

Did I care? Did I f**k! It was wonderful!

Yet my first solo tour finished where it was always going to end – in Dublin.

I did three nights back-to-back at the Olympia, a grand old Dublin theatre, over St Patrick's weekend in March 2014. My family were all there. It was the perfect end to a tour that had been everything I could have wished, and more.

I could not have been more proud.

There was more good news to come. John and Sarah, my live agents, told me there was enough demand for tickets for me to do a second leg of the British tour later that year, which was wonderful to learn.

And I also learned that other parts of the world still cared about me too.

My Asian promoters, Midas, were fixing up a tour of China and Southeast Asia later in the year, and packed me off to Asia a few weeks in advance to do interviews and promotion. It was a route that I had trodden with Westlife so many times, and it felt weird and a bit intimidating returning on my own. Would anyone even care, now Westlife were no more?

They did. When I landed in the Philippines, security men were wrestling with 300 or 400 screaming girls waiting for me. I went to sign autographs and sing a couple of songs in a shopping mall, and found 2,000 people going demented. I sang on the final of the Philippines version of *The Voice* and 75 million people tuned in (not all for me, obviously!).

Ah, it is good to know that I am still a thriller in Manila...

Just after I came back from Asia, and while I was writing this book, I celebrated my thirty-fifth birthday. It's the landmark that always used to indicate that you were halfway through your life, your threescore years and ten; but I can't help but feel I have already packed at least two lives into mine.

It has been an incredible life, really. I have crammed in so many unbelievable experiences that I could never even have imagined when I was growing up over the Carlton Café in Castle Street, Sligo.

In particular, I guess I have done two things that seem out of the reach, out of the ken, of most people. I have been a pop star in one of the biggest boy bands in the world, and I have been declared bankrupt owing €23m.

How do I begin to make sense of it all?

Looking back, everything happens for a reason. Ever since I saw Michael Jackson doing 'Man in the Mirror' amidst a city of twinkling lights, I wanted to be a pop star, and I devoted myself single-mindedly to this goal.

I made it – through a lot of hard work; but through a lot of luck as well. I was lucky to meet Kian, Mark, Nicky, and Brian, and lucky that so many things fell into place when they did.

I am especially lucky that my mum grew up in the same little County Mayo village as Louis Walsh. In so many ways I owe everything to her, and to him. And to one fateful phone call.

My pop career can be seen as a white-knuckle rollercoaster journey up the charts and around the world that ended at Croke Park, in Dublin, when I stood in the midst of my own city of twinkling lights.

The property business and the bankruptcy are rather harder to make sense of.

I made some bad mistakes and I was very unlucky. That was the long and short of it. I took bad advice and did things that I never should have, but in truth I still think I was harshly treated where other people were given an escape route.

As Ireland collapsed in the global crash, people owing €1bn or €500m were quietly given IVAs with no publicity while the pop star who was seen as getting ideas above his station went to the wall as the media salivated. Looking back, it is hard to escape the conclusion that I was made an example of.

Well, these things happen. What can you do? It has made me a stronger person, very realistic but also determined to fight back and bounce back. The anger has long gone, because I was the only person that was hurting. Now it is time to look forward.

We are still not out of the woods yet. I am still working with the trustee, still handing over a large portion of my income, and I will be for a while yet. But I have my wife; my kids; a home. As Gillian said, 'You have me, Nicole, Patrick and Shane – what more do you need?'

I'm so proud that all the time Finbarr and I were going through hell on earth with Shafin Developments, we never once blamed each other or turned on one another. All the way through we had each other's backs, as families do.

Life is full of ironies, and some of them are good ones. One of my best friends in Cobham is a renowned heart surgeon, Professor Brendan Madden. When Gillian's parents visited us last year, Brendan noticed that her dad, Michael, wasn't looking well and gave him a check-up.

He kept an eye on him and a few months later he was doing a sextuple-bypass heart operation on him: one of the few times it's been done in the world. He saved his life – which would never have happened had I not gone bankrupt and moved to England.

There is always a bright side, if you look hard enough.

So what is next for me, and for my solo career?

I am proud of my first album but I want to keep going, and growing, and getting better and better. I know I will never be as big as Westlife, because we were a phenomenon, a once-in-a-generation success story.

We achieved so much that at the time we maybe got blasé, but now I think back it is amazing just what we did. Nobody since has seen their first seven singles all go to number one. Maybe nobody ever will.

So no, I can only dream of being as huge as Westlife, but I'd like to keep making records and touring and go to places I haven't gone to as a solo artist yet. I'd like to do well in Europe, and Australia, and South America, and... who knows?

Maybe with my new Nashville tendencies, I could even have a pop at America; the one place that Westlife could never break. Well, a boy can dream. And, as I've learned to my delight, sometimes dreams come true.

But really it's all about the music, and about the songs. I'm still looking for that special number, that great song that might launch my solo career into the stratosphere. It wasn't on *You and Me*. I'm still searching for my very own 'Flying Without Wings' or my 'You Raise Me Up'.

I don't care who writes it. It doesn't matter. It may be a guy who is sitting in a studio in California right now, or in a café in London, or in a bedroom in Berlin.

It could even be me. I know I shall keep trying.

Recently, I was due to support Garth Brooks playing some huge concerts at Croke Park. I was looking forward to it so much, but the shows got cancelled.

Why? It was a combination of objections from locals, and then those objections being handled ineptly by the local authorities. I had an ironic smile at that one. As I said to Finbarr, it all sounded rather familiar...

I love Garth Brooks – I've loved country music ever since I was a boy, listening to my dad's Patsy Cline and Jim Reeves records over the Carlton Café – and when the Croke Park gigs were pulled, I was down and quite angry for a day or two.

But then I snapped out of it. Life is too short to get dragged down by things you can do nothing about; and I think you'll agree, I have survived far worse setbacks than that one. At least I won't lose my house over it!

If I know one thing for sure about my future career, it is that I will always sing. As a bank manager once said:

*'You can sing, can't you?'*

Singing is me; it is what I do. I will be doing no more property developing, thank God, and no more dabbling in things that I don't fully understand. I am a singer, and even if I end up in my sixties crooning in local pubs or at weddings, that is what I will do. I like writing, but singing is like breathing to me.

I think Gillian and I might like to have more kids, because we always wanted a big family, and maybe we aren't done yet. And I think we might return to live in Sligo one day. I have to admit that our relationship with the hometown that we love got a bit bruised along the way. But it is healing.

And will Westlife ever reform?

Ah, well, there's a question.

The honest answer is that I simply don't know. Mark, Kian, Nicky and I were a gang for fourteen years, up for the craic, having impossible adventures and taking on the world, but since we split up, we have hardly seen or spoken to each other.

I went to support Nicky on *Strictly Come Dancing*... but these days, if we do meet up, it is usually by chance. Kian is still a judge on *The Voice of Ireland*, so when I appeared on the show, he and I caught up. I bumped into Mark on a night out in a pub in Sligo and we had a chat over a pint.

When we happen to see each other, we reminisce. Of course we do. We went through so much together. Yet if I am honest it is different now from how it used to be.

I guess that we have grown apart.

It is only natural.

We were a gang, we were brothers; we were Westlife. Nothing, and nobody, can ever take that away from us. But will we ever take a deep breath, get those stools out of storage, and do it all again?

I don't know. Maybe. Maybe not.

For now, I am just grateful to be happy and healthy, in love with Gillian and our three perfect children, Nicole, Patrick and Shane, and making a living from singing songs. At heart, that is all I ever wanted, right from the start.

It's the simple, precious things that mean the most.

# 17

# DID ALL THAT REALLY HAPPEN?

Nothing truly surprises me about my life nowadays. Having had so many crazy highs and crushing lows over the last few years, I guess I feel I am prepared for anything. But what has happened since this book first came out a few short months ago has amazed even me.

I always knew in my heart that I wanted to move back to Sligo one day, but in July 2014, when I was finishing work on the hardback version of this book, that long-term goal seemed like a distant dream. Here are the words I wrote, just a few months ago:

*I think we might return to live in Sligo one day.*

I never imagined that we would be back there by Christmas 2014. I mean, who knew?

How did it happen? Like so many things in my life, by some bizarre combination of chance, luck, taking a gamble – and something that you might call fate, if you happen to believe in that concept. I always have; and now more than ever.

At the end of the summer of 2014, Gillian, the kids and I went off to Sligo for a month. We were missing it, and decided to have a few weeks seeing the family, and also taking in the *Fleadh Cheoil*, a traditional Irish-music festival that was coming to the town.

As we returned, we were bracing ourselves for Castledale finally being sold. We had known for months that it was coming, but that didn't stop it being horribly painful. To me, it was the ultimate reminder of my failure, and what I had put myself and – more importantly – my family through.

The sale had nearly completed a few weeks earlier, but at the last minute the deal had fallen through.

But while we were out in Sligo, staying at my mum and dad's and catching the *Fleadh*, the sale finally happened. As we had expected, Castledale went for a fraction of what we had paid for it – and obviously all of the money went to my bankruptcy trustee.

It was a sad, weird, horrible time, but at least it brought closure to that part of my life. Gillian and I had built our dream home, we had adored living there for eight years, raising our kids, and now we had lost it.

Full stop. At least there was some kind of finality.

It was over, it had gone, and there was nothing that I could do about it. On the day that the sale was confirmed, I said to Gillian, 'Let's leave the kids with Mum and Dad and go for a walk on the beach.'

It was the best idea, and the best walk, that I have ever had.

Gillian and I drove out to Rosses Point. It's a seaside village on a peninsula, about ten minutes outside Sligo town. It has history for us. When I first began dating Gillian, as Westlife were starting out, she was waitressing there in Austies restaurant, and I would drive out to pick her up after her shifts.

Gillian has always loved Rosses Point's vibe and tranquillity – so much so that she had even told me before that she wanted to live there one day. We used to go for long walks down its beach. It was one of our special places.

So that day late last summer, heading out for our walk, Gillian and I drove down the Rosses Point road towards the beach. It was as peaceful as ever. Two-thirds of the way down the road, we saw a huge sign going up outside a house. It must have been ten feet high.

It said: FOR SALE.

'Is that *that* house?' I asked Gillian. Because I remembered, even as a kid, cycling out to Rosses Point and staring up at that particular house, admiring it. It was surrounded by trees and had always looked... magical. 'Is that that house? Isn't that weird?'

We parked the car and walked hand in hand along the beach, as we had done so many times before over the years. The sun burned in the sky; it was a beautiful August day, and the Atlantic stretched to the horizon.

We looked at one another. It was one of those very rare moments when your life seems to stand still for a second.

And it seemed, as we stood there, that everything became clear to us – how much we had been missing Sligo, where we had grown up, where we had met and fallen in love, where we had wanted to raise our kids.

It was our home. It always would be.

'Shall we have a look at that house?' asked Gillian.

The idea took root in our heads as we walked on down the beach.

At the end of the afternoon, we drove back to my parents' house and we talked it over. 'Let's have a look at the property auctioneer's website,' I suggested. 'What harm can that do?'

The house was on the market for what seemed a very reasonable price. Houses in the Rosses Point area come up so rarely that when they do, they're not on the market for long.

The house looked beautiful, but so many ugly thoughts raced through my mind. I had been hit so badly by property. I had been declared bankrupt. I had lost my home. Plus my relationship with Sligo right now was still so rocky and unsure.

Did we dare to take a deep breath and... try again?

For the next three or four weeks, Gillian and I did nothing. We hung out at the *Fleadh* and talked ourselves in and out of looking at the house fifty times as we agonized over what to do.

My heart was trying to persuade me to go for it. Gillian and I have always loved water and the ocean, and had even imagined that we'd live by the sea one day, but I had guessed that it would be when we were pensioners, as I had assumed – before everything crumbled to dust – that we would be living in Castledale for decades.

This house in Rosses Point seemed to have it all. But was it too good to be true? And had it come up too soon?

My decision point came a few days later, at a funeral. The mother of my heart-surgeon friend from Cobham, Brendan, had died, and as I stood in the church in Dublin, reflecting on life and loss and living, the raging argument in my head finally resolved itself.

*Look, sometimes things are just so final. We are all going to die one day. You know what? Every day is precious. Life is for living. Chances don't come along all that often. Why not ring up and look at the house?* That night, back in Sligo, I suggested to Gillian that we take a look. We said it again: what harm could it do?

The next morning, I rang the auctioneer. It happened to be a guy that I used to know, although I hadn't seen him in years. He was quite surprised to hear from me, but when we got down to talking about the house, he could not have been more enthusiastic.

We fixed up to see it a few days later. As we waited on our appointment, I agonized over what I might be about to do.

To say the least, I was still very badly bruised – emotionally and financially – from my dealings in property. I had put so much hope into deals and promises, only to have them all fall through.

What would the auctioneer think of me making a bid? What would the owner make of it? Would they trust me? Because I had to accept, in Sligo, that being Shane Filan carried a certain stigma right now.

Would they even take me seriously?

But my doubts fell away the second that Gillian and I walked through the front door to view the place. I couldn't help but think of a line in one of my favourite movies, *Jerry Maguire*, where Renée Zellweger tells Tom Cruise, 'You had me at hello.'

This house had the same effect on us.

*If there's any way I can do this, I'm doing it*, I thought. *This could be our home for the rest of our lives.* The house was less than a third of the size of Castledale, but it just felt perfect for us. That didn't mean that I thought we would get it. I figured there would be many potential buyers who wanted this house – and, after my recent financial travails, most of them would have a lot bigger budgets than me.

Once, maybe, Shane Filan might have been the favourite to buy a place like this. Not any more. Gillian and I thanked the auctioneer for showing us around and left it there, with no firm offer on the table.

After a month in Sligo, we returned to Cobham. When we got back to the house, it was clear from the looks on Gillian, Nicole, Patrick and Shane's faces that they were not happy to be back. In truth, neither was I.

A penny dropped for me – but really it was something that I had known all along.

'You really don't want to be here, do you?' I asked them. It was a silly question, to which I already knew the answer. It had been grand living in London, and it had been good to us… but it was not Sligo.

Gillian and I spent a long time doing the sums to work out if we could afford Rosses Point – a home that cost a lot less than a detached house in London. We decided that we could. Fingers crossed. My solo career was going great so far, my first album had done well and I had a month-long live tour in Southeast Asia coming up.

Later that week, I called the auctioneer and made him an offer on the house at Rosses Point. He thanked me and said he would be in touch. He was true to his word. A few days later, he called back with the news that the owner of the house had accepted our offer.

How had this happened? Even within the context of my roller-coaster life, this was an amazing turn of events. It was almost too much to take in.

Gillian was so happy, and the kids could not have been more excited to learn that we were moving back to Sligo. All that I could think was: *Thank God we decided to go listen to some traditional music!*

We had not yet exchanged on the house when, a few days later, I flew out to Asia to embark on the month-long live tour. These were my first international solo shows, and while I felt excited to be flying out to play for crowds on my own rather than as part of Westlife, I was also very apprehensive.

The first dates, in Indonesia and Vietnam, went great, but what I had not expected was that I would feel so cripplingly homesick. For whatever reason, it was the worst I had ever suffered it.

Every day after I had spoken to Nicole, Patrick and Shane on the phone I felt like bawling. They sounded as upset as I was, and Gillian said they were really missing me. The last three weeks of the tour before I would see them again seemed to stretch into eternity.

We had a show in Ho Chi Minh City, and then I had a three-day break until the next gig in Beijing. Before the Vietnam show, I was moaning and giving out to my tour manager, Liam, when he cut me dead.

'Why don't you go home, then?' he asked.

'Huh?'

'You have three days off before Beijing. You can just about do it.'

*Life is for living. Chances don't come along all that often.*

I eagerly agreed.

I came off stage in Vietnam at half past ten and was on a flight by midnight. The time difference meant I landed in London at 1 p.m. the next day and was at home in Cobham by the time Gillian was picking the kids up from school.

I had told Gillian I was making my flying visit home – but not Nicole, Patrick or Shane. Some things work best as surprises. Waiting in the house, I called Gillian's mobile to chat to the kids in the car.

'How are you doing?' I asked them. 'How was school?' The usual craic. They all sounded so miserable as they passed the phone between them and complained how much they were missing me.

By the time they pulled through our gates, I was hiding in the driveway. They still hadn't seen me as I crept up to the car and peered in the back window at them slumped in a row, fed up, their feet up on the backs of the front seats.

'What would you say if I could come home and see you soon?'

'Oh, Daddy, we would love that!'

I tapped on the car window.

The noise was incredible. The three of them screamed their heads off. Nicole was going crazy and Patrick looked set to burst with excitement. In no time they were out of the car, on top of me, and I was flattened on the driveway. I hit the ground like a bad wrestler.

I thought I was going to cry with happiness. In fact, I think that I did. It was a special moment that I will never forget.

We had a couple of days hanging out and then I was back to Asia for the show in Beijing and a load more dates in China and Hong Kong. I was playing to a couple of thousand people per night and the crowds were brilliant. When the tour ended with scenes of hysteria in the Philippines – always such a historic place for Westlife – it was another of those moments when I thought, *Yes! I can do this solo thing!* Back in London, I finally held a finished copy of the hardback of this book in my hands. I felt proud, but my emotions were all over the place. Reading it back, a big part of me felt worried that I had given away far too much and left myself way too open.

*Shit, I've put my whole f\*\*king life out there! What are people going to make of it?*

Because writing this book was draining and difficult for me – but it was also cathartic. It helped to make sense of the chaos that my life had become. In a funny (not ha-ha) way, it was my counsellor, and it helped to see me through.

As I held the book, I remembered one time, just as I was finishing writing, when I was in Sligo and I offered to read my mum and dad some of it. They were keen. So I tried to read them the chapter where I went bankrupt, but I had to stop – my voice would not work. I was about to bawl. It was too painful, too raw.

But, maybe for that reason, when the book came out, in October 2014, it got a great reception. I was doing signings at meet-and-greets, and I lost count of how many fans told me they loved how honest I had been, and even that it had inspired them to get through their own tough times.

It made me glad that I had followed my instincts. Because I think that if you're going to write a book like this, you have to tell your whole story – warts and all.

One nice thing that happened after the hardback came out was that, out of the blue, I heard from Brian. He sent me a text, thanking me for being fair in what I had said about him in the book.

What could I say? I texted him back and told him: 'I was just telling it like it was, buddy. I hope you're well.'

All the time I was doing TV and magazine interviews to promote the book's publication, I knew that our big move into Rosses Point was about to happen. In fact, Gillian had already gone ahead of me to Sligo to get everything ready.

It was so exciting, and yet I made a conscious decision not to talk about it to the press beforehand. So many interviewers were asking me if I thought I would ever go home to Sligo, and I was just giving them vague answers, saying that I hoped I would and I was working hard towards it.

Why? It just didn't feel right to announce it. Not yet. So much had gone wrong in recent years that I didn't want to say anything until I actually had the keys in my hand. The move felt like it was going to be so precious and I didn't want to jinx it.

Also, the return to Sligo wasn't in the book – because we hadn't found the house until after the manuscript had gone to print – and I didn't want to grab headlines and look as if I was announcing it to try to sell copies. I knew some people would be cynical and say I had timed it all very conveniently.

Well, I didn't want to be wrongly accused of that. It was all too obvious, too predictable. I didn't want to be that particular cliché. I knew the time would come to talk about my homecoming – and I guess this chapter is it.

When the book promotional tour was all done, I flew back to Dublin. My dad met me and drove me down to Sligo. He always loves to pick me up from the airport and have a good old catch-up on the way home, and that day we had one of the all-time great father-and-son chats.

The weird thing was that it turned out that my dad had looked at the very same house I had just bought in Rosses Point twenty-four years earlier; the last time it had come up for sale. He had thought it was a great place, but he and my mum had decided to stay in town, and so they had raised all of us kids in the Carlton Café on Castle Street – but I could just as easily have grown up in the house I was about to move into! What a coincidence...

It made it feel even more like that word again – fate.

As the miles fell away behind us, my dad and I talked about all the crazy stuff that has happened to me – the highs of the fame with Westlife, the lows of my bankruptcy. We stopped off for burgers and chips at Supermacs, as we have done so many times over the years.

And as we ate our chips, I realised exactly what this drive felt like for me. It felt like coming home. Not just home to Sligo – home to where I belonged. Where we belonged.

The moving-in day was wonderful. The kids were in seventh heaven, and Gillian and I had to keep pinching ourselves to make sure that this really was happening and we actually were back in Sligo.

After the hell we had been through, we were all beyond excited to be home. Yet at the same time, I knew that it was going to be a difficult transition. We had been through the wringer and there was a lot of pain, tears, heartache, anger and shame that I went through as Shafin collapsed and we lost our home.

I'm still not out of the financial woods yet. I am no longer bankrupt, but I still have a year to go of paying half of my income to the trustee, who pays it on to the banks and to anybody to whom I owe money personally.

I won't pretend that I am destitute, but the wealth of the Westlife years feels a long, long time ago. Everything is different now. I'm not the millionaire pop star who bought the Carlton Lodge house outright, for cash. I have a loan on my home and I will work hard to pay it off, just like the next guy. What more can I do? I have to live my life.

If I have learnt one thing in the last few years, it is this: you can't keep everyone happy. It can't be done. The important thing for me is I am rebuilding my life – my family's life.

The first stage of that is that we are back in Sligo. Gillian and I wanted that more than anything. I mean, we are Irish, our kids are Irish, and we want them to grow up here, with the same relaxed background and way of life that we had.

The kids started their new schools straight away and fitted in like they had never been away. As for me, after just a week in Rosses Point, I was back on the road again. It was time for the second leg of my solo UK tour, which my agents had fixed up after the first lot of dates sold out, and I was off to play thirty-three shows in forty-four days.

I am really enjoying the live dates I'm playing now. I'm performing in halls and theatres to a couple of thousand people and the shows are intimate and have a real intensity. They feel like proper gigs; the kind of gigs I've never played before.

Westlife never did these kinds of shows. We started off in huge arenas – after all, on our very first tour we played ten Wembleys! It may seem like I'm doing things backwards, but the gigs that I'm playing now are a new experience for me, and I am loving them.

Would I like to be playing the big arenas again one day? Of course! But venues like Wembley Arena are where the huge stars like Westlife and One Direction and Justin Timberlake belong. I'm not a huge star today; I'm nowhere near it. I haven't had the songs or the success. I'm just feeling my way.

Of course, I am still Shane Filan *from* Westlife and I always will be; Westlife never really goes away. Just before the end of my solo tour, I was checking Twitter to see fans' reactions to my gigs when I saw a trending headline: *#westlifereform*

Huh? What the f**k was that?

It turned out that a British tabloid – the *Sun*, I think – had run a 'world exclusive' that Simon Cowell's record label Syco had started talks with the band about getting together again to make an album at the end of 2015, with a tour the following year.

A mysterious 'source' then told other papers that: 'There have been some very, very early informal conversations, but any firm decisions are a long way off in the future.'

Well, I hate to let the facts get in the way of a good story, but there have been no conversations between band members about reforming Westlife. Zero. Zilch. Nada.

Like I said before in this book, Mark, Kian, Nicky and I are not talking about anything, let alone getting together again. We haven't fallen out; it's just the way we are.

We are all just doing our own thing, trying to build up our new lives after Westlife. The last time we were all together was in Kehoe's pub in Dublin, almost three years ago, the day after our farewell Croke Park gig.

We always had that camaraderie that all great bands need, but we were never really best friends outside the group, and that's become clearer to me since the band ended. I suppose we just have our own lives now.

We don't even send each other Christmas cards. We never did, really. I remember one year, quite early on, when Kian handed us all a Christmas card and we all laughed at him. Kian told us all, 'F\*\*k you!' and that was that. That was the end of Westlife and Christmas cards...

So will Westlife ever reform? The answer is still the same. Maybe. Maybe not. Because if I have learned one thing in recent years, it's that I cannot predict the future.

The last date of my solo tour – and my seventieth gig of 2014 – was in Sligo, at the Knocknarea Arena. It was a charity gig for the Donal Parsons Trust, which is a charity to benefit a local lad suffering from neuroblastoma, the same rare form of cancer that Niamh had. It was a heartbreaking story and I really wanted to help the family. It was a fantastic gig – a home gig – and a great way to finish the tour.

So, right now, I'm totally focusing on my solo career; I'm all about working on my second album, with a brand-new team around me. I am writing songs again, feeling my way to a sound I can call my own, and Louis and I are very excited about this year.

I'm writing my next album in very different circumstances to my first, thankfully, and I'm really interested to see where my lyrics will take me this year. And I'm still searching for that killer song.

That's what I really want – a famous song, a huge tune that people think about as soon as they hear my name. I want to be in the right place at the right time when a song like that comes along.

Every singer wants those huge hits. I'm no different.

That's my dream, and I'll keep working towards it. If it comes true... fantastic! And if it doesn't? Well, my life is still amazing right now, far better than I dared to think might be possible in the dark, dark days of just a few years ago.

I survived it all, I came out the other side, and now Gillian, Nicole, Patrick, Shane and I are back in Sligo, the home we love, in the house where I hope Gillian and I will grow old together. I'm already imagining the photos of me walking Nicole out of the front door on her wedding day...

After everything, I'm a huge believer that what is meant to be is meant to be. Now and then I reflect on the rollercoaster life I have lived so far, and I ask myself: *Did all that really happen?* It did, and it led me to where I am now, which is a very happy, contented, excited and hopeful place. I'm sure there are many more twists and turns to come but, for now, that is the extraordinary story of my life to date.

That is My Side of Life.

# ACKNOWLEDGEMENTS

I would like to thank everybody named and pictured in this book who has helped to get me to where I am today. First of all, of course, my parents Peter and Mae, my brothers and sisters Finbarr, Peter, Yvonne, Liam, Denise and Mairead, Gillian's family, my extended family, and all of our friends in Sligo and Cobham.

To the people who stood by me when things got rough: Louis Walsh, Alan McEvoy, Liam McKenna, Joanne Byrne, John Giddings, Sarah Sherlock and Steve Levitt.

To my live tour promoters and my band and crew who travel the world with me, and above all, to my fans – without you, there is no me.

To everybody at Virgin Books who helped to put this book together, especially my co-writer, Ian Gittins, for his many trips to Cobham, and my editor Yvonne Jacob, for her patience, understanding and local knowledge of the west of Ireland.

And finally, always and forever, thank you to Gillian, Nicole, Patrick and Shane for helping me to keep smiling through it all. I love you so much – you're everything to me.

The following charities are very close to my heart. If you would like to find out more, or if you wish to make a donation, please visit:

www.niamhsnextstep.com
www.donalparsonstrust.com
www.childline.ie

# INDEX

(the initials SF refer to Shane Filan)